THE FIRST YEAR OF LATIN

The First Year of Latin

Based On

Caesar's War with the Helvetii

BY
Walter B. Gunnison
AND
Walter S. Harley

Armfield Academic Press

THE FIRST YEAR OF LATIN

Originally published in 1902. This edition copyright © 2007 by

ARMFIELD ACADEMIC PRESS
www.armfieldacademicpress.com

ISBN-13: 978-0-9795051-2-6
ISBN-10: 0-9795051-2-7

Library of Congress Control Number: 2007929777

CONTENTS

TEXTS

APPENDIX

GLOSSARIES

MAPS

PREFACE

The plan of *The First Year of Latin* is the result of practical experience in the classroom. It aims in the most direct manner to prepare the pupil at the end of the year to continue the reading of Caesar. While a general survey of the essential features of the Latin grammar is made, only those parts are emphasized which are needed. With few exceptions the words and phrases are taken directly from Caesar's *War with the Helvetii*, and by their frequent repetition a sufficient vocabulary is established to simplify the reading of Caesar in the second year.

Special attention is given to reviews. At short intervals a lesson is made up of questions on the new forms and constructions of the lessons immediately preceding it, together with a repetition of the new words and such sentences of Caesar as will be used later. The earlier review lessons contain sentences for sight-reading, based on the review vocabulary. In the later lessons connected passages covering chapters 1-12 of *The War with the Helvetii* replace these. Throughout the book the plan is to give individual forms and constructions first, and then to mass them in review when the last of a series is reached. For example, at the end of each mood, voice or tense system, the whole mood, voice or tense system is reviewed. The different uses of a case are presented separately, as needed; and in the last lessons they are brought together.

Many classes may find it possible to complete the lessons before the close of the year. For such, the remaining chapters of *The War with the Helvetii* (13-29) have been annotated, and sentences to be turned into Latin have been based upon them. Those who wish, at the end of Lesson 73, to pass directly to the reading of Book II will be prepared to do so.

Though the book has been divided into lessons, these must not be understood to mean daily portions. Conditions vary too much to make a division into such portions practicable.

The authors wish especially to recognize the valuable assistance given to them by the careful and full criticisms made during the revision of these pages by Professor Isaac Bronson Burgess, of the University of Chicago, and by Dr. Sidney G. Stacey, of the Erasmus Hall High School.

BROOKLYN, N.Y., *August 1, 1902*

THE FIRST YEAR OF LATIN

INTRODUCTION

The Introduction is chiefly for reference. In preparation for Lesson I, section 3 should be learned, and sections 8, 9, 10, 11 and 13 should be read. Other sections will be referred to as they become of use.

1. The Latin Language.—Latin was the language of the ancient Romans, whose literature in part has come down to us. After the downfall of the Roman government in 476 A.D., Latin for centuries was the language of church and state in Europe. Though no longer spoken as a national language, it is the parent of the modern languages of Italy, France, Spain and Portugal. It is the source of the majority of our English words, and of the terms of law, medicine and natural science in all European languages.

2. The Alphabet.—(a) The Latin Alphabet has the same letters as the English, omitting **j** and **w**.

(b) The vowels are **a, e, i, o, u** and **y**. **i** is a consonant (English **j**) between two vowels, and at the beginning of a word whose second letter is a vowel: **ēius, iam.**

(c) The consonants are—

Mutes: **b, p, t, d, c, k, q, g.**
Liquids: **l, m, n, r.**

Spirants: **h, f, s.** s is also a sibilant.

Double consonants: **x**(*cs* or *gs*) and **z**(*ds*).

i and **v** are semi-vowels.

3. PRONUNCIATION.—Latin is now pronounced chiefly according to the so-called Roman method, which is given here:

(*a*) *Vowels.* A vowel is either long or short. In this book long vowels are marked thus (ˉ).

LONG.	SHORT.[1]
ā is like *a* in *father:* **lātus.**	**a** is like *a* in *artistic:* **castra.**
ē " *e* " *they:* **dē.**	**e** " *e* " *net:* **eam.**
ī " *i* " *machine:* **līber.**	**i** " *i* " *pin:* **itinera.**
ō " *o* " *rode:* **tōtus.**	**o** " *o* " *obey:* **homō.**
ū " *u* " *rule:* **ūna.**	**u** " *u* " *pull:*[2] **duo.**

The sound of **y** is like the German *ü*, which has no exact English equivalent.

(*b*) *Diphthongs.*[3]

ae is like *ai* in *aisle:* **prae.**	**ui,** sounded like *we*, occurs
au " *our* " *our:* **audiō.**	chiefly in **cui** (*kwee*) and
oe " *oi* " *oil:* **proelium.**	**huic** (*hweek*).

(*c*) *Consonants.*

c is like *c* in *can:* **cēdō.**

g   "   *g* " *get:* **rēgem.**

i   "   *y* " *yet:* **hūius.**

s   "   *s* " *son* or *this:* **hostis.**

t   "   *t* " *ten:* **tertia.**

---

[1] The short vowels have the same quality of sound as the long, but take half the time : ā = ăă.

[2] u in **qu-**, and sometimes in **gu-** and **su-** before a vowel, has the sound of *w*.

[3] **ei,** like *ei* in *eight*, and **eu** like *eh´-oo*, occur in a few words.

v is like *w* in *wet:* **nāvis.**

x " *x* " *ax:* **lēx.**

bs and **bt** are like *ps* and *pt:* **urbs, obtinent.**

ch is like *k*.

Other consonants are sounded as in English.

NOTE.—Latin words are sometimes pronounced as if they were English. This is called the English method. According to a method known as the Continental, the vowels have the same sounds as given in the Roman method, while the consonants are sounded as in the language of the learner.

4. SYLLABLES.—(*a*) A Latin word has as many syllables as it has vowels and diphthongs: **vic-tō-ri-a,** *victory;* **proe-li-um,** *battle;* **a-qui-la,** *eagle;* **hū-ius,** *of this.*

(*b*) In dividing a word into syllables a single consonant between two vowels is to be written with the second: **lo-cus,** *place.* Compound words are to be separated into their component parts: **ab-est,** *he is away.*

(*c*) The next to the last syllable is called the *penult;* the one before the penult is the *antepenult.*

5. QUANTITY OF VOWELS.—The *quantity* of a vowel refers to its length; that is, to the time occupied in pronouncing it. Quantity must be learned chiefly by observation, but in many cases the following rules will determine it:

(*a*) A vowel is short before **nd, nt, h** or another vowel[1]: **fŭnditor,** *slinger;* **portănt,** *they carry;* **nĭhil,** *nothing;* **dĭēs,** *day.*

(*b*) A vowel is generally long before **gm, gn, nf, ns,** and **i** (consonant): **māgnus,** *great;* **īnfrā,** *below;* **oriēns,** *rising;* **hūius,** *of this.*

---

[1] With exceptions.

(*c*) A vowel produced by contraction is long: **nīl** from **nihil,** *nothing.*

(*d*) Diphthongs are long: **nauta,** *sailor.*

6. QUANTITY OF SYLLABLES.—(*a*) A syllable is short if it contains a short vowel not followed by two or more consonants: **nu-me-rus,** *number;* **vi-a,** *way.*

(*b*) A syllable is long by nature if it contains a long vowel or a diphthong: **a-mī-cus,** *friend;* **tu-bae,** *trumpets.*

(*c*) A syllable is long by position if it contains a short vowel followed in the same word by **x** or **z,** or by any two consonants except a mute with **l** or **r: nox,** *night;* **noc-tēs,** *nights.* A syllable, therefore, may be long in quantity, even though its vowel is short.

7. ACCENT.—(*a*) A word of two syllables is accented on the first: **car'-rus,** *cart;* **pu'-er,** *boy.*

(*b*) A word of more than two syllables is accented on the penult, if that is long; otherwise, on the antepenult: **a-mī'-cus,** *friend;* **im-pe'-ri-um,** *command.*

(*c*) **-que** and a few other words, which are never used by themselves and are called *enclitics,* require the accent to fall on the last syllable of the word to which they are attached: **tēla'que.**

8. PARTS OF SPEECH.—In Latin, as in English, there are eight parts of speech: *nouns, adjectives, pronouns, verbs, adverbs, prepositions, conjunctions* and *interjections.* The last four are sometimes called *particles,* " little parts " of speech. Participles are adjective forms of the verb. There is no article in Latin.

9. DECLENSION.—Nouns, pronouns and adjectives

are inflected or declined; that is, they take different endings to show the *case*, *number*, and in many instances the *gender* of the word. In English the relation of a noun to other words of a sentence is not determined by a special ending, except in the possessive case; the objective is the same in form as the nominative. In Lat'n the objective of many words differs from the nominative; thus, the objective form for boy is **puerum,** while the nominative is **puer.** Special endings are used to show relations which in English require prepositions: thus, *of the boy* is **puerī;** *to the boy,* **puerō.**

10. CASES.—Declined words have six cases: the *nominative, vocative, genitive, dative, accusative* and *ablative.*

LATIN.   GENERAL ENGLISH EQUIVALENTS.

Nominative: Nominative (Case of the subject).
Vocative: "   used in address (Case of address).
Genitive: Objective with *of*, or the possessive.
Dative: "   with *to* or *for* (Case of the indirect object).
Accusative: "   after a verb or preposition (Case of the direct object).
Ablative: "   with *from, by, with, in*, etc.

The vocative is spelled like the nominative in all Latin words, except in the singular of some nouns and adjectives in **-us,** as explained in section 57.

Some names of towns and a few other words have in the singular another case, called the *locative*, denoting the place *where.* It is equivalent to the English objective with *in* or *at.*

11. NUMBER AND GENDER.—The numbers are the *singular* and the *plural;* the genders are the *masculine*, the *feminine*, and the *neuter*. In Latin many words are masculine or feminine which in English are neuter: **pēs,** *foot*, masculine; **manus,** *hand*, feminine. ·

12. GENERAL RULES FOR GENDER.—(*a*) Nouns denoting males, and most names of rivers, winds and months are masculine: **fīlius,** *son;* **Iūlius,** *Julius;* **Rhēnus,** *Rhine;* **auster,** *south wind ;* **Mārtius,** *March.*

(*b*) Nouns denoting females and most names of countries, towns, islands and trees are feminine: **fīlia,** *daughter;* **Iūlia,** *Julia;* **Gallia,** *Gaul;* **Rōma,** *Rome;* **Mona,** *Isle of Man ;* **pirus,** *pear tree.*

13. FIVE DECLENSIONS.—There are five declensions, distinguished by the ending of the genitive singular, which in the first declension is **-ae;** second, **-ī;** third, **-is;** fourth, **-ūs;** fifth, **-ĕī.**

14. CONJUGATION.—Verbs are inflected or conjugated to show the voice, mood, tense, number and person.

15. VOICE. MOOD. TENSE.—In Latin there are two voices: the *active* and the *passive;* three moods: the *indicative*, the *subjunctive* and the *imperative;* six tenses: the *present*, the *imperfect*, the *future*, the *perfect*, the *pluperfect* and the *future perfect*. The numbers and persons are the same as in English.

16. VERBAL NOUNS AND ADJECTIVES.—The conjugation of the verb includes also certain verbal nouns: the *infinitives*, the *gerund* and the *supine;* and verbal adjectives: the *participles* (including the *gerundive*).

17. PRINCIPAL PARTS.—Certain forms of a verb are

called its *principal parts*, because from them all the other forms can be derived. For a verb in the active voice, they are the first person of the present indicative, the present infinitive, the first person of the perfect indicative and the supine. Thus for **laudō,** *I praise*, the principal parts are **laudō, laudāre, laudāvī, laudātum.**

18. STEMS OF THE VERB.—A stem of a verb is a fixed part to which are added certain letters indicating number and person, and sometimes others denoting mood and tense. Verbs have three stems: the *present*, the *perfect* and the *supine*. The present stem is found by dropping **-re** of the present infinitive active: **laudāre, laudā-;** the perfect stem, by dropping **-ī** of the perfect indicative active: **laudāvī, laudāv-;** the supine stem, by dropping **-um** of the supine: **laudātum, laudāt-.**

19. FOUR CONJUGATIONS.—There are four conjugations, distinguished by the final letter (*characteristic*) of the present stem. The first is sometimes called the **ā**-conjugation, the second the **ē**-conjugation, the third the **ĕ**-conjugation, the fourth the **ī**-conjugation, because the present stems end in **ā, ē, ĕ** and **ī**, respectively.

LESSON I

Tho First Declension (Singular).—The Nominative Case.

Learn the sounds of the vowels and consonants in section 3. Read sections 8, 9, 10, 11 and 13.

20. THE GENITIVE SINGULAR.—The first declension includes all words whose genitive singular ends in -ae. The nominative, except in some words of Greek origin, ends in -a.

21. GENDER.—Nouns of the first declension are feminine, except a few that denote male beings, and the names of some rivers, which are masculine (12, *a*).

22. BASE.—The base of a declined word is that part of it which is the same in all its cases. It may be found in all declensions by dropping the ending of the genitive singular. A word is declined by adding the endings to the base.

23. MODEL NOUN

Porta, F., *gate.* Base: **port-.**

	Singular	Endings.
Nominative [1]	porta, *a gate* [2]	-a
Genitive	portae, *of a gate*	-ae
Dative	portae, *to* or *for a gate*	-ae
Accusative	portam, *a gate*	-am
Ablative	portā, *from, by, with, in, a gate*	-ā

subject
possession
indirect obj.
direct obj.

[1] The vocative, being like the nominative, is omitted in this and the following models. See 10.

[2] The word may be translated *gate, a gate,* or *the gate.*

(handwritten top margin)
① Vocabulary
memorize: - nominative singular
- genitive singular
- gender
- meaning (English)

24. *(handwritten: nouns)*   **VOCABULARY**   *(handwritten: adjectives)*

porta, -ae,[1] F., *gate.*
prōvincia, -ae, F., *province.*
rīpa, -ae, F., *bank* (of a river).
terra, -ae, F., *land, country.*
via, -ae, F., *road, way.*
Gallia, -ae, F., *Gaul* (now called France).
Helvētia, -ae, F., *Helvetia* (now called Switzerland).
Sēquana, -ae, F. or M., the *Seine.*

alta, *high, deep.*
dīvīsa, *divided.*
lāta, *broad.*
longa, *long.*
māgna, *large, great.*
parva, *small.*
et, conj., *and.*
est, (*he, she, it*) *is.*

Decline the nouns and adjectives like **porta.** Decline together **via longa.**

NOTE.—Give careful attention to the length of vowels (3) and to accent (7). Do not accent the last syllable of a word. Mark the long vowels (¯) in all written work. *(handwritten margin: See "Topical Lectures")*

(handwritten: L esp. Ablative sing.)

25.   MODEL SENTENCE

Porta est alta: *The gate is high.*

Notice that **porta** is in the nominative case and is the subject.

26. RULE I.—*The subject of a finite[2] verb is in the nominative case.*

27.   TRANSLATE INTO ENGLISH   *(handwritten: (Do all.))*

1. Viae.   2. Prōvinciae.   3. Terram.   4. Prōvinciam.   5. Lāta terra.   6. Rīpa lāta.   7. Viā.   8. Viā Helvētiae. 9. Parvae prōvinciae.   10. Sēquana est longa.   11. Prōvincia est māgna.   12. Rīpa est lāta.   13. Via est longa

---

[1] The genitive singular is given in the vocabularies to show to which declension a word belongs (13).
[2] A *finite* verb is a verb in the indicative, subjunctive or imperative mood.

(handwritten bottom margin)
                                    in case, gender and number
① — adjective must agree w/ noun it modifies.
① — word order is flexible

et lāta. 14. Gallia est māgna terra.[1] 15. Helvētia est parva. 16. Gallia est dīvīsa.

28. TRANSLATE INTO LATIN *(Do all except #4)*

1. For the broad land. 2. Of the deep Seine. 3. A road of Helvetia. 4. By the bank of the Seine. 5. The bank is high. 6. The province is a small country.[1] 7. The country is Helvetia. 8. Helvetia is divided.

LESSON II

The First Declension (Plural).

Read and apply sections 4, 5, 6, and 7, *a, b.*

29. MODEL NOUN

	Plural.	*Endings.*
N.	port**ae**, *gates*	-ae
G.	port**ārum**, *of gates*	-ārum
D.	port**īs**, *to* or *for gates*	-īs
Ac.	port**ās**, *gates*	-ās
Ab.	port**īs**, *from, by, with, in, gates*	-īs

30. VOCABULARY

amīcitia, -ae, F., *friendship.* nauta, -ae, M., *sailor.*
littera, -ae, F., *letter* (of alpha- victōria, -ae, F., *victory.*
bet); pl. *letter* (epistle). nōn, adv., *not.*
sunt, (*they*) *are.*

Decline the nouns of 24 and 30 in both numbers.

---

[1] A predicate nominative (94).

31.   MODEL SENTENCES

1. **Porta est alta:** *The gate is high.*
2. **Portae sunt altae:** *The gates are high.*

Notice that the verb is changed to agree in number with the subject; and that each adjective has the same number and case as its noun.

32. RULE II.—*A finite verb agrees with its subject in number and person.*

TRANSLATE

33. 1. Nautārum. 2. Victōriārum. 3. Litterārum. 4. Amīcitiā nautae. 5. Victōria nautārum. 6. Rīpās. 7. Litterās. 8. Litterīs. 9. Longīs rīpīs. 10. Parvae portae. 11. Rīpae sunt lātae. 12. Viae sunt longae et lātae. 13. Gallia et Helvētia sunt terrae. 14. Prōvinciae sunt nōn māgnae. 15. Litterae nōn sunt parvae.

34. 1. By the victories. 2. Of the small countries. 3. By the.letter of the sailor. 4. For the friendship of the provinces. 5. The victory of Helvetia is great. 6. The countries are small. 7. The banks are not high.

LESSON III

**The First Conjugation: Present Indicative Active.
The Accusative Case.**

Read sections 14 to 19.

35. PERSONAL ENDINGS OF PRESENT INDICATIVE ACTIVE.—In the indicative mood there are six tenses (15). The present indicative active is conjugated by adding to the present stem (18) certain endings to denote person and number. These *personal* endings are:

	Singular.	Plural.
First Person,	-ō, *I*	-mus, *we*
Second Person,	-s, *you (thou)*	-tis, *you*
Third Person,	-t, *he (she, it)*	-nt, *they*

36. The first conjugation includes all verbs whose present infinitive active ends in -āre.

37. MODEL VERB

Laudō, *I praise.* Present stem: **laudā-.**

PRES. IND.	PRES. INF.	PERF. IND.	SUPINE.
PRIN. PARTS : laudō,	laudāre,	laudāvī,	laudātum.

PRESENT INDICATIVE ACTIVE.

Singular.	Plural.
1. laudō, *I praise.*[1]	laudāmus, *we praise.*
2. laudās, *you praise.*[2]	laudātis, *you praise.*
3. laudat, *he (she, it) praises.*	laudant, *they praise.*

NOTE.—Final -ā- of the stem disappears before the ending -ō in the first person, and becomes short before -t and -nt in the third person (5, *a*).

38. VOCABULARY

cōpia, -ae, F., *supply;* pl. *troops, forces.*

Messāla, -ae, M., *Messala* (name of a Roman officer, 61 B.C.).

Belgae, -ārum, M., *Belgae, Belgians* (inhabitants of northern Gaul).

Celtae, -ārum, M., *Celts* (inhabitants of central Gaul).

---

[1] Or, *I am praising* (progressive form); *I do praise* (emphatic form).
[2] Or, *thou praisest.*

cōnfīrmō, -āre, -āvī, -ātum, *establish, strengthen, affirm.*
laudō, -āre, -āvī, -ātum, *praise.*
nūntiō, -āre, -āvī, -ātum, *announce, report.*
pācō, -āre, -āvī, -ātum, *subdue, conquer.*
portō, -āre, -āvī, -ātum, *carry, bring.*

Inflect (decline or conjugate) the words in 38.

39. MODEL SENTENCES

1. **Messālam laudant:** *They praise Messala.*
2. **Celtae Messālam laudant:** *The Celts praise Messala.*
3. **Messāla nautās laudat:** *Messala praises the sailors.*

Notice that **Messālam** and **nautās** are in the accusative case and are objects of the verb; that the subject is expressed by the personal ending if no other subject is found (sentence 1); that the verb stands last, a common position in Latin prose.

40. RULE III.—*The direct object of a verb is in the accusative case.*

TRANSLATE

41. 1. Portant, nūntiant, cōnfīrmant. 2. Pācāmus, portāmus. 3. Cōnfīrmās, nūntiās. 4. Portātis, pācātis. 5. Belgae victōriam nūntiant. 6. Cōpiās laudāmus. 7. Celtae amīcitiam cōnfīrmant. 8. Messāla māgnam prōvinciam pācat. 9. Nauta litterās portat. 10. Celtās et Belgās laudātis. 11. Cōpiam frūmentī[1] portās. 12. Cōpiae nōn sunt nautae.

42. 1. He carries, subdues, establishes. 2. You (pl.) announce, establish. 3. They praise, establish. 4. We subdue the small provinces. 5. I am carrying a long letter. 6. You (pl.) praise Messala and the sailors. 7. The

---

[1] *of grain.*

sailor announces a great victory. 8. You (sing.) are establishing friendship. 9. He is subduing Helvetia.

LESSON IV

The Second Conjugation : Present Indicative Active.
The Genitive With Nouns.—Prepositions.

43. The second conjugation includes all verbs whose present infinitive active ends in -ēre. Review 35.

44. MODEL VERB

Moneō, *I advise, I warn.* Present stem: **monē-.**
PRINCIPAL PARTS: moneō, monēre, monuī, monitum.

PRESENT INDICATIVE ACTIVE.

Singular.	*Plural.*
moneō, *I advise.*[1]	monēmus, *we advise.*
monēs, *you advise.*	monētis, *you advise.*
monet, *he,* etc., *advises.*	monent, *they advise.*

In which forms is -e- short? Why? See 5, *a.*

45. VOCABULARY

causa, -ae, F., *cause.*
fuga, -ae, F., *flight.*
silva, -ae, F., *forest.*
nostra, possessive pron.,[2] *our.*

Aquītānia,-ae, F., *Aquitania* (a part of Gaul).
Garumna,-ae,M. or F.,the *Garonne* (a river of Gaul).

habeō, habēre, habuī, habitum, *have.*
iubeō, iubēre, iussī, iussum, *order, command.*
moneō, monēre, monuī, monitum, *advise, warn.*
moveō, movēre, mōvī, mōtum, *move.*

---

[1] See page 12, footnote 1.   [2] Used as an adjective.

persuādeō, -suādēre, -suāsī, -suāsum, *persuade.*
pertineō, -tinēre, -tinuī, ——,[1] *extend.*
videō, vidēre, vīdī, vīsum, *see.*

Inflect all words in 45.

46. MODEL SENTENCES

1. **Nautae terram Belgārum vident:** *The sailors see the country of the Belgians, or the Belgians' country.*
2. **Aquītānia ā Garumnā ad Hispāniam pertinet:** *Aquitania extends from the Garonne to Spain.*

Notice that **Belgārum** is in the genitive case, limiting **terram** like an English possessive; that **Garumnā** is in the ablative, governed by the preposition **ā** (*from*); and that **Hispāniam** is in the accusative case, governed by the preposition **ad** (*to*).

47. RULE IV.—*A noun (or pronoun) limiting another noun and not meaning the same person or thing is in the genitive case.*

48. RULE V.—*The accusative and ablative cases, like the objective case in English, may be used with prepositions.*

49. The most common prepositions are:

WITH THE ACCUSATIVE.	WITH THE ABLATIVE.
ad, *to, near*	**ā, ab,**[2] *away from, from, by*
ante, *before*	**cum,** *with, in company with*
circum, *around*	**dē,** *down from, from, concern-*
in, *into*	*ing*
inter, *between, among*	**ē, ex,**[2] *out of, from*
per, *through, over*	**in,** *in, on*

---

[1] The supine, the fourth word of the principal parts, is sometimes wanting.
[2] ā and ē are used only before consonants ; ab and ex, before vowels or consonants.

post, *after, behind*   prō, *before, in front of, in be-*
prope, *near*   *half of*
propter, *on account of*   sine, *without*
trāns, *across*

NOTE.—As a rule, *place to which* is denoted by **ad** or **in**
(*into*) with the accusative; *place from which* by **ab, dē** or
ex with the ablative; *place in which* by **in** (*in*) with the
ablative: *ad* **Hispāniam,** *ā* **Garumnā,** *in* **silvā.** This rule
is explained in section 446.

50. ORDER OF WORDS.—The relation of words in a
Latin sentence is indicated by the endings, not by the
order as in English. Therefore the order of words in
the two languages is generally different. A common
order in Latin is: 1. The subject, preceded or followed by its modifiers. 2. Modifiers of the predicate.
3. The predicate. The tendency is to put the most
emphatic word first.

TRANSLATE

51. 1. Iubēmus, persuādēmus. 2. Movētis. 3. Persuādēs,
movēs. 4. Iubent, persuādent. 5. Celtae māgnam terram habent. 6. Terra Celtārum est māgna. 7. Terra
Celtārum ā Belgīs ad Aquītāniam pertinet. 8. Messāla
litterās nautae habet. 9. Longās et lātās viās Belgārum
vidēmus. 10. Via est per prōvinciam ad Aquītāniam. 11.
Nautās Messālae monet. 12. Vidēs lātās silvās Helvētiae.
13. Causa fugae Celtārum est victōria Messālae.

52. 1. We see, move. 2. You (pl.) order, persuade.
3. He is ordering, is reporting. 4. They extend, move.
5. The Seine has broad banks. 6. The sailors see the
flight of the troops. 7. (There) are long roads through
our province. 8. A large forest extends from Spain to
the province. 9. We have large forces. 10. They announce the causes of victory.

LESSON V

The Second Declension: Nouns in *-us* and *-um*. The Dative of Indirect Object.

53. GENITIVE SINGULAR.—The second declension includes all words whose genitive singular ends in **-ī**. The nominative ends in **-us, -er, -ir** or **-um**.

54. GENDER.—Nouns of the second declension are masculine, except those in **-um**, which are neuter.[1]

55. MODEL NOUNS

Amīcus, M., *friend.* Base: **amīc-.**				
	Singular.	*Plural.*	ENDINGS.	
			Sing.	*Plur.*
N.	amīc**us,** *a friend*	amīc**ī,** *friends*	**-us**	**-ī**
G.	amīc**ī,** *of a friend*	amīc**ōrum,** *of friends*	**-ī**	**-ōrum**
D.	amīc**ō,** *to or for a friend*	amīc**īs,** *to or for friends*	**-ō**	**-īs**
Ac.	amīc**um,** *a friend*	amīc**ōs,** *friends*	**-um**	**-ōs**
Ab.	amīc**ō,** *from,* etc., *a friend*	amīc**īs,** *from,* etc., *friends*	**-ō**	**-īs**

Bellum, N., *war.* Base: **bell-.**				
N.	bell**um,** *war*	bell**a,** *wars*	**-um**	**-a**
G.	bell**ī,** *of war*	bell**ōrum,** *of wars*	**-ī**	**-ōrum**
D.	bell**ō,** *to or for war*	bell**īs,** *to or for wars*	**-ō**	**-īs**
Ac.	bell**um,** *war*	bell**a,** *wars*	**-um**	**-a**
Ab.	bell**ō,** *from,* etc., *war*	bell**īs,** *from,* etc., *wars*	**-ō**	**-īs**

What cases of this declension have the same endings?

---

[1] A few nouns in **-us,** that rarely occur, are feminine.

2

56. Nouns in -ius and -ium have in the genitive -iī or -ī, with the accent of the nominative : fīlius, *a son,* fīliī or fīlī, *of a son;* impe′rium, *command,* impe′riī or impe′rī, *of command.*

57. VOCATIVE.—Nouns of the second declension in -us have the vocative singular in -e: amīce, *friend, O friend.* But fīlius, *son,* and proper names in -ius have the vocative singular spelled like the base, with the accent of the nominative: fī′lī, *O son,* Mercu′rī (from Mercurius), *O Mercury.*

58.   VOCABULARY

fīlia, -ae, F., *daughter.*[1]
fīlius, -ī, M., *son.*
amīcus, -ī, M., *friend.*
equus, equī, M., *horse.*
lēgātus, -ī, M., *lieutenant ambassador.*
nūntius, -ī, M., *messenger, message.*
pāgus, -ī, M., *district, canton.*

Gallī, -ōrum, M., *Gauls* (inhabitants of Gallia).
Aquītānī, -ōrum, M., the *Aquitani* (inhabitants of Aquitania).
bellum, -ī, N., *war.*
oppidum, -ī, N., *town.*
pīlum, -ī, N., *javelin.*

dō, dare,[2] dedī, datum,[2] *give.*
pūgnō, -āre, -āvī, -ātum, *fight.*

Inflect the words in the vocabulary.

TRANSLATE

59. 1. Lēgātī. 2. Equōrum, equīs. 3. Lēgātīs, nūntiīs, fīliābus. 4. Nūntiō, fīliō. 5. Per[3] nūntium. 6. In-

---

[1] Fīlia has the form fīli-ābus in the dative and ablative plural, to avoid confusion with the same cases of fīlius.
[2] Contrary to rule, -a- is short in dare and datum. The present tense is dō, dās, dat, damus, datis, dant.   [3] See 49.

ter¹ equōs. 7. Cum¹ Gallīs, cum fīliō. 8. Equī amīcōrum.
9. Pāgī, pāgōs. 10. Ad oppidum. 11. In¹ oppida.
12. In¹ oppidīs. 13. Pīlō, pīlōrum. 14. Ante¹ bellum.

60. 1. Of the son, of the daughter. 2. With² the
sons, with² the daughters. 3. For the Gauls. 4. Among²
the lieutenants. 5. For the friend of the lieutenant and
of Messala. 6. In the wars of the Germans. 7. The
javelins of the sailor.

61. DEFINITION.—An indirect object is the object to
or for which anything is given, said or done.

62. MODEL SENTENCES

1. **Lēgātus fīliae litterās dat:** *The lieutenant gives his
   daughter* (or *to his daughter*) *a
   letter.*
2. **Belgae Gallīs victōriam nūntiant:**
   *The Belgians report the victory
   to the Gauls.*

In these sentences, notice that
the indirect objects **fīliae** and
Gallīs are in the dative case.

63. RULE VI.—*The indirect object of a verb is in the dative case.*

Lēgātus

TRANSLATE

64. Amīcus lēgātō equum dat.
2. Fīliīs et fīliābus lēgātōrum equōs
dant. 3. Amīcī fīlī et fīliae³ sunt in Germāniā.⁴ 4. Messāla nūntium videt. 5. Helvētia in quattuor⁴ pāgōs est

---

¹ See 49. ² Use a Latin preposition. See 49. ³ Genitive.
⁴ Words not found in the lesson vocabularies will be found in the general vocabulary at the end of the book.

dīvīsa.   6. Persuādet amīcō.[1]   7. Persuādent amīcīs.
8. In oppidīs Celtārum sunt equī et pīla.   9. Causam bellī
nūntiāmus.

65. 1. I see the horses of the Gauls in the forest.
2. You have a letter for the son of the sailor.   3. The lieutenant subdues the Aquitani.   4. The sons of the lieutenant
report the victory to Messala.   5. They are fighting with
the forces of the Aquitani.   6. We persuade the Gauls.

LESSON VI

The Third and Fourth Conjugations: Present Indic-
ative Active.—The Ablative of Means.

66. The third conjugation includes all verbs whose
present infinitive active ends in -ĕre.

67.   MODEL VERB

Regō, *I rule.*   Present stem: regĕ-.
PRINCIPAL PARTS: regō, regere, rēxī, rēctum.

PRESENT INDICATIVE ACTIVE.	
Singular.	*Plural.*
regō, *I rule.*	regimus, *we rule.*
regis, *you rule.*	regitis, *you rule.*
regit, *he,* etc., *rules.*	regunt, *they rule.*

NOTE.—The final -e of the stem disappears before -ō in

---

[1] The verb *persuade* in Latin governs the dative of indirect object. We
should expect the accusative of the direct object, but to the Roman mind
persuādeō meant, *I give a persuasive reason* to some one.

the first person singular, becomes -u- before -nt, and -i-
before the other endings.

68. The fourth conjugation includes all verbs whose
present infinitive active ends in -īre.

69.   MODEL VERB

Audiō, *I hear.*   Present stem: **audī-**.

PRINCIPAL PARTS: audiō, audīre, audīvī, audītum.

<table>
<tr><td colspan="2" align="center">PRESENT INDICATIVE ACTIVE.</td></tr>
<tr><td align="center">Singular.</td><td align="center">Plural.</td></tr>
<tr><td>audiō, I hear.</td><td>audīmus, we hear.</td></tr>
<tr><td>audīs, you hear.</td><td>audītis, you hear.</td></tr>
<tr><td>audit, he, etc., hears.</td><td>audiunt, they hear.</td></tr>
</table>

NOTE.—In the third person plural the letter -u- stands
between the stem and the ending. How does the quantity
of -i- before the endings differ in the third and fourth conjugations?

70.   VOCABULARY

fossa, -ae, F., *ditch.*

tuba, -ae, F., *trumpet.*

gladius, -ī, M., *sword.*

mūrus, -ī, M., *wall.*

Rhēnus, -ī, M., *the Rhine.*

castra, -ōrum, N., *camp* (sing. *fortress*).

proelium, -ī, N., *battle.*

sīgnum, -ī, N., *signal, standard.*

continenter, adv., *continually.*

contendō, -tendere, -tendī, -tentum, *strive, fight, hasten.*

dīvidō, -videre, -vīsī, -vīsum, *divide, separate.*

gerō, gerere, gessī, gestum, *carry on, wage* (*war*), *do.*

incendō, -cendere, -cendī, -cēnsum, *set fire to, burn.*

incolō, -colere, -coluī, ——, *inhabit, dwell.*

regō, regere, rēxī, rēctum, *rule.*

audiō, audīre, audīvī, audītum, *hear.*

mūniō, mūnīre, mūnīvī, mūnītum, *fortify.*
veniō, venīre, vēnī, ventum, *come.*

TRANSLATE

71. 1. Proelia, proeliīs.   2. Tubae, tubā.   3. Mūrōrum.
4. Fossārum.   5. Gladium, gladiō, gladiīs.   6. Sīgnī, sīgna.
7. Ad castra.   8. In castra.   9. In castrīs.   10. Incendit,
mūnit, venit.   11. Incenditis, geritis, mūnītis.   12. Veniunt,
dīvidunt.   13. Contendimus, incolimus, venīmus.

72. 1. Of the camp.   2. Of the battle.   3. For the
camp of the troops.   4. You inhabit.   5. We fortify.
6. They inhabit the towns.   7. He hears a signal.   8. You
are coming to the town.   9. The Garonne separates the
towns.

73.   MODEL SENTENCES

1. **Sīgnum tubā dat:** *He gives the signal with a trumpet.*
2. **Lēgātus castra mūrō et fossā mūnit:** *The lieutenant
   fortifies the camp with a wall and a ditch.*

With what is the signal given?   With what is the
camp fortified?   **Tubā, mūrō** and **fossā,** in these sentences, are ablatives of *means* or *instrument.*

74. RULE VII.—*The means or instrument of an action
is expressed by the ablative without a preposition.*

TRANSLATE

75. 1. Helvētiī [1] oppida incendunt.   2. Sīgna proelī audiō.
3. Rōmānī [1] gladiīs et pīlīs pūgnant.   4. Mūrus castrōrum
ad rīpam nōn pertinet.   5. Cōpiae Rōmānōrum sunt in
castrīs.   6. Cōpiae Rōmānōrum in castra veniunt.   7. Hel-

---

[1] See general vocabulary.

vētiī proeliīs cum Germānīs[1] contendunt. 8. Belgae cum Germānīs continenter bellum gerunt. 9. Lēgātus cum pāgīs Helvētiae bellum gerit. 10. Germānī trāns Rhēnum[1] incolunt. 11. Aquītānī et Belgae et Celtae Galliam incolunt. 12. Gallōs ab Aquītānīs Garumna dīvidit. 13. Gallōs ā Belgīs Mātrona[1] et Sēquana dīvidit.[2]

76. 1. You hear the letter. 2. The trumpets, swords and standards are in the camp. 3. The sailor fights with a sword and a javelin. 4. The Germans are fortifying the town with a wall. 5. We (do) not inhabit a province of the Romans.

Tuba

LESSON VII—REVIEW

77. 1. What is meant by base (22)? 2. How is the noun declined (22)? 3. How is the present tense conjugated (35)? 4. Inflect the model words in Lessons I–VI. 5. What use has been given for each of the cases? 6. What is an indirect object (61)?

---

[1] See general vocabulary.
[2] The verb is singular, for the two subjects form one boundary.

78. Review Vocabulary [1]

amīcitia	fīlius	inter	portō
causa	gladius	per	pūgnō
cōpia	lēgātus	post	habeō
fīlia	mūrus	prope	iubeō
fossa	nūntius	propter	moneō
fuga	pāgus	trāns	moveō
littera	bellum	ā, ab	persuādeō
nauta	castra	cum	pertineō
porta	oppidum	dē	videō
prōvincia	pīlum	ē, ex	contendō
rīpa	proelium	prō	dīvidō
silva	sīgnum	sine	gerō
terra	continenter	et	incendō
tuba	nōn	cōnfīrmō	incolō
via	ad	dō	regō
victōria	ante	laudō	audiō
amīcus	circum	nūntiō	mūniō
equus	in	pācō	veniō

Mention some English words derived from the above. Thus, from **porta** we have *portal;* from **portō,** *portable,* *export, import,* etc. Consult an English dictionary that gives the Latin words from which English words come. ·

Review Sentences

79. 1. Gallia est dīvīsa. 2. Celtae amīcitiam cōnfīrmant. 3. Terra Celtārum ā Belgīs ad Aquītāniam per-

---

[1] In arranging the vocabularies, nouns are placed first, in the order of their declensions ; verbs last, in the order of their conjugations ; the other words following in the usual order of the parts of speech. Exceptions are made in some cases to emphasize related words.

tinet.   4. Aquītānī et Belgae et Celtae Galliam incolunt.
5. Belgae cum Germānīs contendunt.   6. Germānī trāns
Rhēnum incolunt.   7. Gallōs ab Aquītānīs Garumna, ā
Belgīs Mātrona et Sēquana dīvidit.   8. Helvētia in quattuor pāgōs est dīvīsa.   9. Helvētiī oppida incendunt.
10. Helvētiī proeliīs cum Germānīs contendunt.   11. Belgae cum Germānīs continenter bellum gerunt.

80.   **Sight Reading**

1. Nautās moneō.   2. Amīcīs persuādēmus.   3. Tubās
audītis.   4. Via per oppidum est longa.   5. Rhodanus[1]
prōvinciam nostram ab Helvētiīs dīvidit.   6. Gallī oppida inter Rhēnum et Rhodanum habent.   7. Helvētiī
ad rīpam Rhodanī veniunt.   8. Nūntius litterās ab prōvinciā ad Aquītāniam portat.   9. Cōpiae gladiīs et pīlīs
prope silvam contendunt.   10. Lēgātus cōpiās mūnīre[2]
castra iubet.   11. Vīdēmus sīgna Gallōrum, quī[3] in castra
veniunt.   12. Gladiī, quōs[4] Rōmānī habent, sunt parvī.

---

[1] **Rhodanus, -ī,** M., the *Rhone.*   [2] *to fortify.*   [3] *who.*   [4] *which.*

Sīgnum

LESSON VIII

Adjectives of the First and Second Declensions.
Agreement of Adjectives.

81. DECLENSION OF ADJECTIVES.—Latin adjectives have different endings to denote gender, number and case. Some are declined in the masculine like **amīcus,** in the feminine like **porta** and in the neuter like **bellum.** Such adjectives are said to be of the first and second declensions.

82. For adjectives in **-us, -a, -um,** the model is **māgnus, māgna, māgnum,** *great, large.* Base: **māgn-.** Learn the declension of this word in Appendix (11), giving the three forms of the nominative, then the three of the genitive and so on.

83.   VOCABULARY

angustus, -a, -um, *narrow.*
bonus, -a, -um, *good.*
cotīdiānus, -a, -um, *daily.*
dēnsus, -a, -um, *dense.*
multus, -a, -um, sing. *much;* pl. *many.*
reliquus, -a, -um, *remaining, the rest of.*

Adjectives given in section 24:
altus -a, -um.
lātus, -a, -um.
parvus, -a, -um.
longus, -a, -um.
māgnus, -a, -um.
ferē, adv., *almost.*

    dūcō, dūcere, dūxī, ductum, *lead.*
    praecēdō (prae + cēdō), -cēdere, -cessī, -cessum,
                (*go before*), *excel, surpass.*

Decline together **parvus gladius, bonus nauta, longum bellum.**

84.   Model Sentences

1. **Bonus amīcus habet longum pīlum:** *The good friend has a long javelin.*
2. **Parva fīlia altōs mūrōs videt:** *The little daughter sees the high walls.*
3. **Bonus nauta longa pīla habet:** *The good sailor has long javelins.*
4. **Parvī fīliī bonōs nautās vident:** *The little sons see the good sailors.*

In these sentences, notice that each adjective agrees with its noun in *gender, number* and *case;* that is, if the noun is in the masculine singular accusative, the ending of the adjective must denote the masculine singular accusative. The ending of the adjective is not always the same as that of the noun, as seen in 3, **bonus nauta,** and 4, **bonōs nautās.** **Nauta** and **nautās,** of the first declension, being masculine (by exception), require the masculine forms of the adjective, **bonus** and **bonōs,** which are of the second declension.

85. Rule VIII.—*An adjective agrees with its noun in gender, number and case.*

86. Attributive and Predicate Adjectives.— 1. **Nauta longum gladium habet:** *The sailor has a long sword.* 2. **Gladius est longus:** *The sword is long.*

When an adjective qualifies a noun directly, as **longum** in the first sentence, it is an *attributive* adjective; when it completes the predicate, as in the second sentence, it is a *predicate* adjective.

87. Possessive Pronouns.—The possessive pronouns **meus, mea, meum,** *my,* **tuus, tua, tuum,** *thy, your,*

and **suus, sua, suum,** *his, her, its, their,* are declined
like **māgnus.**[1]

Notice the four meanings of **suus.** It will not be
difficult to determine which meaning is intended in a
sentence, for **suus** as a rule refers to the subject of the
verb. Thus:

1. **Lēgātus suam fīliam videt:** *The lieutenant sees his* (*own*)
daughter.
2. **Fīlia suum amīcum videt:** *The daughter sees her* (*own*)
friend.

In the first sentence **suam** is translated *his,* for
lēgātus, to which it refers, is masculine, but it is of the
feminine gender, because it modifies **fīliam** (Rule VIII);
in the second **suum,** *her,* for **fīlia** is feminine.

There are two other possessive pronouns, which are
given in 92.

TRANSLATE

88. 1. Bonō amīcō. 2. Bonīs amīcīs. 3. Multōrum
proeliōrum. 4. Longī mūrī. 5. Multae causae. 6. Par-
vum fīlium. 7. Bonī fīlī. 8. Tua pīla. 9. Per dēnsās
silvās. 10. Mea amīcitia. 11. Trāns suam prōvinciam.
12. Cum bonō nautā.

89. 1. Silvae māgnī pāgī sunt dēnsae. 2. In dēnsā
silvā sunt multī equī. 3. Angusta via est inter silvam et
Rhodanum. 4. Rōmānī māgna castra movent. 5. Cōpiae multīs gladiīs et pīlīs pūgnant. 6. Lēgātō suam
fīliam in mātrimōnium[2] dat. 7. Helvētiī reliquōs Gallōs
praecēdunt. 8. Ferē cotīdiānīs proeliīs cum Germānīs
contendunt.

---

[1] And are used as adjectives.   [2] *in marriage.*
[3] Modifies **cotīdiānīs.**

90. 1. Daily battles.   2. The-rest-of the sailors.
3. To the narrow road.   4. Many friends praise the good
sailors.   5. He fights with a small sword and a long
javelin.   6. We establish friendship with the-rest-of the
Gauls.   7. He sees your sword in the narrow road.   8. Messala gives a long letter to his daughters.   9. They are
coming into the large town of the Belgians.   10. The
walls of the town are high.

Gladil

LESSON IX

**The Second Declension: Nouns in *-er* and *-ir*.—Ad-
jectives in *-er*.   Present Indicative of *sum*.—Predicate Noun.**

91. Some nouns of the second declension have lost
the termination **-us** in the nominative, and end in **-er**
or **-ir.**

MODEL WORDS

	Puer, M., *boy.* Base: **puer-**		**Ager, M., *field.*** Base: **agr-**		**Vir, M., *man.*** Base: **vir-**	
	SING.	PLUR.	SING.	PLUR.	SING.	PLUR.
N.	puer	puerī	ager	agrī	vir	virī
G.	puerī	puerōrum	agrī	agrōrum	virī	virōrum
D.	puerō	puerīs	agrō	agrīs	virō	virīs
Ac.	puerum	puerōs	agrum	agrōs	virum	virōs
Ab.	puerō	puerīs	agrō	agrīs	virō	virīs

How does the declension of **ager** differ from that of **puer**?

92. The termination **-us** of the masculine singular is wanting in some adjectives of the first and second declensions, and in the possessive pronouns **noster, nostra, nostrum,** *our,* and **vester, vestra, vestrum,** *your.* Learn in the Appendix (11) the declension of **līber, lībera, līberum,** *free,* and of **noster.**

93. PRESENT INDICATIVE OF **sum,** *I am.*

PRIN. PARTS: **sum, esse, fuī.** Present stem: **es-.**	
Singular.	*Plural.*
sum,[1] *I am.*	**sumus,**[1] *we are.*
es, *thou art, you are.*	**estis,** *you are.*
est, *he (she, it) is.*	**sunt,**[1] *they are.*

94. PREDICATE NOUN.—A noun in the predicate used

---

[1] In the forms **sum, sumus** and **sunt, e-** of the stem **es-** has been dropped.

with an intransitive verb or a verb in the passive voice
and meaning the same person or thing as the subject
is a predicate noun:—**Cōnsidius est lēgātus:** *Considius
is a lieutenant.* The use with a passive verb will be
llustrated in 105.

95. RULE IX.—*A predicate noun agrees with the subject in case.*

96. VOCABULARY

ager, agrī, M., *field.*	**vesper, -ī,** M., *evening.*
arma, -ōrum, N., *arms.*	**vir, -ī,** M., *man.*
frūmentum, -ī, N., *grain;*	**līber, -a, -um,** *free.*
pl. *standing grain, crops.*	**mātūrus, -a, -um,** (*early*), *ripe.*
perīculum, -ī, N., (*trial*),	**miser, -a, -um,** *wretched.*
peril, danger.	**noster, nostra, nostrum,** *our.*
puer, -ī, M., *boy.*	**vester, vestra, vestrum,** *your.*

sīgnifer, -ī, M. (**sīgnum**), *standard-bearer.*
līberī, -ōrum, M., *children* (free members of a household).
puerī, -ōrum, M., *children* [1] (with regard to age).

dēfendō, -fendere, -fendī, -fēnsum, *defend, protect.*

TRANSLATE

97. 1. Multī virī ex agrīs veniunt. 2. Nostrī[2] ad vesperum pūgnant. 3. Haeduī amīcīs Helvētiōrum agrōs
dant. 4. Perīculum sīgniferī vidēmus, et eum[3] dēfendimus.
5. Sīgniferī sīgna in castra portant. 6. Estis fīliae līberī
virī. 7. Sumus amīcī miserōrum virōrum in oppidō.
8. Vestrī līberī sunt māgnō[4] in perīculō. 9. Reliquī virī

---

[1] Words similar in meaning are called *synonyms.*
[2] **Nostrī,** the masculine plural of **noster,** is often used without a noun
with the meaning *our men, our forces.* [3] *him.*
[4] When a preposition and an adjective are used with the same noun, the
adjective often stands first.

oppidum dēfendunt. 10. Frūmenta in agrīs mātūra nōn
sunt. 11. Puerīs persuādētis. 12. Reliquīs armīs puerōs
defendit.

98. 1. The men of the small town protect the children.
2. The Haedui bring grain for our (men). 3. The long
walls extend to the fields. 4. The arms of the Romans
are swords and javelins. 5. You are a free man and the
sòn of a free man. 6. He leads the troops out of the
camp. 7. We are free. 8. Our fields are broad. 9. I am
a standard-bearer of the Celts.

Sīgnum

LESSON X

Present Indicative Passive (Conj. I–IV).—The Ablative of the Agent.

99. PASSIVE ENDINGS.—The present indicative passive is formed in general by adding to the present
stem the following personal endings [1]:

-r, *I*	**-mur**, *we*
-ris (or **-re**), *you* (*thou*)	**-minī**, *you*
-tur, *he, she, it*	**-ntur**, *they*

[1] Note these exceptions : In the first person singular **-r** is added to the
corresponding active form. In the third conjugation, final **e** of the stem
becomes **i** before **-tur, -mur, -minī**, and **u** before **-ntur**. See also 5, *a*.

100.   MODEL VERBS

PRESENT INDICATIVE PASSIVE.	
Singular.	*Plural.*
laudor, *I am praised.*	laudāmur, *we are praised.*
laudāris (-re), *you are praised.*	laudāminī, *you are praised.*
laudātur, *he*, etc., *is praised.*	laudantur, *they are praised.*
moneor, *I am advised.*	monēmur, *we are advised.*
monēris (-re), *you are advised.*	monēminī, *you are advised.*
monētur, *he*, etc., *is advised.*	monentur, *they are advised.*
regor, *I am ruled.*	regimur, *we are ruled.*
regeris (-re), *you are ruled.*	regiminī, *you are ruled.*
regitur,[1] *he*, etc., *is ruled.*	reguntur, *they are ruled.*
audior, *I am heard.*	audīmur, *we are heard.*
audīris (-re), *you are heard.*	audīminī, *you are heard.*
audītur, *he*, etc., *is heard.*	audiuntur, *they are heard.*

In the same way, conjugate the passive of **portō, videō, dūcō, mūniō.**

101.   VOCABULARY

lingua, -ae, F., (*tongue*), *language.*

nātūra, -ae, F., *nature.*

fīnitimī, -ōrum, *neighbors.*

locus, -ī, M.(pl. loca, -ōrum), *place.*

populus, -ī, M., *people, nation.*

iugum, -ī, N., *yoke, ridge.*

ūnus, -a, -um, *one.* (For declension, see App., 12.)

sub, prep with acc. and abl., *under.*[2]

---

[1] See footnote on page 32.

[2] **Sub** is used with the accusative to denote *motion* toward ; with the ablative to denote *rest* in a place.

3

appellō, -āre, -āvī, -ātum, *call* (by name), *name*.
expūgnō (ex + pūgnō, 58),[1] *capture* (a town by storm).
vāstō, -āre, -āvī, -ātum, *lay waste, devastate.*
contineō (con + teneō), -tinēre, -tinuī, -tentum,
(*hold together*), *bound, hem in, restrain.*
abdūcō (ab + dūcō, 83),[1] *lead away.*
mittō, mittere, mīsī, missum, *send.*
relinquō, relinquere, relīquī, relīctum,
leave behind; passive, *be left, remain.*

102.   TRANSLATE

1. Portāris, iubēris, dūceris. 2. Continēmur, dūcimur.
3. Dantur, mūniuntur. 4. Datur, mūnītur, iubētur.
5. Continēminī, dūciminī. 6. You are seen, sent, called.
7. He is led, ordered. 8. They are bounded. 9. They are
led away. 10. It remains.

103.   MODEL SENTENCES

1. **Nautae victōriam nūntiant:** *The sailors report the victory.*
2. **Victōria ā nautīs nūntiātur:** *The victory is reported
by sailors.*

Notice that **nautae**, the subject in the first sentence,
is in the ablative in the second. The ablative here
denotes the doer or agent of the action, and answers the
question, By whom? The ablative so used may be
called the *ablative of the agent.*

104. RULE X.—*With a passive verb the person by
whom an action is done is expressed by the ablative with
ā or ab.*

105. The passive verbs with which a predicate noun
may be used (94) are those meaning *to be named, called,
chosen, made* and the like:

---

[1] Principal parts the same as those of the simple verb.

Ariovistus ā populō Rōmānō[1] **amīcus appellātur:** *Ariovistus is called friend by the Roman people.*

TRANSLATE

106. 1. Celtae nostrā linguā Gallī appellantur. 2. Celtās[2] Gallōs[3] appellāmus. 3. Fīnitimī Helvētiōrum pācantur. 4. Sīgnum ab Helvētiīs vidētur. 5. Cōpiae Rōmānōrum sub iugum[4] ab Helvētiīs mittuntur. 6. Relinquitur ūna per Sēquanōs via. 7. Castra mūrō et fossā ā lēgātō mūniuntur. 8. Agrī Haeduōrum vāstantur, līberī abdūcuntur, oppida ab fīnitimīs expūgnantur. 9. Locī nātūrā Helvētiī continentur. 10. Amīcī appellāmur.

107. 1. The lieutenant is warned by his son. 2. Many messengers are sent to the camp. 3. The horses are led into the broad field. 4. The town is captured by the-rest-of the Belgians. 5. The towns are fortified by high walls. 6. The forest is devastated by the Aquitani. 7. The boys are named Marcus and Julius. 8. We are defended by the nature of the place.

LESSON XI

The Third Declension: Nouns in *-l, -o, -r.*—**Imperfect Indicative of** *sum.*—**The Dative of the Possessor.**

108. GENITIVE AND GENDER.—The third declension includes all words whose genitive singular ends in **-is.** The gender may be masculine, feminine or neuter.

---

[1] **Rōmānus,** when used with **populus,** follows it.
[2] Direct object.   [3] Predicate accusative.
[4] The **iugum** referred to consisted of two spears set upright in the ground with another placed across them. A conquered army was made to pass under this, to indicate submission.

109. NOMINATIVE SINGULAR.—In some words of the third declension, as in those of 110, the nominative singular has no case-ending. It may be the same as the base (22), as in **cōnsul** and **mercātor.** It may be a modified form, as in **legiō,** which drops a final **-n-** of the base, or **pater,** in which **-e-** appears before final **-r.**

110.   MODEL NOUNS

Cōnsul, M., consul. Base: cōnsul-	Legiō, F., legion. legiōn-	Mercātor, M., trader. mercātor-	Pater, M., father. patr-	END-INGS.
Singular.	*Singular.*	*Singular.*	*Singular.*	
N. cōnsul	legiō	mercātor	pater	—
G. cōnsulis	legiōnis	mercātōris	patris	-is
D. cōnsulī	legiōnī	mercātōrī	patrī	-ī
Ac. cōnsulem	legiōnem	mercātōrem	patrem	-em
Ab. cōnsule	legiōne	mercātōre	patre	-e
Plural.	*Plural.*	*Plural.*	*Plural.*	
N. cōnsulēs	legiōnēs	mercātōrēs	patrēs	-ēs
G. cōnsulum	legiōnum	mercātōrum	patrum	-um
D. cōnsulibus	legiōnibus	mercātōribus	patribus	-ibus
Ac. cōnsulēs	legiōnēs	mercātōrēs	patrēs	-ēs
Ab. cōnsulibus	legiōnibus	mercātōribus	patribus	-ībus

Māter, *mother,* and **frāter,** *brother,* are declined like **pater.**

111.   IMPERFECT INDICATIVE OF **sum.**

Singular.	*Plural.*
eram, *I was.*	**erāmus,** *we were.*
erās, *you were.*	**erātis,** *you were.*
erat, *he (she, it) was.*	**erant,** *they were.*

112.   VOCABULARY

cōnsilium, -ī, N., *plan.*

cōnsul, -is, M., *consul.*

Caesar, Caesaris, M., *Caesar.*

Pīsō, Pīsōnis, M., *Piso* (a Roman name).

homō, hominis, M., *man, human being.*[1]

legiō, -ōnis, F., *legion.*

mercātor, -ōris, M., *trader, merchant.*

multitūdō, multitūdinis, F. (multus), *great number.*

pater, patris, M., *father.*

septentriōnēs, -um, M., *the north.*

saepe, adv., *often.*

commeō, -āre, -āvī, -ātum, *go back and forth, resort.*

vergō, vergere, ——, ——, *incline, slope, lie.*

Decline prīma legiō, bonus cōnsul.

113.   TRANSLATE

1. Legiōne cōnsulis. 2. Patrēs mercātōrum. 3. Multidūdinem hominum. 4. Cum Caesare et legiōnibus. 5. Ad septentriōnēs. 6. For the merchant and the neighbors. 7. To (**ad**) the consuls, Piso and Messala. 8. By the man. 9. By the plan.

114.   MODEL SENTENCES

1. **Cōnsul multās legiōnēs habet:** *The consul has many legions.*

2. **Cōnsulī multae legiōnēs sunt:** *The consul has (to the consul there are) many legions.*

Both sentences are to be translated the same way. Possession may be expressed by **habeō** (*have*), as in sentence 1, or by **sum** with a dative, as in sentence 2. If **sum** is used, the possessor is in the dative (**cōnsulī**) and the thing possessed in the nominative (**legiōnēs**). The

---

[1] Synonyms: **homō** means *man* distinguished from lower animals; **vir** (91) means *man* distinguished from woman.

dative so used is called the *dative of the possessor* and is
to be translated as the subject of *have* in English.

115. RULE XI.—*The dative of the possessor is used
with the verb* **sum.**

TRANSLATE

116. 1. Mārcus Messāla et Marcus Pīsō erant cōnsulēs.[1]
2. Pater Casticī erat amīcus populī Rōmānī.   3. Ad Belgās

Legiōnārius
(Soldier of a legion)

mercātōrēs nōn saepe commeant.
4. Gallia vergit ad septentriōnēs.
5. Multitūdō hominum erat in Helvētiā.   6. Ūna legiō[2] erat in Galliā.
7. Caesar in Galliam contendit et ad
Genāvam pervenit.[3]   8. Ūnā legiōne[4]
Caesar longum mūrum et fossam
perdūcit.[4]   9. Cōnsilium erat Helvētiīs.   10. Meō frātrī sunt multī equī.
11. Mercātōribus erant Rōmāna arma.

117. 1. Caesar was commander-in-
chief[6] of many legions.   2. Caesar had
many legions.   3. A great number
of men capture the towns.   4. The
towns are captured by a great number of men.   5. The province is sub-

dued by the consul.   6. We were traders in Aquitania.
7. The brothers of the consul have many plans.[7]   8. You
were the standard-bearers of the Roman legions.

---

[1] Rome for about five centuries B.C. was a republic.   There were two
presidents, called consuls, elected annually.

[2] The Roman army was divided into legions.   A legion varied in number
of men, but in Caesar's time consisted of about 3,600.

[3] **pervenit** = **per** + **venit,** *comes through, arrives.*

[4] **perdūcit** = **per** + **dūcit,** *leads through ;* with **fossam** and **mūrum** it
may be translated *constructs.*   [5] See 74.   [6] **imperātor.**   [7] Translate
sentence 7 in two ways.

LESSON XII

**Third Declension: Neuter Nouns in -*men* and -*us*.—
Imperfect Indicative (Conj. I).**

118. Genitive and Gender.—Before declining a
noun, note carefully its *genitive* and *gender*. The genitive is important because it shows the base (22). The
gender should be noted because a neuter noun requires
different endings from a masculine or feminine in the
accusative singular, and the nominative and accusative
plural.

119.   Model Nouns

Flūmen, n., *river.* Base: **flūmin-**	Tempus, n., *time.* tempor-	Opus, n., *work.* oper-	Endings.
Singular.	*Singular.*	*Singular.*	
N. flūmen	tempus	opus	—
G. flūminis	temporis	operis	-is
D. flūminī	temporī	operī	-ī
Ac. flūmen	tempus	opus	—
Ab. flūmine	tempore	opere	-e
Plural.	*Plural.*	*Plural.*	
N. flūmina	tempora	opera	-a
G. flūminum	temporum	operum	-um
D. flūminibus	temporibus	operibus	-ibus
Ac. flūmina	tempora	opera	-a
Ab. flūminibus	temporibus	operibus	-ibus

120. Formation of the Imperfect Indicative.—
The imperfect tense of the indicative is formed by add-

ing to the present stem a *tense-sign* and the personal endings. The sign of the imperfect tense is -ba-. The personal endings are those given in sections 35 and 99, except that -m is used instead of -ō in the first person singular active: Active, **laudā-ba-m**; passive, **laudā-ba-r.**

121. THE IMPERFECT INDICATIVE.

ACTIVE.		PASSIVE.	
I was praising, I praised.		*I was praised.*	
laudābam	laudābāmus	laudābar	laudābāmur
laudābās	laudābātis	laudābāris (-re)	laudābāminī
laudābat	laudābant	laudābātur	laudābantur

Conjugate the imperfect of **dō,**[1] **portō** and **nūntiō.**

122. USE OF THE IMPERFECT TENSE.—The imperfect indicative represents action as going on in past time: *Caesar was praising,* or *Caesar praised* (**laudābat**) *his troops.* It may express repeated or customary action: *Caesar kept praising,* or *used to praise* (**laudābat**) *his troops.* It is also used in descriptions: **Flūmen erat inter Belgās et Celtās.** *A river was between the Belgians and the Celts.* (See also 176.)

123. VOCABULARY

annus, -ī, M., *year.*
flūmen, flūminis, N., *river.*
nōmen, nōminis, N., *name.*
genus, generis, N.. *race, tribe.*
opus, operis, N., *work, fortification.*

tempus, temporis, N., *time.*
altitūdō, -inis, F. (altus), *height, depth.*
coniūrātiō, -ōnis, F., *conspiracy.*
celeriter, adv., *quickly.*

---

[1] For the quantity of -a- in the present stem of **dō,** see footnote 2, page 18.

ēnūntiō (**ē** + **nūntiō**, 38), (*speak out*), *disclose, report.*
vocō, -āre, -āvī, -ātum, *call.*
revocō (**re** + **vocō**), *call back, recall.*

TRANSLATE

124. 1. Revocābāmus, ēnūntiābāmus. 2. Ēnūntiābātis, pācābant. 3. Commeābam. 4. Portābātur, dabantur. 5. Portābās, portābāris. 6. Puerum appellābat. 7. Nōmen oppidī erat Genāva. 8. Altitūdō flūminis est parva. 9. Helvētiī cum fīnitimīs amīcitiam cōnfīrmābant. 10. Ariovistus amīcus populī Rōmānī appellābātur. 11. Propter tempus annī nōn pūgnābant. 12. Nostrī ab opere revocābantur. 13. Multa genera hominum erant in Galliā. 14. Helvētiī oppidum celeriter expūgnābant. 15. Coniūrātiōnem Helvētiīs ēnūntiābat. 16. Helvētia continētur flūmine Rhēnō, quī¹ agrum Helvētium² ā Germānīs dīvidit.

125. 1. The name of the tribe. 2. By the conspiracy. 3. We were recalled. 4. You (pl.) were called. 5. The boys were carrying trumpets and swords. 6. The grain was not given. 7. The Seine and Marne were rivers of Gaul. 8. Gaul extends from³ the Rhone river. 9. The camp is fortified by the work of the troops. 10. The towns were quickly stormed. 11. The lieutenants recalled our men from³ the work. 12. The conspiracy was reported to the Celts. 13. Marcus and Titus were Roman names.

LESSON XIII—REVIEW

126. 1. Inflect the model words in Lessons VIII–XII. 2. Conjugate the present and imperfect indicative of **sum.** 3. How do adjectives agree (85)? 4. After

---

¹ *which.* ² **Helvētius** (or **Helvēticus**), **-a, -um,** proper adj., *Helvetian ;* **Helvētiī, -ōrum,** the *Helvetii ;* **Helvētia, -ae,** *Helvetia* (the country).
³ Use a Latin preposition.

what verbs is a predicate noun used (94, 105)? 5.
How is possession expressed in Latin (114)?

127. Review Vocabulary

lingua	mercātor	dēnsus	ferē
nātūra	pater	lātus	saepe
annus	altitūdō	longus	sub
fīnitimī	coniūrātiō	māgnus	appellō
locus	homō	mātūrus	commeō
populus	legiō	multus	ēnūntiō
ager	multitūdō	parvus	expūgnō
puer	septentriōnēs	reliquus	vocō
sīgnifer	flūmen	ūnus	revocō
vesper	nōmen	līber	vāstō
vir	genus	miser	contineō
arma	opus	meus	dūcō
cōnsilium	tempus	tuus	abdūcō
frūmentum	altus	suus	dēfendō
iugum	angustus	noster	mittō
perīculum	bonus	vester	praecēdō
cōnsul	cotīdiānus	celeriter	relinquō
			vergō

Mention English derivatives.

128. Review Sentences

1. Angusta via est inter silvam et Rhodanum.
2. Helvētiī reliquōs Gallōs praecēdunt. 3. Ferē cotīdiānīs proeliīs cum Germānīs contendunt. 4. Celtae nostrā
linguā Gallī appellantur. 5. Sīgnum ab Helvētiīs vidētur.
6. Cōpiae Rōmānōrum sub iugum ab Helvētiīs mittuntur. 7. Relinquitur ūna per Sēquanōs via. 8. Agrī Haeduōrum vāstantur, līberī abdūcuntur, oppida ab Helvētiīs
expūgnantur. 9. Undique[1] locī nātūrā Helvētiī conti-

---

[1] **undique,** adv., *on all sides.*

nentur. 10. Mārcus Messāla et Mārcus Pīsō erant cōnsulēs. 11. Pater Casticī erat amīcus populī Rōmānī.
12. Ad Belgās mercātōrēs nōn saepe commeant. 13. Gallia
vergit ad septentriōnēs. 14. Ūna legiō erat in Galliā.
15. Caesar in Galliam contendit et ad Genāvam pervenit.
16. Legiōne Caesar longum mūrum et fossam perdūcit.
17. Frūmenta in agrīs mātūra non erant.

129. **Sight Reading**

1. Legiōnēs reliqua loca vāstābant. 2. Locus erat
idōneus[1] castrīs. 3. Flūmen est nōn longum. 4. Multa
et[2] longa flūmina sunt in Galliā. 5. Puerī erant in perīculō. 6. Nostrae legiōnēs erant in armīs extrā[3] castra.
7. Reliquī Gallī ab Helvētiīs laudābantur. 8. Helvētiī
Rōmānās cōpiās sub iugum mittunt. 9. Coniūrātiōnem
Gallōrum mercātōrēs, quī ā prōvinciā Rōmānā veniunt,
ēnūntiant. 10. Segusiāvī[4] sunt extrā prōvinciam trāns
Rhodanum prīmī.[5]

Pīlum

LESSON XIV

**Imperfect Indicative (Conj. II-IV).—Apposition.—
Review of Nominative Case.**

130. The second conjugation forms the imperfect
like the first (120): **monē-ba-m.**

---

[1] **idōneus, -a, -um,** *suitable.* [2] Do not translate **et.** [3] **extrā,** prep.
with acc., *outside of.* [4] A tribe on the west side of the Rhone.
[5] **prīmus, -a, -um,** *first.*

ACTIVE. *I was advising, I advised.*		PASSIVE. *I was advised.*	
monēbam	monēbāmus	monēbar	monēbāmur
monēbās	monēbātis	monēbāris (-re)	monēbāminī
monēbat	monēbant	monēbātur	monēbantur

131. The third conjugation lengthens the final **-e-** of the stem, before the tense-sign: **regē-ba-m.**

ACTIVE. *I was ruling, I ruled.*		PASSIVE. *I was ruled.*	
regēbam	regēbāmus	regēbar	regēbāmur
regēbās	regēbātis	regēbāris (-re)	regēbāminī
regēbat	regēbant	regēbātur	regēbantur

132. The fourth conjugation inserts **-ē-** before the tense-sign, and shortens the final **-ī-** of the stem (69): **audiē-ba-m.**

ACTIVE. *I was hearing, I heard.*		PASSIVE. *I was heard.*	
audiēbam	audiēbāmus	audiēbar	audiēbāmur
audiēbās	audiēbātis	audiēbāris (-re)	audiēbāminī
audiēbat	audiēbant	audiēbātur	audiēbantur

Conjugate the imperfect of **habeō** (45), **mittō** (110), **mūniō** (70).

133. DEFINITION.—A noun added to another noun or pronoun to explain or describe it, and meaning the same person or thing, is called an *appositive.*

134.   MODEL SENTENCES

1. **Cassius cōnsul cum Gallīs contendēbat:** *Cassius, the consul, was fighting with the Gauls.*

2. **Puerī Cassium cōnsulem vidēbant:** *The children saw Cassius, the consul.*

3. **Patrem Cassī cōnsulis vidēbant:** *They saw the father of Cassius, the consul.*

In these sentences, **cōnsul** is used as an appositive to explain **Cassius** and is put in the same case.

135. RULE XII.—*A noun in apposition with another or a pronoun agrees with it in case.*

NOTE.—Later it will be seen that a phrase or a clause as well as a single word may be in apposition with a noun or a pronoun.

136. VOCABULARY

concilium, -ī, N., *council, assembly.*

hīberna, -ōrum, N., *winter-quarters.*

pābulum, -ī, N., *fodder.*

explōrātor, -tōris, M., *scout.*

imperātor, -tōris, M., *commander-in-chief.*

decimus, -a, -um, *tenth.*

perītus, -a, -um, *experienced, skilful.*

satis, adv., *sufficiently, enough*

semper, adv., *always.*

hiemō, -āre, -āvī, -ātum, *pass the winter.*

dīmittō (dī + mittō, 101), *send away, dismiss.*

ēdūcō (ē + dūcō, 83), *lead out.*

suppetō (sub + petō), -petere, -petīvī, -petītum, *be on hand.*

TRANSLATE

137. 1. Veniēbant, incendēbant, incolēbant. 2. Vidēbāmus, dūcēbātis, dēfendēbās. 3. Iubēbātur. vidēbāmur, dēfendēbāminī. 4. Caesar imperātor in Galliam contendēbat. 5. Legiō quam¹ habēbat erat decima. 6. Relinquē-

---

¹ *which.*

bātur ūna per Sēquanōs via. 7. Helvētiī agrōs Haeduōrum, amīcōrum populi Rōmānī, vāstābant. 8. Castra
semper mūniēbantur. 9. Trēs¹ legiōnēs quae² circum
Aquilēiam hiemābant, ex hībernīs ēdūcit. 10. Caesar
suōs³ ā proeliō continēbat. 11. Pābulī satis māgna cōpia nōn suppetēbat. 12. Celeriter concilium dīmittēbātur.
13. Pūblius Cōnsidius, quī perītus habēbātur,⁴ cum explōrātōribus mittēbātur.

138. 1. I was led, you were seen, he was sent. 2. We
contended, you (pl.) inhabited. 3. The town was fortified.
4. They moved the camp from that⁵ place. 5. Caesar sent
Considius, the lieutenant, with scouts. 6. He quickly
dismissed the council. 7. Caesar's forces were restrained
from battle. 8. Three legions were led out of winter-
quarters. 9. They were reporting the victory to the Belgians, a nation of Gaul.

139.   Review of the Nominative Case

The nominative case may be used as follows:

1. As the subject of a finite verb (26).

2. In the predicate with—

   (a) certain intransitive verbs meaning *be,
   become, seem,* etc. (94.)

   (b) certain passive verbs meaning *be made, be
   called, chosen, named,* etc. (105.)

3. In apposition with another nominative. (135.)

ILLUSTRATIONS:

   1. **Caesar erat imperātor.**

   2. **Caesar appellābātur imperātor.**

   3. **Caesar imperātor ab amīcīs laudābātur.**

---

¹ *three.*   ² *which.*   ³ Supply **mīlites.**   ⁴ *was held,* in the sense
of *was considered.*   ⁵ **eō.**

LESSON XV

Third Declension (continued).—The Ablative of Specification.

140. NOMINATIVE SINGULAR.—Some nouns of the third declension form the nominative singular by adding -s to the base. The base may end in -b, -p, -d, -t, -c or -g. Bases ending in -d or -t drop these letters in the nominative: **lapis,** *stone,* for **lapids,** from base **lapid-;** **mīles,** *soldier,* for **mīlits,** from base **mīlit-.** Bases in -c or -g have -x in the nominative, for **cs** and **gs = x** (2, *c*): **dux,** *leader,* for **ducs,** from base **duc-; rēx,** *king,* for **rēgs,** from base **rēg-.**

141. Learn the declension of **lēx, mīles, prīnceps, cīvitās** and **caput,** in Appendix (4, 5).

142. VOCABULARY

numerus, -ī, M., *number.*	**Dumnorīx, -īgis,** M., *Dumno-*
auctōritās, -tātis, F., *influ-*	*rix.*
ence.	**Orgetorīx, -īgis,** M., *Orgetorix.*
cīvitās, -tātis, F., *state, tribe.*	**virtūs -tūtis,** F. (**vir**), (*manli-*
lēx, lēgis, F., *law.*	*ness*), *virtue, valor.*
pāx, pācis, F., *peace.*	**caput, capitis,** N., *head.*
mīles, mīlitis, M., *soldier.*	**apud,** prep. with acc., *among.*
prīnceps, prīncipis, M., *chief.*	

convocō (con + vocō 123), *call together.*

143. MODEL SENTENCE

Gallī et Belgae linguā et lēgibus differunt [1]: *The Gauls and Belgians differ in language and laws.*

---

[1] From **differō,** *differ.*

In what *respect* do the Gauls and Belgians differ? **Linguā** and **lēgibus**, which answer this question, are called *ablatives of specification*.

144. RULE XIII.—*The ablative of specification is used to denote that in respect to which anything is true.*

TRANSLATE

145. 1. Apud Helvētiōs erat prīnceps, Orgetorīx nōmine. 2. Auctōritās Orgetorīgis erat māgna. 3. Ad cīvitātēs mittēbātur. 4. Cum cīvitātibus pācem et amīcitiam cōnfīrmābat. 5. Mīlitum māgnum numerum habēbat. 6. Mīlitēs conveniēbant.[1] 7. Lēgātōs ad Dumnorīgem, Haeduum, mittēbant. 8. Caesar prīncipēs Haeduōrum, quōrum[2] māgnam cōpiam[3] in castrīs habēbat, convocābat. 9. Numerus capitum erat decem. 10. Vidēmus capita equōrum. 11. Helvētiī reliquōs Gallōs virtūte praecēdunt. 12. Pīlum et gladius erant mīlitī.

146. 1. The chiefs of the Haedui were called together by Caesar. 2. Ambassadors were sent to Dumnorix, the Haeduan. 3. They send Orgetorix to the tribes. 4. Peace was established with the-rest-of the tribes. 5. Many soldiers came from the province. 6. Dumnorix surpassed many men in influence among the Haedui. 7. The Romans did not surpass the Helvetians in number of soldiers.

---

[1] **conveniēbant** = con (*together*) + **veniēbant**.
[2] *of whom.*   [3] *number.*

LESSON XVI

Future Tense (Conj. I, II).—*Sum* : Future Tense.

147. FORMATION OF THE FUTURE INDICATIVE.—The future tense of the first and second conjugations is formed by adding to the present stem the tense-sign **bi-** and the personal endings (35, 99). In the first person singular, **-i-** of the tense-sign disappears before the ending **-ō**; in the third person plural it becomes **-u-**; and in the second person singular passive it becomes **-e-**.

148.
THE FUTURE INDICATIVE.

ACTIVE.		PASSIVE.	
I shall [1] *praise.*		*I shall be praised.*	
laudābō	laudābimus	laudābor	laudābimur
laudābis	laudābitis	laudāberis (-re)	laudābiminī
laudābit	laudābunt	laudābitur	laudābuntur

149.

ACTIVE.		PASSIVE.	
I shall advise.		*I shall be advised.*	
monēbō	monēbimus	monēbor	monēbimur
monēbis	monēbitis	monēberis (-re)	monēbiminī
monēbit	monēbunt	monēbitur	monēbuntur

Conjugate the future of **dō, imperō, portō** and **habeō.**

---

[1] I, or we, *shall* praise ; you, he, or they, *will* praise.

4

150.   Future Tense of **sum.**

erō, *I shall be.*	erimus, *we shall be.*
eris, *you will be.*	eritis, *you will be.*
erit, *he (she, it) will be.*	erunt, *they will be.*

151.   VOCABULARY

memoria, -ae, F., *memory.*
dux, ducis, M., *leader, guide.*
rēx, rēgis, M., *king.*
eques, equitis, M., *horseman.*
obses, obsidis, M. F., *hostage.*[1]

pedes, peditis, M., *foot-soldier.*
salūs, salūtis, F., *safety.*
fortiter, adv., *bravely.*
atque, conj., *and, and also.*[2]
sed, conj., *but.*

teneō, -ēre, -uī, tentum, *hold.*
memoriā teneō, (*hold in memory*), *remember.*

TRANSLATE

152.   1. Nūntiābunt.   2. Iubēbis.   3. Vocābitis, vocā-biminī.   4. Vidēbimus, vidēbimur.   5. Castra movēbuntur. 6. Equitēs proeliīs cum Gallīs fortiter pūgnābunt.   7. Obsidēs Ariovistō, rēgī Germānōrum, dabuntur.   8. Caesar equōs peditibus dabit.   9. Ā Rōmānīs virtūs Helvētiōrum memoriā tenēbitur.   10. Cassius bellō cum Helvētiīs dux Rōmānōrum erit.   11. Explōrātōrēs erunt māgnō in perī-culō.   12. Populus Rōmānus Ariovistum rēgem atque amīcum appellābit.   13. Cōnsilia bellī ā ducibus nōn ēnūntiābuntur.

153.   1. I shall see, give, report.   2. You will call, carry, have.   3. They will be seen.   4. The victory will be

---

[1] A hostage was a person given by one nation to another, to be held as a pledge of good faith.
[2] When **atque** connects two words, it emphasizes the second.

reported. 5. You will be considered[1] skilful. 6. The Helvetians will not give hostages to the Romans. 7. The leaders will remember the first victory of our horsemen. 8. The valor of the Gauls will be praised, but they will be subdued by the Roman leader. 9. The hostages are seeking[2] safety by flight, and will be in the forest.

Eques

LESSON XVII

Third Declension (continued).—The Ablative of Time.

154. Special Singular Endings.—Some nouns of the third declension have in the singular the following endings:

Acc. -im or -em (nāvis, puppis, sēmentis, turris).

Abl. -ī or -e (avis, cīvis, classis, collis, fīnis, īgnis, nāvis, orbis, puppis, sēmentis, turris).

Abl. ī (neuters in -e, -al or -ar).

155. Special Plural Endings.—The following nouns

---

[1] **habeo.** See 137, 13.   [2] **petunt.**

have -ium in the genitive plural, and -ēs or -īs in the accusative plural:

1. Nouns in -is or -ēs, having the same number of syllables in the nominative and genitive singular.[1]

2. Most nouns in -ns or -rs.

3. Monosyllables in -s or -x, following a consonant. Neuters in -e, -al or -ar have -ium in the genitive plural and -ia in the nominative and accusative plural.

156. Learn the declension of **hostis, nāvis, mōns, nox, cubīle** and **animal** in Appendix (6, 7).

157.   **VOCABULARY**

hōra, -ae, F., *hour*.

vigilia, -ae, F., *watch* (a fourth of the night).

aestās, -tātis, F., *summer*.

animal, -is, N., *animal*.

Arar, Araris (acc. -im; abl. -ī), M., the *Saone* (a river of Gaul).

fīnis, -is, M., *end, limit;* pl. *territory*.

hostis, -is, M., *enemy*.

nāvis, -is, F., *ship*.

mare, maris, N., *sea*.

mōns, montis, M., *mountain*.

pōns, pontis, M., *bridge*.

pars, partis, F., *part, side, direction*.

nox, noctis, F., *night*.

duo, duae, duo, *two*. (For declension see App., 14.)

proximus, -a, -um, *nearest, next*.

tertius, -a, -um, *third*.

quārtus, -a, -um, *fourth*.

īnfluō (in + fluō, *flow*), -fluere, -fluxī, -fluxum, *flow into*.

158.   MODEL SENTENCES

1. **Prīmā hōrā castra movēbantur:** *At the first hour the camp was moved.*

---

[1] Nouns having the same number of syllables in the nominative and genitive singular are called *parisyllabic*.

2. **Ūnā aestāte Caesar duo bella gerēbat:** *Caesar carried on two wars in one summer.*

The ablatives **hōrā** and **aestāte** denote *time*. The former answers the question *When?*, the latter, the question *Within what time?*

159. RULE XIV.—*The ablative is used to denote time when or within which.*

160. TRANSLATE

1. Gallia est dīvīsa in partēs trēs. 2. Ūnam partem incolunt Belgae. 3. Helvētiī in Germānōrum fīnibus bellum gerunt. 4. Ūnā ex[1] parte Helvetia flūmine Rhēnō continētur; alterā[2] ex[1] parte monte Iūrā. 5. Fīnēs Helvētiōrum sunt angustī. 6. Ex Genāvā pōns ad Helvētiōs pertinet. 7. Pontem, quī erat ad Genāvam, Caesar iubet rescindī.[3] 8. Flūmen est Arar, quod[4] per fīnēs Haeduōrum et Sēquanōrum in Rhodanum īnfluit. 9. Quārtā horā cum prīmīs nāvibus Britanniam attigit.[5] 10. Tertiā vigiliā legiōnēs trēs ē castrīs ēdūcēbat. 11. Hostēs[6] ad flūmen Axonam contendēbant, quod erat post nostra castra. 12. Proximā nocte castra movēbō. 13. Mare altīs montibus continēbātur.

161. 1. The enemy had winter-quarters near[7] the Saone river. 2. The war was carried on with[8] a great number of soldiers. 3. The soldiers are coming through the territory of the Sequani. 4. (At) that[9] time Dumnorix was chief of the tribe. 5. The leaders of the enemy heard the plan of the messenger in the first watch. 6. Many ani-

---

[1] *on.* See page 31, footnote 4. [2] *another.* [3] *to be destroyed.*
[4] *which.* [5] *reached.* [6] The plural **hostēs** is to be translated *enemy*.
[7] **prope** (49). [8] See 74. [9] **eō.**

mals will be in the fields in the summer. 7. The enemy's horsemen will have[1] good horses. 8. The night is divided into watches.

Nāvis

LESSON XVIII

Gender in the Third Declension. — Future Tense (Conj. III, IV).

162. GENDER.—The gender of nouns o the third declension may be determined partly by the general rules (12). The following special rules will be helpful, though there are important exceptions to each:

1. Masculine: Nouns in -ō, -or, -ōs, -er, -ĕs (gen. -idis, -itis).

2. Feminine: Nouns in -ās, -ēs (gen. -is), -is, -ūs, (gen. -ūdis, -ūtis), -x, -s (following a consonant), -dō, -gō, -iō.

3. Neuters: Nouns in a, c, e, l, n, t, ar, ur, us (gen. -eris, -oris).

---

[1] See 115.

163. In the future of verbs of the third and fourth conjugations, the tense-sign **-bi-** (147) is not found. The tenses are formed by adding the personal endings to a modified form of the present stem. The ending of the first person singular in the active voice is **-m.**

THE FUTURE INDICATIVE.

164.   THIRD CONJUGATION.

ACTIVE.		PASSIVE.	
I shall rule.		*I shall be ruled.*	
regam	regēmus	regar	regēmur
regēs	regētis	regēris (-re)	regēminī
reget	regent	regētur	regentur

165.   FOURTH CONJUGATION.

ACTIVE.		PASSIVE.	
I *shall hear.*		*I shall be heard.*	
audiam	audiēmus	audiar	audiēmur
audiēs	audiētis	audiēris (-re)	audiēminī
audiet	audient	audiētur	audientur

Conjugate the future of **dūcō** and **mūniō.**

166.   VOCABULARY

auxilium, -ī, N., *aid;* pl. *auxiliary forces.*
Ōceanus, -ī, M., *ocean.*
vīcus, -ī, M., *village.*

collis, -is, M., *hill.*
ubi, adv., *where, when.*
quod, conj., *because.*

petō, petere, petīvī, petītum, *seek, ask.*
pōnō, pōnere, posuī, positum, *place, pitch (a camp).*

TRANSLATE

167. 1. Incolēmus, veniēmus, dīvidēmus.   2. Contendē-
tis, mittēminī, defendēminī.   3. Mūniam, veniēs, dūcet.
4. Vocābor, vidēbor, dēfendar.   5. Nocte ad oppidum veniet.
6. Dux legiōnēs et auxilia ad collem mittet.   7. Locus ab
mīlitibus, quī ex prōvinciā veniunt, mūniētur.   8. Tribus[1]
annīs vīcī et oppida ab Helvētiīs incendentur.   9. Quod
perīculum māgnum est, hostēs fugā salūtem petent.
10. Collis, ubi castra ponentur, nōn est altus.   11. Bellum in Galliā gerētur, quod Helvētiī sunt hostēs populī
Rōmānī.   12. Aquītānia ad eam[2] partem Ōceanī, quae est
ad Hispāniam pertinet.

168. 1. You (sing.) will defend, be defended.   2. You
(pl.) will lead, be led.   3. We shall fortify, contend, lead.
4. They will be led away.   5. The wars will be carried on.
6. The fields of the Belgians will be inhabited.   7. Caesar
will give a part of the village to the Gauls.   8. The auxiliary forces will be in the winter-quarters across the
Rhone, where (there) is much grain.   9. The Sequani
will seek aid from[3] Caesar, because Ariovistus, the king
of the Germans, is in their territory.   10. We shall persuade the soldiers.

LESSON XIX—REVIEW

169. 1. Inflect the model words in Lessons XIV–XVIII.
2. How is the imperfect tense formed (120)?   3. How
does the future of the first and second conjugations
differ from the future of the third and fourth (163)?
4. What nouns have **-ium** in the genitive plural (155)?

---

[1] *three.*   [2] *that.*   [3] **ā.**

5. What is the difference between a predicate noun and a noun in apposition ?

170.   Review Vocabulary

hōra	aestās	collis	semper
memoria	auctōritās	fīnis	apud
vigilia	cīvitās	hostis	atque
auxilium	imperātor	nāvis	quod
concilium	mōns	animal	sed
hīberna	pars	caput	ubi
numerus	pōns	mare	convocō
pābulum	prīnceps	decimus	hiemō
vīcus	salūs	perītus	teneō
dux	virtūs	proximus	dīmittō
lēx	eques	quārtus	ēdūcō
nox	mīles	tertius	īnfluō
pāx	obses	fortiter	petō
rēx	pedes	satis	suppetō
			pōnō

171.   Review Sentences

1. Trēs legiōnēs, quae [1] circum Aquilēiam hiemābant, ex hībernīs ēdūcit. 2. Caesar suōs ā proeliō continēbat. 3. Pābulī satis māgna cōpia nōn suppetēbat. 4. Pūblius Cōnsidius, quī [2] perītus habēbātur, cum explōrātōribus mittēbātur. 5. Cum cīvitātibus pācem et amīcitiam Orgetorīx cōnfīrmābat. 6. Caesar prīncipēs Haeduōrum, quōrum [3] māgnam cōpiam in castrīs habēbat, convocat. 7. Helvētiī reliquōs Gallōs virtūte praecēdunt. 8. Gallia est dīvīsa in partēs trēs. 9. Ūnam partem incolunt Belgae. 10. Helvētiī in Germānōrum fīnibus bellum gerunt. 11. Ūnā ex parte Helvētia flūmine Rhēnō continētur, alterā ex parte monte Iūrā. 12. Ex Genāvā pōns ad Helvētiōs

---

[1] *which.*   [2] *who.*   [3] *of whom.*

pertinet. 13. Pontem, quī[1] erat ad Genāvam, Caesar iubet rescindī. 14. Flūmen est Arar, quod[1] per fīnēs Haeduōrum et Sēquanōrum in Rhodanum īnfluit. 15. Helvētiī legātōs ad Dumnorīgem Haeduum mittunt.

172.   Sight Reading

1. Ūnam partem Galliae Aquītānī incolunt. 2. Ūna pars continētur Garumnā flūmine, Ōceanō, fīnibus Belgārum. 3. Belgae pertinent ad īnferiōrem[2] partem flūminis Rhēnī. 4. Aquītānia ā Garumnā flūmine ad Pȳrēnaeōs montēs et ad eam partem Ōceanī quae[1] est ad Hispāniam pertinet. 5. Dumnorīx Helvētiīs erit amīcus, quod ex eā[3] cīvitāte Orgetorīgis fīliam in mātrimōnium dūcet. 6. Is[4] pāgus appellābātur Tigurīnus. 7. Cīvitās Helvētia in quattuor pāgōs dīvīsa est. 8. Allobrogēs, quī[5] trāns Rhodanum vīcōs habēbant, ad Caesarem veniunt. 9. Legiōne, quam[1] habet, atque mīlitibus, quī[5] ex prōvinciā convenient, ā Genāvā ad montem Iūram, quī[1] fīnēs Sēquanōrum ab Helvētiīs dīvidit, Caesar mūrum et fossam perdūcet. 10. Trēs cōpiārum partēs Helvētiī trāns flūmen dūcēbant.

LESSON XX

The Perfect Indicative Active.—Irregular Adjectives of the First and Second Declension.

173. ENDINGS OF THE PERFECT INDICATIVE ACTIVE. —The *perfect stem* is found by dropping -ī of the perfect indicative active, the third of the principal parts (17): **laudāv-ī, monu-ī, rēx-ī, audīv-ī.** The perfect indicative active is conjugated by adding to the perfect stem the following endings:

---

[1] *which.*   [2] *lower.*   [3] *that.*   [4] *this.*   [5] *who.*

Singular.	Plural.
-ī, *I*	-imus, *we*
-istī, *you*	-istis, *you*
-it, *he*, etc.	-ērunt, or -ēre, *they*

174.   THE PERFECT INDICATIVE ACTIVE.

I have praised, or *I praised*.

laudāvī	laudāvimus
laudāvistī	laudāvistis
laudāvit	laudāvērunt (-ēre)

I have advised, or *I advised*.

monuī	monuimus
monuistī	monuistis
monuit	monuērunt (-ēre)

I have ruled, or *I ruled*.

rēxī	rēximus
rēxistī	rēxistis
rēxit	rēxērunt (-ēre)

I have heard, or *I heard*.

audīvī	audīvimus
audīvistī	audīvistis
audīvit	audīvērunt (-ēre)

175.   PERFECT INDICATIVE OF **sum.**

fuī, *I have been, was.*	fuimus, *we have been, were.*
fuistī, *you have been, were.*	fuistis, *you have been, were.*
fuit, *he has been, was.*	fuērunt (-ēre), *they have been, were.*

Conjugate the perfect indicative active of **dō, persuādeō, dīvidō, mūniō** and **veniō.**

176.   MODEL SENTENCES

1. **Rhēnum nōn vīdimus:** *We have not seen the Rhine.*
2. **Haeduī, quod Helvētiī agrōs vāstābant, lēgātōs ad Caesarem mīsērunt:** *The Haedui sent ambassadors to Caesar, because the Helvetii were devastating (their) fields.*

The Latin perfect may be translated in two ways: (1) It may be equivalent to the English present perfect (with *have*), and may be called the *present perfect:* **vīdimus,** sentence 1. (2) It is more frequently equivalent to the English past tense, and may be called the *historical perfect:* **mīsērunt,** sentence 2.

The historical perfect is used to state the main events of the past; the imperfect frequently states subordinate events, or what was true when the main events occurred: **Caesar in castra vēnit; litterās portābat.** *Caesar came into the camp;* (at the time when he came) *he was carrying a letter.*

177. IRREGULAR ADJECTIVES.—Nine adjectives have the ending **-īus** (for **-ī, -ae, -ī**) in the genitive singular, and **-ī** (for **-ō, -ae, -ō**) in the dative singular of all genders. They are:

alius, -a, -ud, *another, other.*	**sōlus, -a, -um,** *alone, only.*
alter, -era, -erum, *the other.*	**tōtus, -ā, -um,** *whole.*
neuter, -tra, -trum, *neither.*	**ūllus, -a, -um,** *any.*
nūllus, -a, -um, *not any, no.*	**ūnus, -a, -um,** *one, alone.*
uter, -tra, -trum, *which (of two) ?*	

178. In the other cases of the singular and in the plural these words are declined [1] like **māgnus, līber** or **noster,** except **alius,** which is as follows:

---

[1] See Appendix (12).

M.	F.	N.
alius	alia	aliud
alīus	alīus	alīus
aliī	aliī	aliī
alium	aliam	aliud
aliō	aliā	aliō

Decline **alter equus, neutra fīlia, tōtum flūmen, ūnus nauta.**

179. VOCABULARY

familia, -ae, F., *household,* **Dīvicō, -ōnis,** M., *a leader of*
 retainers. *the Helvetii.*
iūdicium, -ī, N., *judgment,* **ita,** adv., *so, thus.*
 trial.

agō, agere, ēgī, āctum, (*drive*), *do, act, plead, discuss.*
cōgō (con + agō), **cōgere, coēgi, coāctum,** *bring together, compel.*
committō (con + mittō, 101), *join* (battle), *commit, permit.*
vincō, vincere, vīcī, victum, *conquer.*

TRANSLATE

180. 1. Vēnī, vīdī, vīcī. 2. Habuistī, habuistis. 3. Mūnī-vimus, mūnīvistis. 4. Pūgnāvit, pūgnāvērunt. 5. Ūnīus nāvis. 6. Alterum sīgnum. 7. Prōvinciae tōtī. 8. Con-iūrātiō tōtīus Galliae. 9. Caesar ante oppidum castra posuit. 10. Helvētiī aliud cōnsilium habuērunt nūllum. 11. Dīvicō ita cum Caesare ēgit.[1] 12. Orgetorīx fuit prīnceps Helvētiōrum et cīvitātī persuāsit. 13. Orgetorīx ad iūdicium suam familiam coēgit. 14. Caesar proelium commīsit. 15. Multī hominēs ē castrīs Helvētiōrum ad Rhēnum fīnēsque Germānōrum contendērunt.

---

[1] *plead.*

181. 1. We have seen, have given. 2. You have called, have persuaded. 3. They came, conquered. 4. For another boy. 5. With one soldier. 6. In the other part of the village. 7. The tribe will join battle with Orgetorix. 8. The chiefs brought together their retainers, a great number of men. 9. We have been soldiers. 10. There were many animals in the fields. 11. The enemy pitched the camp at night. 12. Neither horseman surpassed the footman in valor. 13. Orgetorix had a large household.

LESSON XXI

The Relative Pronoun *qui.*—Agreement of the Relative.—Sentences and Clauses.

182. DEFINITION.—A *relative* pronoun refers or relates to some preceding noun or pronoun called its *antecedent.* In Latin the relative pronoun is **quī,** *who, which* or *that.*

	SINGULAR.			PLURAL.		
	M.	F.	N.	M.	F.	N.
N.	quī	quae	quod,	quī	quae	quae,
			who, which or *that.*			
G.	cūius	cūius	cūius,	quōrum	quārum	quōrum,
			whose, of whom or *of which.*			
D.	cui	cui	cui,	quibus	quibus	quibus,
			to or *for whom* or *which.*			
Ac.	quem	quam	quod,	quōs	quās	quae,
			whom, which or *that.*			
Ab.	quō	quā	quō,	quibus	quibus	quibus,
			from (etc.) *whom* or *which.*			

183. MODEL SENTENCES

1. **Celtae, quī Gallī appellantur, ūnam partem incolunt:** *The Celts, who are called Gauls, inhabit one part.*
2. **Germānī, quōrum rēx erat Ariovistus, trāns Rhēnum incolēbant:** *The Germans, whose king was Ariovistus, were living across the Rhine.*

In these sentences notice that **quī** and **quōrum** are of the same gender, number and person as the antecedents **Celtae** and **Germānī**. **Quī** is in the nominative case not because **Celtae** is, but because it is the subject of **appellantur**.

184. RULE XV.—*A relative pronoun agrees with its antecedent in gender, number and person, but its case depends on the structure of the clause in which it stands.*

185. SENTENCES.—With regard to form, sentences may be *simple, complex* or *compound,* as in English.

The above model sentences are *complex,* for they consist each of two clauses, a principal or independent, and a subordinate or dependent. The clauses of a complex sentence may be connected by a relative pronoun, a relative adjective or a subordinate conjunction.

186. CLAUSES.—Clauses may be used as nouns, adjectives or adverbs.

(*a*) A *noun-clause,* or substantive clause, is one that is used as a noun, being the subject of a verb, object of a verb, in apposition with a noun or pronoun, etc.

(*b*) An *adjective-clause* is one that modifies a noun or pronoun. The relative clauses in 183 are illustrations.

(c) An *adverb-clause* is one that modifies a verb, adjective or other adverb. Noun-clauses and adverb-clauses will be illustrated later.

187. VOCABULARY

obaerātus, -ī, M., *debtor.*
iter, itineris, N., *journey, march, road.*
lēgātiō, -ōnis, F., *embassy.*
nātiō, -ōnis, F., *race, nation.*
novus, -a, -um, *new.*
quī, quae, quod, *who, which or that.*

condūcō (con + dūcō, 83), *bring together.*
conscrībō (con + scrībō, *write*), -scrībere, -scrīpsī, -scrīptum, *enroll, enlist.*

NOTE.—Iter is declined thus: iter, itineris, itinerī, iter, itinere; pl. itinera, etc.

TRANSLATE

188. 1. Oppidum quod mūnītur. 2. Ēques cui sīgnum dant. 3. Eques cui persuāsī. 4. Nāvēs quae sunt Caesarī. 5. Itinera quae vīdistis. 6. Mīlitēs quibus auxilium dabitur. 7. Rēx quem vīdistī. 8. Belgae quōs laudābāmus. 9. Nauta cūius nāvis est in[1] marī. 10. Puerī quōrum pater erit dux. 11. Prōvincia quam incolimus. 12. Mīlitēs quibus persuāsimus. 13. Tuba quā sīgnum datur. 14. Nātiōnēs quibuscum[2] contendunt. 15. Erant duo itinera ex Helvētiā. 16. Orgetorīx suōs obaerātōs, quōrum māgnum numerum habēbat, condūxit. 17. Duae legiōnēs, quās Caesar in Galliā conscrībit, ad oppidum mittentur. 18. In itinere persuādet Casticō, cūius pater rēx in Sēquanīs fuerat.[3] 19. Helvētiī lēgātōs ad Caesarem mittunt, cūius lēgātiōnis Dīvicō prīnceps fuit, quī bellō Cassiānō dux fuerat.[3]

---

[1] *on.* [2] With the ablative of the relative pronoun, the preposition **cum** may be attached as an enclitic (7, c). [3] *had been,*

189. 1. The hostage whose brother will come. 2. For the boy whom they praise. 3. The towns which are fortified. 4. The sailors whose ship is new. 5. The man with ¹ whom we came. 6. Into the forests which we see. 7. Across the river which is deep. 8. The traders whom you will not persuade. 9. The enemy hold the mountain which you see near the river. 10. There were many new ships that carried the soldiers. 11. We are defended by a great number of the soldiers whom you praise.

LESSON XXII

The Demonstrative Pronouns *is* and *īdem.*

190. DEFINITION.—A *demonstrative* pronoun points out the noun or pronoun to which it refers. One of the demonstratives is **is, ea, id,** *that, he, she* or *it.* Another is **īdem (is + dem), eadem, idem,** *the same.* Learn the declension of these two words as given in the Appendix, section 19.

191. USES OF **is.**—(*a*) There is no special pronoun of the third person, but **is** may be used as such: **Lēgātī ad eum veniunt:** *Ambassadors come to him.*

(*b*) When used as personal pronouns, the forms of **is** do not refer to the subject of the sentence, but to some other person or thing: **Prīnceps ēius amīcum vīdit:** *The chief saw his* (some other person's) *friend.* **Suus** (87) is used in referring to the subject: **Prīnceps suum amīcum vīdit:** *The chief saw his own friend.*

(*c*) Demonstrative pronouns when used as adjectives

---

¹ See note 2, page 64.

agree in gender, number and case with the noun they modify: **id flūmen, īdem vīcus, ea legiō.**

(*d*) **Is** (or **īdem**) is often used as the antecedent, or in agreement with the antecedent, of a relative pronoun: **Eī quī castra dēfendunt:** *Those who defend the camp.* **Ea legiō quae est in castrīs:** *That legion which is in the camp.*

192. **VOCABULARY**

> **mors, mortis,** F., *death.*
> **is, ea, id,** *that, he,* etc.
> **īdem, eadem, idem,** *the same.*
> **ob,** prep. with acc., (*against*), *on account of, for.*

respondeō, -spondēre, -spondī, -spōnsum, *reply, answer.*

Decline **id flūmen, ea legiō, īdem puer.**

TRANSLATE

193. 1. Per eōs. 2. Cum eīs, ab eīs. 3. Ob eam causam, ob eās causās. 4. In eō itinere. 5. Is pāgus. 6. Eōdem tempore. 7. Māgna eōrum pars. 8. In eam partem. 9. Eādem tubā. 10. Eadem oppida. 11. Eōrum itinerum. 12. Eaedem lēgātiōnēs. 13. Eārundem legiōnum. 14. Idem[1] Caesar audit. 15. Īdem Dīviciācus Haeduus respondet. 16. Eādem legiōne quam habēbat. 17. Is bellum gessit. 18. Orgetorīx id[2] eīs[3] persuāsit. 19. Orgetorīx eī suam fīliam dat. 20. Post eius mortem Helvētiī convēnērunt. 21. Ab eīsdem nostra cōnsilia ēnūntiantur. 22. Caesar eōdem itinere, quō hostēs ierant,[4] ad eōs contendit. 23. Germānī sunt eīdem quibuscum Helvētiī contendērunt.

---

[1] Notice that **i** is short in the neuter of **idem**, but long in the masculine. [2] Direct object of **persuāsit**; translate *of this.* [3] How is **eīs** related to **persuāsit?** [4] *had gone.*

194. 1. Of that number. 2. For that nation. 3. By those nations. 4. Across those rivers. 5. Out of those fields. 6. The same conspiracy. 7. Of those tribes. 8. Of the same laws. 9. To the same man. 10. That road is near. 11. That boy, whom we saw in the forest, is the son of the chief. 12. The Helvetians fortified their (own) towns. 13. The Helvetians were devastating their (the Haeduans') fields. 14. Caesar will enroll a new legion, which he will lead into Gaul.

LESSON XXIII

The Present Subjunctive (of Conj. I and *sum*).—The Subjunctive of Purpose.

195. FORMATION OF THE PRESENT SUBJUNCTIVE.— The subjunctive mood has four tenses: the *present, imperfect, perfect* and *pluperfect*. In the first conjugation the present is formed by adding the personal endings to the present stem with its final -ā- changed to -e- (-ē-): active, **laude-m·** passive, **laude-r**.

196. MODEL VERB

THE PRESENT SUBJUNCTIVE (CONJUGATION I).

ACTIVE.		PASSIVE.	
laudem	laudēmus	lauder·	laudēmur
laudēs	laudētis	laudēris (-re)	laudēminī
laudet	laudent	laudētur	laudentur

Conjugate the present subjunctive of **appellō** and **dō**.

PRESENT SUBJUNCTIVE OF **sum.**

Singular.	Plural.
sim	sīmus
sīs	sītis
sit	sint

197. USES OF THE SUBJUNCTIVE.—The subjunctive is used to express action (1) as willed: **laudēmus,** *let us praise;* (2) as desired: **laudēmur,** *may we be praised;* (3) as possible: **laudētur,** *he may be praised.* No one meaning can be given for subjunctive forms. In independent clauses or sentences, the present may be translated as in the illustrations just given; in dependent clauses, by *may, should, would* or as explained in 198 and elsewhere.

198. MODEL SENTENCES

1. **Caesar venit (veniet) ut mīlitēs laudet:** *Caesar is coming (will come) to praise (that he may praise) the soldiers.*
2. **Caesar mittit (mittet) legiōnem quae (= ut ea) agrōs vāstet:** *Caesar sends (will send) a legion to devastate the fields.*
3. **Mīlitēs pūgnant (pūgnābunt) nē oppidum expūgnētur:** *The soldiers fight (will fight) that the town may not be taken.*
4. **Bellum gerēmus nē sit rēx:** *We shall wage war that he may not be king.*

(*a*) Sentence 1. For what purpose does Caesar come? In English we may answer *to praise, that he may praise, for the purpose of praising.* In Latin prose the answer is not expressed by the infinitive, as may be done in English (*to praise*), but often by a clause beginning with **ut,** etc., and having its verb in the subjunctive. Such a clause is called a *purpose clause* or a *final clause*.

(*b*) Sentence 2. Instead of **ut, quī** may be used when there is an antecedent. **Quī** then is equivalent to **ut** + a demonstrative (**is, ea, id**).

(*c*) Sentences 3 and 4. To express negative purpose (*that—not*), **nē** is used.

Note.—These clauses are all adverbial (186, *c*).

199. RULE XVI.—*The subjunctive mood is used to express purpose with* **ut, nē, quī** *or* **quō** (456).

200. <center>**VOCABULARY**</center>

ut (utī), conj., *that, in order that, as.*
nē, conj., (*lest*), *that—not.*

oppūgnō (ob + pūgnō, 58), *fight against, attack.*

TRANSLATE

201. 1. Mittitur ut sit imperātor. 2. Mittimur ut pācem cōnfīrmēmus. 3. Cōnsulēs nōn mittuntur ut obsidēs dent.
4. Cōnscrībiminī ut in prōvinciā pūgnētis. 5. Rōmānī in Helvētiam venient ut eam partem Galliae pācent. 6. Imperātor mīlitēs convocat ut nova sīgna eīs det. 7. Rauracī sua oppida incendunt, nē ab hostibus oppūgnentur.
8. Tum Ariovistus partem suārum cōpiārum, quae castra oppūgnet, mittit. 9. Eōdem tempore mercātōrēs ad eōs commeābant. 10. Eaedem cīvitātēs Germānōs virtūte praecēdent.

202. 1. I shall come to announce the victory. 2. He will come to announce the victory. 3. We shall come to spend-the-winter.[1] 4. We shall send men to carry the

---

[1] hiemō.

grain. 5. They are fortifying the towns that they may not be in great peril. 6. The king will send a messenger that you may be recalled. 7. You are sent by the consul to attack the villages by night.

LESSON XXIV

The Present Subjunctive (Conj. II - IV).—Noun-clauses with *ut* and *nē.*

203. In the second and fourth conjugations the letter -a- (-ā-) is added to the present stem before the personal ending: **mone-a-m, mone-a-r; audi-a-m, audi-a-r.** In the third conjugation the final -e- of the stem is changed to -a- (-ā-) before the personal ending: **rega-m, rega-r.**

204. MODEL VERBS

THE PRESENT SUBJUNCTIVE (CONJUGATIONS II–IV).

ACTIVE.		PASSIVE.	
moneam	moneāmus	monear	moneāmur
moneās	moneātis	moneāris (-re)	moneāminī
moneat	moneant	moneātur	moneantur
regam	regāmus	regar	regāmur
regās	regātis	regāris (-re)	regāminī
regat	regant	regātur	regantur
audiam	audiāmus	audiar	audiāmur
audiās	audiātis	audiāris (-re)	audiāminī
audiat	audiant	audiātur	audiantur

Conjugate the present subjunctive of **videō, dūcō** and **mūniō.**

205.   VOCABULARY

iniūria, -ae, F., *injustice, in-*   nōbilitās, -tātis, F., *nobility,*
  jury, wrong.   *the nobles.*
maleficium, -ī. N., *harm.*   Catamantāloedēs, -is, M., a
rēgnum, -ī, N. (rēx), *royal*   chief of the Sequani.
  power, kingdom.   -que, conj., *and.*
sēmentis, -is, F., *sowing.*

occupō, -āre, -āvī, -ātum, *seize.*
prohibeō (prō + habeō), -ēre, -uī, -itum, *keep off, hinder.*
timeō, -ēre, -uī, ——, *fear.*
exūrō (ex + ūrō), -ūrere, -ussī, -ūstum, *burn up.*

206.   MODEL SENTENCES

1. **Casticō, ut rēgnum occupet, persuādet:** *He persuades
   Casticus to seize the royal power.*
2. **Casticō, ut rēgnum occupet, persuādētur:** *Casticus is
   persuaded* (literally, it is persuaded to Casticus) *to seize
   the royal power.*
3. **Timeō nē sit rēx:** *I fear that he will be king.*
4. **Timeō ut sit rēx:** *I fear that he will not be king.*

(*a*) A clause beginning with **ut** or **nē** and having its
verb in the subjunctive may be the object of verbs
meaning *advise, command,*[1] *induce, permit, persuade,* etc.
See sentence 1.

(*b*) If these verbs are in the passive, the *clause* becomes the subject, and the noun which we should
expect to be the subject becomes the indirect object,
as in sentence 2.

---

[1] Except **iubeō** ; see 233.

(c) Verbs meaning *fear* are followed by object-clauses with **ut** or **nē**, but **nē** means *lest*, or *that*, while **ut** means *that not*.

TRANSLATE

207. 1. Monet eum nē proelium committat.   2. Timet nē Caesar eōs vincat.   3. Timet ut Caesar eōs vincat. 4. Mīlitēs pūgnant nē collis ab hostibus teneātur.   5. Germānīs, quī trāns Rhēnum incolunt, persuādētur ut in Galliam veniant.   6. Orgetorīx coniūrātiōnem nōbilitātis facit[1] et cīvitātī persuādet, ut dē fīnibus suās cōpiās ēdūcant.[2]   7. Helvētiī sēmentēs māgnās faciunt[3] ut in itinere cōpia frūmentī suppetat.   8. In itinere persuādet Casticō, Catamantāloedis fīliō, Sēquanō, ut rēgnum in cīvitāte suā occupet.   9. Persuādent Rauracīs et Tulingīs et Latobrīgīs, fīnitimīs, ut oppida sua vīcōsque[4] exūrant.   10. Dumnorīx Sēquanōs monet, nē itinere Helvētiōs prohibeant; Helvētiōs, ut sine maleficiō et iniūriā fīnēs Sēquanōrum trānseant.[5]

208. 1. The traders come to see the camp, which extends from the river to the mountain.   2. The nobles will wage war in order that Gaul may be free.   3. We fear that our friends will not hear.   4. We fear that the nobles[6] will seize the royal power.   5. I shall persuade Piso and Galba to defend the camp.   6. Piso and Galba will be persuaded to defend the camp.   7. Many horsemen will be sent to keep off the enemy.

---

[1] *is making.*   [2] Plural, because **cīvitātī** is a collective noun.
[3] *are making.*   [4] **que** is an enclitic (7, *c*) and is attached to the second of the two words which it connects.   It must therefore be translated *before* the word to which it is attached: **gladius pīlumque,** *the sword and the javelin.*   [5] *pass through.*
[6] Use a singular noun.

LESSON XXV

Adjectives of the Third Declension.—The Genitive with Adjectives.

209. NOMINATIVE SINGULAR.—A few adjectives of the third declension have a different form for each gender in the nominative singular, and are called *adjectives of three endings :* **ācer, ācris, ācre.** Many have one form for the masculine and feminine, and another for the neuter. These are called *adjectives of two endings :* **fortis, forte.** Some have the same form for all genders, and are called *adjectives of one ending:* **potēns.**

210. ENDINGS.—Most adjectives of the third declension, except comparatives, have **-ī** in the ablative singular, **-ium** in the genitive plural, **-īs** (**-ēs**) in the accusative masculine and feminine plural, and **-ia** in the nominative and accusative neuter plural.

Learn from the Appendix (13), the declension of the following model adjectives:

> **ācer, ācris, ācre,** *sharp, active.* Base: **ācr-.**
> **fortis, forte,** *brave.* Base: **fort-.**
> **potēns,** *powerful.* Base: **potent-.**
> **vēlōx,** *swift.* Base: **vēlōc-.**

211.   VOCABULARY

praeda, -ae, F., *booty, plunder.*

īnstitūtum, -ī, N., *custom.*

supplicium, -ī, N., *punishment.*

equester, -tris, -tre (**equus**), *of the cavalry.*

facilis, -e, *easy.*

difficilis, -e, *difficult.*

gravis, -e, *heavy, severe.*

74   THE FIRST YEAR OF LATIN

cupidus, -a, -um, *eager, de-*   omnis, -e, *all, every.*
sirous.
recēns, -entis, *new, late, recent.*

dēpōnō (dē + pōnō, 166), *lay down, deposit;* with **memoriam,** *blot out.*

212.   MODEL SENTENCE

Orgetorīx erat cupidus rēgnī: *Orgetorix was desirous of royal power.*

In this sentence **rēgnī,** a noun in the genitive, completes the meaning of the adjective **cupidus.**

213. RULE XVII.—*The genitive is used to complete the meaning of many adjectives denoting* desire, knowledge, memory, fullness, power *and their opposites.*

TRANSLATE

214. 1. Facile iter. 2. Facilī itinere. 3. Potēns nātiō. 4. Per potentēs nātiōnēs. 5. Ab fortī puerō. 6. Ab fortibus puerīs. 7. Recēns victōria. 8. Recēns proelium. 9. Ante recentem victōriam. 10. Gravēs gladiī. 11. Omne frūmentum. 12. Omnia sua oppida. 13. Eōrum omnium. 14. Cum omnibus cōpiīs. 15. Gallia omnis. 16. Gallī omnēs linguā, īnstitūtīs, lēgibus differunt.[1] 17. Mīlitēs erant perītī bellī. 18. Praeda erit fortibus virīs.[2] 19. Legiō fuit cupida praedae. 20. Peditēs erant vēlōcēs et fortēs. 21. Iter per Sēquanōs erat angustum et difficile: iter per prōvinciam nostram, facile. 22. Ariovistus dē[3] omnibus obsidibus, quī apud eum sunt, grave supplicium sūmit.[4] 23. Rōmānī cum Germānīs equestrī proeliō contendēbant. 24. Caesar recentium iniūriārum memoriam

---

[1] *differ.*   [2] See 115.   [3] *upon.*   [4] *inflicts.*

nōn dēpōnet. 25. Casticus rēgnum occupābit ut cīvitās sit potēns. 26. Timēmus nē perīculum sit māgnum.

215. 1. Among the swift horses 2. Near the brave horsemen. 3. Many cavalry battles. 4. The men have been brave. 5. The boy was carrying a heavy sword. 6. The boy had[1] a heavy sword. 7. We are all desirous of victory. 8. The mountain will be held by the active troops, for they are skilled in warfare.[2] 9. I fear that the journey is difficult. 10. Orgetorix will persuade the same neighbors to fortify their winter-quarters.

LESSON XXVI—REVIEW

Caesar, Book I, Chapter i (begun)

216. 1. What are the personal endings of the perfect indicative active? 2. How is the perfect indicative active formed? 3. The present subjunctive? 4. Give the nine adjectives whose genitive singular ends in **-īus.** 5. Decline **quī, is, īdem, tōtus** and the model adjectives of Declension III. 6. Conjugate the present subjunctive of the model verbs. 7. How does the relative pronoun agree with its antecedent? 8. After what adjectives is the genitive case used? 9. How is purpose expressed in Latin? 10. Give a classification of clauses. 11. State one use of the noun-clause.

217. Review Vocabulary

familia	sēmentis	difficilis	-que
iniūria	alius	fortis	occupō
praeda	alter	gravis	oppūgnō

---

[1] See 115.　　　[2] **bellum.**

obaerātus	neuter	omnis	prohibeō
īnstitūtum	nūllus	potēns	respondeō
iūdicium	sōlus	recēns	timeō
maleficium	tōtus	vēlōx	agō
rēgnum	ūllus	is	cōgō
supplicium	uter	īdem	committō
mors	cupidus	quī	condūcō
lēgātiō	novus	ita	conscrībō
nātiō	ācer	ob	dēpōnō
iter	equester	ut (utī)	exūrō
nōbilitās	facilis	nē	vincō

218.   Review Sentences

1. In itinere persuādet Casticō, cūius pater rēx in Sēquanīs fuerat. 2. Orgetorīx obaerātōs suōs, quōrum māgnum numerum habēbat, condūxit. 3. Helvētiī lēgātōs ad Caesarem mittunt, cūius lēgātiōnis Dīvicō prīnceps fuit, quī bellō Cassiānō dux Helvētiōrum fuerat. 4. Orgetorīx coniūrātiōnem nōbilitātis facit et cīvitātī persuādet, ut dē fīnibus suās cōpiās ēdūcant. 5. Helvētiī sēmentēs māgnās faciunt, ut in itinere cōpia frūmentī suppetat. 6. In itinere persuādet Casticō, Catamantāloedis fīliō, Sēquanō, ut rēgnum in cīvitāte suā occupet. 7. Persuādent Rauracīs et Tulingīs et Latobrīgīs, fīnitimīs, ut oppida sua vīcōsque exūrant. 8. Sēquanī obsidēs dant, nē itinere Helvētiōs prohibeant; Helvētiī, ut sine maleficiō et iniūriā fīnēs Sēquanōrum trānseant. 9. Tum Ariovistus partem suārum cōpiārum, quae castra oppūgnet, mittit. 10. Orgetorīx ad iūdicium omnem suam familiam coēgit. 11. Orgetorīx id eīs persuāsit. 12. Iter per Sēquanōs erat angustum et difficile; iter per prōvinciam, facile. 13. Caesar recentium iniūriārum memoriam nōn dēpōnet.

219. HISTORICAL NOTE.—Caius Julius Caesar, the Roman general, statesman and writer, was born

100 B.C. After an education in Rome and Greece, and a short career in the army, he held several important political offices, the last of which was the consulship for the year 59 B.C. At the close of this year he became governor of Gaul, or ancient France. During the following eight years (58–51) he subdued the tribes of Gaul and also invaded Germany and Britain. The history of these years is contained in eight books, called Commentaries on the Gallic Wars, seven of which were written by himself. The first book begins with a chapter on the geography and people of Gaul, a portion of which is given below.

220. Caesar's Gallic War, I. 1 (begun): The Divisions of Gaul.

Gallia est omnis dīvīsa in partēs trēs; quārum ūnam[1] incolunt Belgae, aliam[1] Aquītānī, tertiam[1] quī ipsō-rum[2] linguā Celtae, nostrā Gallī appellantur. Hī[3] om-nēs linguā, īnstitūtīs, lēgibus inter sē[4] differunt. Gallōs ab Aquītānīs Garumna flūmen, ā Belgīs Mātrona et Sē- 5 quana dīvidit.

Notes and Vocabulary
[1] ūnam, aliam and tertiam agree with partem, which is implied.
[2] ipsōrum, *their own*, gen. pl. of ipse (257); modifies linguā.
[3] Hī, *these*, nom. pl. of hīc (255) ; subject of differunt.
[4] sē, *themselves*, acc. pl. (350); inter sē, *from one another*.

LESSON XXVII

The Imperfect Subjunctive (Conj. I-IV).—The Imperfect Subjunctive in Clauses of Purpose, etc.

221. Formation of the Imperfect Subjunctive.— The imperfect subjunctive is formed by adding the personal endings to the present active infinitive.[1] This tense may be translated by *might*, *would*, etc., or as explained in 224 and elsewhere.

222. MODEL VERBS

THE IMPERFECT SUBJUNCTIVE

ACTIVE.		PASSIVE.	
laudārem	laudārēmus	laudārer	laudārēmur
laudārēs	laudārētis	laudārēris (-re)	laudārēminī
laudāret	laudārent	laudārētur	laudārentur
monērem	monērēmus	monērer	monērēmur
monērēs	monērētis	monērēris (-re)	monērēminī
monēret	monērent	monērētur	monērentur
regerem	regerēmus	regerer	regerēmur
regerēs	regerētis	regerēris (-re)	regerēminī
regeret	regerent	regerētur	regerentur
audīrem	audīrēmus	audīrer	audīrēmur
audīrēs	audīrētis	audīrēris (-re)	audīrēminī
audīret	audīrent	audīrētur	audīrentur

223. IMPERFECT SUBJUNCTIVE OF **sum.**

Singular.	*Plural.*
essem	essēmus
essēs	essētis
esset	essent

Conjugate the imperfect subjunctive of **dō, pūgnō, teneō, mittō, mūniō.**

---

[1] Or, in regular verbs, by adding the tense-sign **-re-** and the personal endings to the present stem.

224.   MODEL SENTENCES

1. **Mīlitēs pūgnābant** (or **pūgnāvērunt**) **ut castra dēfende-
   rent:** *The soldiers were fighting* (or *fought*) *to defend
   (that they might defend) the camp.*
2. **Persuāsit eīs ut venīrent:** *He persuaded them to come.*
3. **Timuit nē vincerentur:** *He feared that they might be
   conquered.*

In 1 the subordinate clause is adverbial and expresses purpose; in 2 and 3 it is used as a noun (or substantive).

Notice that the subordinate verbs are in the imperfect
tense. The *imperfect* tense is used in such clauses when
the verb in the principal clause is in the *past* tense.
Compare these sentences with those of 198, in which
there is a *present* verb in the subordinate clause when
there is a *present* or *future* verb in the principal clause.

225.   VOCABULARY

mūnītiō -ōnis, F. (**mūniō**),   **turpitūdō, -inis,** F., *disgrace.*
   fortification.   **nōnnūllī, -ōrum,** M., *some.*
suspīciō, -ōnis, F., *suspicion.*   **quālis, -e,** adj., *of what sort?*
timor, timōris, M., *fear.*   *what?*

   impetrō, -āre, -āvī, -ātum, *obtain* (a request).
   supportō (sub + portō, 38), *bring up, supply.*
   vītō, -āre, -āvī, -ātum, *escape, avoid.*
   dēleō, dēlēre, dēlēvi, dēlētum, *blot out.*
   remaneō (re + maneō), manēre, -mānsī, -mānsum,
      remain.
   terreō, -ēre, -uī, -itum, *frighten, alarm.*
   cōgnōscō, -gnōscere, -gnōvī, -gnitum, *learn, ascertain.*
   interclūdō (inter + claudō), -clūdere, -clūsī, -clūsum,
      cut off.
6

TRANSLATE

226. 1. Explōrātor lēgātum monuit nē remanēret. 2. Eī Gallīs persuāsērunt ut oppida sua incenderent. 3. Nōn-nūllī, ut timōris suspīciōnem vītārent, remanēbant. 4. Lē-gātōs ad Dumnorīgem mīsērunt, ut ā Sēquanīs impe-trārent. 5. Ariovistus prope Caesarem castra posuit, ut frūmentō,[1] quod ex Haeduīs supportārētur,[2] eum inter-clūderet. 6. Caesar explōrātōrēs mīsit, quī[3] cōgnōscerent quālis esset[2] nātūra montis. 7. Equitēs, ut turpitūdi-nem fugae virtūte dēlērent, omnibus in locīs pūgnāvērunt. 8. Ariovistus cōpiās mīsit, quae[3] nostrōs terrērent et mū-nītiōne prohibērent. 9. Vītāvimus gravia pīla quae ā pe-ditibus mittēbantur.[4] 10. Quattuor hōrīs omnia hostium cōnsilia cōgnōscēs.

227. 1. He persuaded the men to be brave. 2. Some feared that grain might not be supplied. 3. To escape the javelins, the trader remained on[5] the hill. 4. We were devastating the fields to terrify the enemy. 5. We shall remain in[5] the village, that we may learn the number of hostages. 6. The Gauls were fortifying the town, that it might not be in peril. 7. The same chief will blot out the tribe's disgrace.

LESSON XXVIII

The Present Infinitive.—The Uses of the Infinitive.— The Subject of the Infinitive.

228. THE INFINITIVE.—The infinitive is a verbal noun. As a noun it may have the uses of the nomina-

---

[1] *from the grain.*   [2] To be translated like the imperfect indica-tive. This subjunctive, which is not one of purpose, will be explained later.   [3] See 199.   [4] *hurled.*   [5] Use Latin preposition **in.**

tive and accusative. As a verb it has voice, tense,
may have a subject or object, and may be modified by
an adverb.

The infinitive has three tenses in each voice: the
present, the perfect and the future. The present
active infinitive has already been mentioned as the second of the principal parts of the verb (17, 36, etc.).

The present passive infinitive is formed by changing·
the final -e of the active to -ī, except in the third conjugation, in which final -ere becomes -ī.

ACTIVE.	PASSIVE.
laudāre, *to praise.*	laudārī, *to be praised.*
monēre, *to advise.*	monērī, *to be advised.*
regere, *to rule.*	regī, *to be ruled.*
audīre, *to hear.*	audīrī, *to be heard.*
esse, *to be.*	

What are the present passive infinitives of **dō, mittō,
mūniō, pōnō, prohibeō, vāstō**?

229.   **VOCABULARY**

castellum, -ī, N., *fort, redoubt.*

comportō (con + portō, 38), *bring together, collect.*
obtineō (ob + teneō), **-tinēre, -tinuī, -tentum,** *hold,
    occupy.*
ascendō, -ere, -ī, ascēnsum, *climb, ascend.*
cōnstituō, -stituere, -stituī, -stitūtum, *put, station, de-
    cide, appoint.*
dīcō, dīcere, dīxī, dictum, *say.*
commūniō (con + mūniō, 70), *strongly fortify.*

230. USES OF THE INFINITIVE.—The infinitive is used chiefly as follows:

I. Without a subject—

1. As the subject of a finite verb (especially **est** or an impersonal verb, 426): **Expūgnāre oppidum est facile:** *To capture the town is easy.*

2. As an object or complement: **Helvētii pācem cōn- firmāre cōnstituunt:** *The Helvetians decide to establish peace.*

In the latter use the infinitive completes the meaning of certain verbs which imply another action of the same subject. Thus, in the last example, the *establishing* as well as the *deciding* is done by the Helvetians. This is called the *complementary* infinitive, and is used in connection with verbs meaning *can, wish, dare, resolve, begin, ought, seem, hasten, hesitate,* etc.

231. II. With the subject-accusative—

1. As the subject of a finite verb : **Dicitur collem esse altum:** *It is said that the hill is high.*

2. As an object or complement: (*a*) **Oppidum expūg- nārī dīcunt:** *They say that the town is captured.* (*b*) **Agrum esse māgnum vidēmus :** *We see that the field is large.*

In the last three examples, **collem, vīcum** and **agrum** are the subjects of the infinitives; the "infinitive clause" **collem esse altum** is the subject of **dīcitur;** **vīcum expūgnārī** is the object of **dīcunt;** and **agrum esse māgnum** is the object of **vidēmus.** In such examples the infinitive represents the indicative in Latin and is translated by that mood in English.

NOTE.—The infinitive with or without a subject-accuative may also be used in apposition with another word, or as a predicate nominative.

232. III. With a subject-nominative— The infinitive is sometimes used with the meaning of the imperfect indicative. It then has its subject in the nominative case, as **dīcere** in the following: **Haeduī frūmentum comportārī dīcere**: *The Haedui kept saying that the grain was being collected.* This is called the *historical* infinitive.

233. RULE XVIII.—*The subject of the infinitive (except the historical infinitive) is in the accusative case.*

RULE XIX.—*The infinitive with subject-accusative is used with verbs meaning* say, know, think, perceive, *etc.; also with* **iubeō,** command, **vetō,** forbid, **prohibeō,** prevent, **sinō,** allow, **cōgō,** compel, **cupiō,** desire, **volō,** wish, *etc.*

TRANSLATE

234. 1. Frūmentum comportārī dīcunt. 2. Nostra cōnsilia hostibus ēnūntiārī dīcit. 3. Dumnorīx māgnum numerum mīlitum habēre dīcitur. 4. Obsidēs nōn dare cōnstituimus. 5. Dīviciācum vocārī iubet. 6. Caesar Labiēnum montem ascendere iubet. 7. Cōnsidius dīcit montem, quem Caesar ā Labiēnō occupārī voluerit,[1] ab hostibus tenērī. 8. Helvētiōs angustōs fīnēs habēre dīxērunt. 9. Hīs[2] Helvētiī persuādēre nōn poterant.[3] 10. Caesar castella commūnit, ut Helvētiōs prohibēre possit.[4] 11. Ūna pars, quam[5] Gallōs[5] obtinēre dīcitur, ā flūmine Rhodanō pertinet. 12. Orgetorīgem causam dīcere[6] coēgērunt.

---

[1] *wished.*   [2] Why is **hīs** in the dative?   [3] *were able.*   [4] *may be able.*
[5] **quam** is the object of **obtinēre, Gallōs** the subject.   [6] *plead.*

235. 1. Our plan is to establish friendship. 2. We report (that) the redoubt is strongly fortified. 3. The road is said to be broad. 4. It is said (that) the town is defended. 5. We learn (that) the Haedui are bringing grain to the camp. 6. Caesar ordered the camp to be pitched. 7. I have decided to see the fort.

LESSON XXIX

Tho Present Participle.—The Gerund.—The Gerundive.—The Present System.

236. Participles.—There are four participles, two in the active voice (the *present* and the *future*) and two in the passive (the *perfect* and the *juture*, or *gerundive*).

The present participle may be translated by the English present active participle. It is formed by adding **-ns** (**-ēns** in the fourth conjugation) to the present stem: **laudāns**, *praising;* **monēns**, *advising;* **regēns**, *ruling;* **audiēns**, *hearing.*

237. The present participle is declined like **potēns** (210). In the ablative singular the ending is **-e**, but when the participle is used simply as an adjective, it is **-ī**.

238. The participle is a verbal *adjective.* Like an adjective, it agrees with a noun or pronoun in gender, number and case. Like a verb, it may take an object and be modified by an adverb: **Mīlitēs collem celeriter ascendentēs vīdimus:** *We saw the soldiers quickly climbing the hill.*

239. The Gerund.—The gerund is a neuter verbal

noun, equivalent in meaning to an English verbal noun in *-ing:* **cupidus videndī**, *desirous of seeing*. It is found in the genitive, dative, accusative and ablative singular, the present infinitive being used for the nominative.

The gerund is formed by adding to the present stem **-nd-** (**-end-** in the fourth conjugation) and the endings of the second declension: laud**andī**, mon**endī**, reg**endī**, aud**iendī**.

GEN. laud**andī**, *of praising*.
DAT. laud**andō**, *to* or *for praising*.
Acc. laud**andum**, *praising* (used chiefly with **ad**).
ABL. laud**andō**, *with* or *by praising*.

240.   MODELS OF THE GERUND

1. **Homō cupidus regendī**, *a man desirous of ruling* (or *eager to rule*).
2. **Pūgnandī causā**,[1] *for-the-purpose of fighting*.
3. **Ad oppūgnandum**, *for attacking, to attack*.
4. **Caesar in quaerendō**[2] **reperiēbat**[3]: *Caesar found upon inquiring*.

NOTE.—The gerund seldom takes an object, the gerundive construction being used instead. See 242.

241. THE GERUNDIVE.—The gerundive is a verbal *adjective*, declined in both numbers like **māgnus**. It is formed by adding **-ndus** (**-endus** in the fourth conjugation) to the present stem: laud**andus**, mon**endus**, reg**endus**, aud**iendus**.

The gerundive may be translated in different ways. Thus, **laudandus** may mean *to be praised, deserving to be*

---

[1] The ablative **causā** follows a genitive and means *for the purpose, for the sake.* [2] **quaerō, quaerere, quaesīvī, quaesītum**, *search for, inquire.* [3] **reperiō, reperīre, repperī, repertum**, *find, discover, learn.*

praised, but when used as an attributive adjective it is rendered, like the gerund, by an English verbal in *-ing*, as in the following models.

242.   MODELS OF THE GERUNDIVE

1. **Cupidus amicōrum laudandōrum,** *desirous of praising friends (of friends to-be-praised).*
2. **Pācis petendae causā,** ⎰ *for the purpose of seeking peace*
3. **Ad pācem petendam,** ⎱   *(for peace to be sought).*
4. **Expūgnandō oppidō,** *by capturing the town.*

Notice that the nouns in these models are translated as the objects of the gerundives, though the gerundives have the adjective agreement with the nouns.   Another way of expressing model 1 is **cupidus amīcōs laudandī,** in which **laudandī** is a gerund having amīcōs as its object.   This construction, however, is seldom used.

243. GERUND AND GERUNDIVE COMPARED.—The gerund is a verbal noun, found only in the singular neuter, and belongs to the active voice; the gerundive is a verbal adjective, found in both numbers and all genders, and belongs to the passive voice.

The beginner will have no difficulty in distinguishing the singular of the gerundive from the gerund, if he applies this test: *the gerundive agrees with a noun or pronoun ; the gerund governs it.*

244.   VOCABULARY

animus, -ī, M., *mind, spirit.*
· **cupiditās, -tātis,** F., *desire.*
facultās, -tātis, F., *ease, opportunity, means.*

tēlum, -ī, N., *javelin, spear.*
parātus, -a, -um, *ready, prepared.*
sīc, adv., *so.*

coniūrō (con + iūrō, *swear*), āre, -āvī, -ātum, *conspire*.
dēlīberō, -āre, -āvī, -ātum, *deliberate*.
dēspērō (dē + spērō, *hope*), -āre, -āvī, -ātum, *despair*.
effēminō, -āre, -āvī, -ātum, *weaken, enfeeble*.
fleō, flēre, flēvī, flētum, *weep*.
sūmō, sūmere, sūmpsī, sūmptum, *take, assume*.

What are the present participle, gerund and gerundive of effēminō, obtineō, sūmō and mūniō?

245. Abstract Nouns.—Many abstract nouns—that is, nouns denoting a quality—are derived from adjectives. Some abstract nouns have the suffix -tās: facultās, *ease*, from facilis, *easy ;* cupiditās, *desire,* from cupidus, *desirous*. Other illustrations are hūmāni-tās (hūmānus, homō), nōbili-tās (nōbilis), alti-tūdō (altus), multi-tūdō (multus), amīci-tia (amīcus, *friendly*).

Translate

246. 1. Mīlitēs dēspērantēs dē pūgnā. 2. Caesarī petentī. 3. Dīviciācus flēns auxilium ā Caesare petit. 4. Helvētiī flentēs pācem petēbant. 5. Helvētiī in nostrōs venientēs tēla mittēbant. 6. Pūgnandī tempus. 7. Hiemandī causā. 8. Vītandae suspīciōnis causā. 9. Ad effēminandōs animōs. 10. Cupidus bellī gerendī. 11. Cupiditās rēgnī obtinendī. 12. Caesar diem [1] ad dēlīberandum sūmit. 13. Caesar cōgnōscit multās esse causās coniūrandī. 14. Decima legiō est parāta ad bellum gerendum. 15. Oppidum nātūrā sīc mūniēbatur, ut ad dūcendum [2] bellum daret [3] facultātem.

247. 1. The boys [4] coming to the village. 2. The men seeing the standard. 3. The river [4] flowing into the sea.

---

[1] *a day.* [2] *prolonging.* [3] A subjunctive of *result* (399).
to be translated, like the indicative. [4] Use nominative case.

4. Desirous of hearing. 5. The desire to see[1] the mountain. 6. For the purpose of praising. 7. For the purpose of carrying grain. 8. By giving grain. 9. Ready to give[1] hostages. 10. Ready to move the camp. 11. Ready to defend the town. 12. They say that the javelins are long and heavy.

248. THE PRESENT SYSTEM.—With the exception of the imperative, all the forms of the verb that are derived from the *present stem* have been given in the preceding chapters. Taken together, these forms constitute *the present system.* For **laudō** they are:

ACTIVE.

	INDICATIVE.	SUBJUNCTIVE.	INFINITIVE.	PARTICIPLE.	GERUND.
Pres.	laud-ō	laude-m	laudā-re	laudā-ns	lauda-ndī
Impf.	laudā-bam	laudā-rem			
Fut.	laudā-bō				

PASSIVE.

Pres.	laudo-r	laude-r	laudā-rī
Impf.	laudā-bar	laudā-rer	
Fut.	laudā-bor		lauda-ndus (Gerundive)

In the same manner, write a table of the forms derived from the present stem of **teneō, mittō, mūniō.**

LESSON XXX

Third Conjugation: Verbs in *iō.*—The Ablative of Manner.

249. A few verbs of the third conjugation end in -**iō**. They are conjugated like **regō**, except that they have

---

[1] Do not translate by an infinitive.

-i before -o and -u- in the present indicative, and also before -a- and -e- in the imperfect indicative, future indicative, present subjunctive, present participle, gerund and gerundive. Learn from the Appendix (30), the present system (except the imperative) of both voices of the model verb—

capiō, capere, cēpī, captum, take.

250.   **VOCABULARY**

audācia, -ae, F., *daring, bold-* **initium, -ī,** N., *beginning.*
  ness.   **calamitās, -tātīs,** F., *disaster,*
cōnātum, -ī, N., *attempt, un-*   *defeat.*
  dertaking.

    capiō, capere, cēpī, captum, *take.*
    faciō, facere, fēcī, factum, *make, do.*[1]
    iaciō, iacere, iēcī, iactum, *throw, hurl.*
    perficiō (per + faciō), -ficere, -fēcī, -fectum, *accomplish,*
      complete.
    iter faciō, *march.*

251.   MODEL SENTENCE

     Cum audāciā ⎱ oppūgnābant: ⎰ *with boldness.*
    Māgnā audāciā ⎰ *They were attack-* ⎱ *with great boldness.*
Māgnā cum audāciā ⎰   *ing*   ⎱ *with great boldness.*

The ablatives here answer the question *How?* They denote the *manner* of attacking, and therefore are called *ablatives of manner.*

---

[1] The passive of the simple verb **faciō** is not used in the present system, but is supplied by the irregular verb **fīō** (39). The gerundive, however, is **faciendus.**

252. RULE XX.—*The manner of an action is expressed by a noun in the ablative with* **cum,** *if there is no modifying adjective ; with or without* **cum** *if there is an adjective.*

TRANSLATE

253. 1. Facimus, iacimus. 2. Faciēbātis, iaciēbātis. 3. Faciēmus, iaciēmus. 4. Iaciunt, iacient. 5. Tēla iaciuntur. 6. Cōnāta perficientur. 7. Iter facitis. 8. Facultās praedae faciendae. 9. Facultās per prōvinciam itineris faciendī. 10. Fīlius ducis capiēbātur. 11. Perficit. 12. Facile est cōnāta perficere. 13. Populus Rōmānus pācem cum Helvētiīs faciet. 14. Hostēs in agrōs fīnitimōrum iter faciunt. 15. Hostēs in nostrōs venientēs tēla iaciēbant. 16. Hīc¹ locus ex calamitāte populī Rōmānī nōmen capiet. 17. Liscus māgnō cum perīculō id faciēbat. 18. Mōns ā nostrīs celeriter capitur. 19. Helvētiīs facultās per prōvinciam itineris faciendī nōn datur. 20. Māgnā cum virtūte bellum gerunt. 21. Ūna Galliae pars initium capit ā² flūmine Rhodanō.

254. 1. I was throwing javelins. 2. You will accomplish the undertaking. 3. The Gauls will build (make) forts, that they may defend their territory. 4. The Helvetians marched through the province doing much harm.³ 5. The name of the place will be derived (taken) from the victory of the Germans. 6. All the hostages were taken. 7. We shall give the enemy an opportunity for (of) fighting. 8. He orders the soldiers to take (up) arms. 9. They say that the Belgians are taking up arms. 10. He persuaded the Belgians to take up arms. 11. I fear that the royal power will be seized.

---

¹ *This.*   ² **initium capit ā** = *begins at.* What is the literal meaning of these words ?   ³ *doing much harm* = *with much harm.*

LESSON XXX.

The Pronouns *hīc, iste, ille* and *ipse.*—Caesar, I. 1
(continued).

255. DEMONSTRATIVE PRONOUNS.—Besides **is** and
īdem (190), there are three other demonstratives : **hīc,
iste** and **ille.**

Hīc, *this;* plural, *these.*

	Singular.			*Plural.*		
	M.	F.	N.	M.	F.	N.
N.	hīc	haec	hōc	hī	hae	haec
G.	hūius	hūius	hūius	hōrum	hārum	hōrum
D.	huic	huic	huic	hīs	hīs	hīs
Ac.	hunc	hanc	hōc	hōs	hās	haec
Ab.	hōc	hāc	hōc	hīs	hīs	hīs

Learn from the Appendix (19), the declension of **iste,
ista, istud,** *that* (*of yours*), and of **ille, illa, illud,** *that*
(*yonder*); *he, she, it.*

256. Hīc puer means *this boy* (*near me*); **iste puer,** *that
boy* (*near you*); **ille puer,** *that boy* (*yonder, near him*).
From this difference in meaning, these pronouns may be
called demonstratives of the first, second and third person,
respectively.

Ille—hīc are sometimes correlative, meaning *the former
—the latter.*

257. INTENSIVE PRONOUN.—**Ipse, ipsa, ipsum,** *himself,
herself, itself,* is called the intensive pronoun, because it
emphasizes the word to which it refers : **Ipse ad castra
vēnit,** *He* (Caesar) *himself came to the camp.* It sometimes

means *very:* **In ipsīs flūminis rīpīs,** *on the very banks of the river.* In the genitive it may mean *his own, their own:—* **Ipsīus cōpiae vīsae sunt :** *His own troops were seen.* Learn the declension of **ipse** in Appendix (20).

258.   VOCABULARY

imperium, -ī, N., *command,* **ipse, ipsa, ipsum,** *himself,* etc.;
control.   *very.*
hūmānitās -tātis, F. (**homō**), **longē,** adv., *far.*
  (*humanity*), *civilization.*   **proptereā (propter + ea),** adv.,
hīc, haec, hōc, *this.*   *on this account, for this reason.*
iste, ista, istud, *that, that* (*of* **proptereā quod,** *for the reason*
  yours).   *that.*
ille, illa, illud, *that* (*yonder*); **vel—vel,** conj., *either—or.*
  he, she, it.

absum (ab + sum), abesse, āfuī, *be away, be distant.*
conciliō, -āre, -āvī, -ātum, (*bring together*), *secure, gain.*
interficiō (inter + faciō), ficere, -fēcī, -fectum, *kill.*
statuō, statuere, statuī, statūtum, (*set up*), *decide.*

Decline **hīc fortis nauta, haec legiō, hōc bellum.**

TRANSLATE

259. 1. Hīc pāgus Lucium Cassium cōnsulem interfēcit.
2. Hī sunt extrā [1] prōvinciam trāns Rhodanum prīmī.
3. Hōrum fortissimī [2] sunt Belgae, proptereā quod ab hū-mānitāte prōvinciae longē absunt. 4. Ille locus. 5. Illud bellum. 6. Illō cōnsiliō. 7. Illa pars equitum tēla iēcit.
8. Fīnitimīs illī agrōs dedērunt. 9. Ipse in Ītaliam māgnīs itineribus contendit. 10 Ipsī in eōrum fīnibus bellum gerunt. 11. Ipsōrum linguā Celtae,[3] nostrā Gallī[3] appel-lantur. 12. Cōnsulēs ipsī. 13. Orgetorīx illīs rēgna con-

---

[1] See 129.   [2] *bravest.*   [3] Predicate nominative.

ciliābit, proptereā quod ipse suae cīvitātis imperium
obtinēbit. 14. Eōdem tempore Caesar per explōrātōrēs
cōgnōvit hostēs esse prope ipsīus castra. 15. Caesar
petit ut vel ipse¹ dē eō² statuat vel cīvitātem statuere
iubeat. 260. 1. This nation, these nations. 2. Of this legion,
of these legions. 3. To this hill, to these hills. 4. By
this sailor. 5. By these lieutenants. 6. That standard
(of yours). 7. That river (yonder) is deep. 8. They
themselves came to Helvetia. 9. Those hostages were
given to the king by the Gauls themselves. 10. Caesar
hears (that) Dumnorix is the very (man).

CAESAR, CHAP. 1 (CONTINUED): THE PEOPLE OF GAUL.

261. Hōrum omnium fortissimī sunt Belgae, proptereā
quod ā cultū¹ atque hūmānitāte prōvinciae longissimē²
absunt, minimēque³ ad eōs mercātōrēs saepe commeant
atque ea quae ad effēminandōs animōs pertinent important;⁴ proximīque sunt Germānīs quī trāns Rhēnum 5
incolunt, quibuscum continenter⁵ bellum gerunt. Quā
dē causā⁶ Helvētiī quoque⁷ reliquōs Gallōs virtūte praecēdunt, quod ferē cotīdiānīs proeliīs cum Germānīs contendunt, cum⁸ aut⁹ suīs fīnibus eōs prohibent aut ipsī
in eōrum fīnibus bellum gerunt. 10

NOTES AND VOCABULARY

¹ cultū, abl. of fourth declension, *refinement.*
² longissimē, adv., *farthest;* modifies absunt.
³ minimē, adv., *least;* minimē saepe, *very seldom.*
⁴ importō (in + portō, 38), *import.*
⁵ continenter, adv., *continually.*
⁶ quā dē causā, *and for this reason.*
⁷ quoque, adv., *also.*
⁸ cum, conj., *when.*
⁹ aut—aut, correlative conj., *either—or.*

¹ Diviciacus. ² Dumnorix.

LESSON XXXII

The Pluperfect and Future Perfect Indicative Active. Synopsis.—Contraction.

262. FORMATION OF PLUPERFECT AND FUTURE PERFECT INDICATIVE ACTIVE.—The pluperfect and future perfect indicative active are formed on the perfect stem, the former by adding the tense-sign -era-, the latter, the tense-sign -eri-: laudāv-era-m, laudāver(i)-o.

The pluperfect is equivalent to the English past perfect, and therefore denotes action completed in past time: *I had praised.* The future perfect, like the English future perfect, denotes action completed in the future: *I shall have praised.*

263.   MODEL VERBS

PLUPERFECT.			
I had praised.	*I had advised.*	*I had ruled.*	*I had heard.*
laudāveram	monueram	rēxeram	audīveram
laudāverās	monuerās	rēxerās	audīverās
laudāverat	monuerat	rēxerat	audīverat
laudāverāmus	monuerāmus	rēxerāmus	audīverāmus
laudāverātis	monuerātis	rēxerātis	audīverātis
laudāverant	monuerant	rēxerant	audīverant

FUTURE PERFECT.			
I shall have [1] *praised.*	*I shall have advised.*	*I shall have ruled.*	*I shall have heard.*
laudāverō	monuerō	rēxerō	audīverō
laudāveris	monueris	rēxeris	audīveris
laudāverit	monuerit	rēxerit	audīverit
laudāverimus	monuerimus	rēxerimus	audīverimus
laudāveritis	monueritis	rēxeritis	audīveritis
laudāverint	monuerint	rēxerint	audīverint

PLUPERFECT AND FUTURE PERFECT OF SUM.	
I had been.	*I shall have been.*
fueram	fuerō
fuerās	fueris
fuerat	fuerit
fuerāmus	fuerimus
fuerātis	fueritis
fuerant	fuerint

Conjugate the pluperfect and the future perfect of oppūgnō, teneō, agō, capiō.

264. SYNOPSIS.—A *synopsis* is a table consisting of one form of each tense, in the same voice, number and person. Write a synopsis of laudō in the second person singular; of regō in the third person singular; and of sum in the third person plural.

265. CONTRACTION.—Forms derived from perfects in

---

[1] You, he, they, *will* have praised.

7

-āvī, -ēvī, -ōvī, sometimes drop **v** and contract the vowels into **ā, ē, ō,** respectively. Forms derived from perfects in **-īvī-** drop **v,** but contraction occurs only with **-is.**

laudāvistī,	contracted into laudāstī.		
laudāvistis,	"	"	laudāstis.
laudāvērunt,	"	"	laudārunt.
laudāveram, etc.,	"	"	laudāram, laudārās, etc.
laudāverō, etc.	"	"	laudārō, laudāris, etc.
audīvistī, etc.	"	"	audīstī, etc.
audīveram, etc.	"	"	audieram, etc.
audīverō, etc.	"	"	audierō, etc.

266. VOCABULARY

angustiae, -ārum (angustus), F., *narrowness, narrow pass.*

Nōrēia, -ae, F., *Noreia* (a town in Gaul).

Bōiī, Bōiōrum, M., *Boii* (a Celtic tribe).

iam, adv., *already, now, by this time.*

ibi, adv., *there, in that place.*

imperō, -āre, -āvī, -ātum, *demand, levy, order, command.*

āvertō (ā + vertō), **-vertere, -vertī, -versum,** *turn aside.*

revertō (re + vertō), etc., *return.*[1]

trādūcō (trāns + dūcō, 83), *lead across, bring over.*

TRANSLATE

267. 1. Habuerat, dīxerat. 2. Cōgnōverat, incenderant. 3. Ēgerit, coēgerimus. 4. Imperāveris. 5. Castra posuerimus. 6. Cōnsidius fuerat cum Crassō. 7. Casticī pater rēgnum obtinuerat. 8. Caesar suōs mīlitēs revocāverit. 9. Mīlitēs ex prōvinciā convēnerant. 10. Mīlitēs, quōs imperāverat, convēnērunt. 11. Hīc pāgus ēius exercitum[2]

---

[1] The present system of **revertō** is not used in the active, but in the passive with active meaning. [2] *army.*

sub iugum mīserat. 12. Iter ab Ararī Helvētiī āverterant.
13. Ibi Helvētiī erunt, ubi Caesar eōs esse cōnstituerit.
14. Bōiī trāns Rhēnum incoluerant et Nōrēiam oppūgnāverant. 15. Ea diēs [1] quam cōnstituerat cum lēgātīs,
vēnit et lēgātī ad eum revertērunt. 16. Helvētiī iam per
angustiās et fīnēs Sēquanōrum suās cōpiās trādūxerant, et
in Haeduōrum fīnēs pervēnerant.

268. 1. I shall have come. 2. You had replied. 3. They
had spent-the-winter near Noreia. 4. We shall have returned to this town through the narrow pass. 5. Caesar
had turned (his) course [2] from the Helvetians. 6. The
same lieutenants had demanded a great number of hostages. 7. They have come for the purpose of importing
grain.[3]

LESSON XXXIII—REVIEW

Caesar, I. 1 (concluded)

269. 1. How is the imperfect subjunctive formed?
2. When is this tense used in a clause of purpose?
3. How does the present passive infinitive differ from
the present active? 4. What is a complementary
infinitive? 5. What construction is used after a verb
meaning *say*, *think*, etc.? 6. How is the present participle formed? 7. The gerund? 8. The gerundive?
9. In what respects does the gerund differ from the
gerundive? 10. What are the tense-signs of the pluperfect and future perfect indicative? 11. Decline
hīc, ille and **audiēns.** 12. Write a synopsis of **iaciō**
in the third person singular, indicative active.

---

[1] *day.*   [2] **iter.**   [3] See 199 and 241.

270.   Review Vocabulary

angustiae	nōnnūllī	dēspērō	cōnstituō
audācia	parātus	effēminō	dīcō
animus	quālis	imperō	interclūdō
castellum	hīc	impetrō	statuō
cōnātum	ille	supportō	sūmō
imperium	ipse	vītō	trādūcō
initium	iam	dēleō	capiō
tēlum	ibi	fleō	faciō
calamitās	proptereā	obtineō	iaciō
cupiditās	sīc	remaneō	interficiō
facultās	aut–aut	respondeō	perficiō
hūmānitās	vel–vel	terreō	commūniō
mūnītiō	comportō	ascendō	absum
suspīciō	conciliō	āvertō	
timor	coniūrō	revertō	
turpitūdō	dēlīberō	cōgnōscō	

271.   Review Sentences

1. Dīviciācus flēns haec ā Caesare petit. 2. Caesar cōgnōscit hās esse causās coniūrandī. 3. Decima legiō est parāta ad bellum gerendum. 4. Helvētiī in nostrōs venientēs tēla iaciēbant. 5. Facultās per prōvinciam itineris faciendī dabātur. 6. Oppidum nātūrā locī sīc mūniēbātur, ut māgnam ad dūcendum bellum daret facultātem. 7. Hīc locus ex calamitāte populī Rōmānī nōmen capiet. 8. Liscus māgnō cum perīculō id faciēbat. 9. Mōns ā nostrīs celeriter capitur. 10. Per explōrātōrēs Caesar montem ā suīs tenērī cōgnōvit. 11. Helvētiī pācem et amīcitiam cōnfīrmāre cōnstituērunt. 12. Hī sunt īdem quibuscum Helvētiī contendērunt. 13. Bōiī trāns Rhēnum incoluerant et Nōrēiam oppūgnāverant. 14. Helvētiī per angustiās et fīnēs Sēquanōrum suās cōpiās trādūxerant. 15. Eī

Gallīs persuāsērunt ut oppida incenderent. 16. Nōnnūllī, ut timōris suspīciōnem vītārent, remanēbant.
17. Caesar explōrātōrēs mīsit, quī cōgnōscerent quālis esset
nātūra montis. 18. Equitēs, ut turpitūdinem fugae virtūte dēlērent, omnibus in locīs pūgnāvērunt. 19. Frūmentum comportārī dīcunt. 20. Helvētiōs fīnēs angustōs
habēre dīxērunt. 21. Orgetorīgem causam dīcere coēgērunt. 22. Caesar petit ut vel ipse dē eō statuat vel cīvitātem statuere iubeat.

CAESAR, I. 1 (CONCLUDED): THE BOUNDARIES OF GAUL.

272. Eōrum ūna pars, quam Gallōs obtinēre dictum
est,[1] initium capit ā flūmine Rhodanō; continētur Garumnā flūmine, Ōceanō, fīnibus Belgārum; attingit[2]
etiam[3] ab[4] Sēquanīs et Helvētiīs flūmen Rhēnum ; vergit ad septentriōnēs. Belgae ab[5] extrēmīs[6] Galliae fīni- 5
bus oriuntur,[7] pertinent ad īnferiōrem partem flūminis
Rhēnī, spectant[8] in septentriōnem et orientem[7] sōlem.[9]
Aquītānia ā Garumnā flūmine ad Pȳrēnaeōs montēs et
eam partem Ōceanī quae est ad Hispāniam pertinet;
spectat inter occāsum[10] sōlis et septentriōnēs. 10

NOTES AND VOCABULARY

[1] **dictum est,** *it has been said* (perf. passive ind.).   Compare 235, II.
[2] **attingō, -tingere, -tigī, -tāctum,** *border upon.*
[3] **etiam,** adv., *even.*
[4] **ab,** *on the side of.*   [5] **ab,** *at.*
[6] **extrēmus, -a, -um,** *farthest.*
[7] **orior** (passive form with active meaning), *rise, begin ;* **oriēns** (237),
rising.
[8] **spectō, -āre, -āvī, -ātum,** *face.*
[9] **sōl, sōlis,** M., *sun.*
[10] **occāsum,** acc. of fourth declen., *setting ;* **occāsum sōlis,** *setting of the
sun, the west.*

LESSON XXXIV

The Perfect Participle.—The Ablative Absolute.

273. SUPINE STEM.—The *supine stem* is found by dropping -um of the supine (17, 18): **laudāt-, monit-, rēct-, capt-, audīt-.**

274. PERFECT PARTICIPLE.—The perfect participle (237) is found only in the passive voice, and is equivalent in meaning to the English perfect passive participle. It is formed by adding **-us, -a, -um,** etc., to the supine stem.

> laudā**tus, -ā, -um,** *praised, having been praised.*
> moni**tus, -a, -um,** *advised, having been advised.*
> rēc**tus, -a, -um,** *ruled, having been ruled.*
> cap**tus, -a, -um,** *taken, having been taken.*
> audī**tus, -a, -um,** *heard, having been heard.*

275. The perfect participle may be used (1) like an appositive adjective, in agreement with a noun or pronoun ; (2) like a predicate adjective, to form the compound tenses of the passive voice (283). The former use is shown in the following:

1. **Mīlitēs, trāns Rhēnum trāductī, castra posuērunt:** *The soldiers, having been led over the Rhine, pitched the camp.*
2. **Fīlia prīncipis, ab hostibus capta, ad castra dūcēbātur:** *The daughter of the chief, having been captured by the enemy, was led to the camp.*

276. ABLATIVE ABSOLUTE.—(*a*) An ablative absolute is a phrase consisting of a noun or pronoun in the

ablative, and a participle, an adjective or another noun in agreement with it. It may therefore be:
1. A noun (or pronoun) + a participle. See models 1–4 in 277.
2. A noun (or pronoun) + an adjective (predicate). See model 5 in 277.
3. A noun (or pronoun) + a noun (predicate). See model 6 in 277.

(b) An ablative absolute often denotes one of the following ideas:
1. Time (*when, after*). See models 1 and 6 in 277.
2. Cause (*because, since*). See model 2 in 277.
3. Concession (*although*).   " "   3 " 277.
4. Condition (*if*).   " "   4 " 277.

277.   MODELS

1. **Proeliō factō:** (*the battle having been fought*), *when* (or *after*) *the battle was fought.* (Time.)
2. **Nostrīs succēdentibus**[1]: (*our men advancing*), *because* (or *since, while, when*) *our men were advancing.* (Cause or time.)
3. **Paucīs**[2] **dēfendentibus:** (*few defending*), *though the de-*
• *fenders were few.* (Concession.)
4. **Datā facultāte:** (*an opportunity having been given*), *if an opportunity should be given.* (Condition.)
5. **Caesare invītō**[3]: (*Caesar being unwilling*), *against Caesar's will.*
6. **Messālā cōnsule:** (*Messala being consul*), *when Messala was consul, in the consulship of Messala.* (Time.)

---

[1] **succēdō (sub + cēdō), -cēdere, -cessī, -cessum,** *come up, advance.*
[2] **paucī, -ōrum** (adj. as noun), *few.*
[3] **invītus, -a, -um,** adj., *unwilling.*

Notice that these phrases when translated literally, as in the parentheses, are equivalent to the English nominative absolute. But it will be found that this is usually not the best equivalent. It is often better to translate by a clause beginning with *when, since* or *if*, etc., the proper word being determined only by the thought of the sentence.

278. Helvētiīs pācātīs, Caesar cum Germānīs contendit : *Having subdued the Helvetians, Caesar fought with the Germans.*

Latin, having no active perfect participle, very often uses the passive in place of it, as in the illustration. To do this, notice that it puts the English object (*Helvetians*) in the ablative case, forming an ablative absolute with the participle (**pācātīs**). The literal meaning of **Helvētiīs pācātīs** is, *the Helvetians having been subdued*, etc., but as Caesar did the action expressed by **pācātīs** as well as by **contendit,** that fact is best expressed by the translation given above.

Note.—The perfect participle of deponent verbs (356) is an exception to this usage, for, having an active meaning, it may be used in agreement with the subject like an English active perfect. This is illustrated in 361, 15.

279. RULE XXI.—*A noun or pronoun in the ablative, with a noun, adjective or participle in agreement with it, may form an ablative absolute.*

280.   **VOCABULARY**

inopia, -ae, F., *scarcity.*   **Allobrogēs, –um,** M., *Allobroges*
praesidium, ī, N., *guard.*   (a tribe near Lake Geneva).

accūsō, -āre, -āvī, -ātum, *accuse.*
exspectō, -āre, -āvī, -ātum, *wait for, expect.*

permoveō (per + moveō, 45), (*move thoroughly*), *influence*.
addūcō (ad + dūcō, 83), (*lead to*), *induce*.
indūcō (in + dūcō, 83), (*lead on*), *induce*.
dispōnō (dis + pōnō, 166), *station*.
iungō, iungere, iūnxī, iūnctum, *join*.
trādō, trādere, trādidī, trāditum, *give up, surrender*.

TRANSLATE

281. 1. Rēgnō occupātō.[1] 2. Hōc proeliō nūntiātō.[1]
3. Armīs trāditīs.[2] 4. Galli hāc ōrātiōne adductī coniūrātiōnem faciunt. 5. Eō opere perfectō,[3] Caesar praesidia
dispōnit. 6. Helvētiī nāvibus iūnctīs [5] flūmen trānseunt.[6]
7. Nostrī sīgnō datō impetum [7] fēcērunt. 8. Convocātīs
prīncipibus, Caesar eōs accūsat. 9. Equitēs ā cīvitāte missī
ad Caesarem vēnērunt. 10. Labiēnus, monte occupātō,
nostrōs exspectābat. 11. Orgetorīx, Messālā et Pīsōne cōnsulibus, rēgnī cupiditāte inductus coniūrātiōnem nōbilitātis
fēcit. 12. Galba frūmentī inopiā permōtus in prōvinciam
contendit et, nūllō hoste prohibente,[4] legiōnem in Allobrogēs perdūxit. 13. Caesar lēgātōs nāvēs exspectāre iussit.
14. Mīlitēs ipsī sunt parātī ad oppūgnandam Nōrēiam.

282. 1. (When) the towns (were) burned, the Helvetians were ready. 2. Induced by the influence of Orgetorix, the Helvetians made peace. 3. (After) all Gaul
(was) subdued, our (forces) were led into the territory of
the Belgae. 4. (Though) the guard (was) small, the enemy did not make an attack. 5. Many villages will be
captured by the troops under the leadership [6] of Labienus.

---

[1] Translate by a clause expressing time.
[2] " " " " condition.
[3] " " " " time, or see 278.
[4] " " " " cause.
[5] See 278. [6] *cross*. [7] *attack*, accusative. [6] *under the leadership of
Labienus = Labienus (being) leader*.

6. The Allobroges say that the guard is expected.   7. Caesar had sent ships to transport¹ the troops.   (Translate the last sentence in two ways.)

LESSON XXXV

The Perfect, Pluperfect and Future Perfect Indicative Passive.—Review of Indicative, Active and Passive.

283. FORMATION OF PASSIVE PERFECT TENSES.— In the passive voice, the perfect, pluperfect and future perfect are formed by combining respectively the present, imperfect and future of **sum** with the perfect participle of the given verb: perfect, **laudātus sum;** pluperfect, **laudātus eram;** future perfect, **laudātus erō.** These tenses, consisting of two words, are called *compound tenses;* other tenses, consisting of one word, may be called *simple tenses.*

284.   MODEL VERBS

PERFECT INDICATIVE PASSIVE.

I have been praised, I was praised.	
laudātus sum	laudātī sumus
laudātus es	laudātī estis
landātus est	laudātī sunt

monitus sum, *I have been advised, I was advised.*
rēctus sum, *I have been ruled, I was ruled.*
captus sum, *I have been taken, I was taken.*
audītus sum, *I have been heard, I was heard.*

¹ **trānsportō** (trāns + portō).

PLUPERFECT INDICATIVE PASSIVE.

I had been praised.	
laudātus eram	laudātī erāmus
laudātus erās	laudātī erātis
laudātus erat	laudātī erant

monitus eram, *I had been advised.*
rēctus eram, *I had been ruled.*
captus eram, *I had been taken.*
audītus eram, *I had been heard.*

FUTURE PERFECT PASSIVE.

I shall have been praised.	
laudātus erō	laudātī erimus
laudātus eris	laudātī eritis
laudātus erit	laudātī erunt

monitus erō, *I shall have been advised.*
rēctus erō, *I shall have been ruled.*
captus erō, *I shall have been taken.*
audītus erō, *I shall have been heard.*

Write a synopsis of the model verbs in the passive voice, indicative mood.

285. AGREEMENT OF THE PARTICIPLE.—The participle agrees with the subject in gender, as well as number and case. For a feminine subject we should have **laudāta sum, laudātae sumus**, etc.; for a neuter, **laudātum est, laudāta sunt.** If a verb has two or more subjects of different genders, the participle is masculine if the subjects denote persons, neuter if they denote things, or it may agree with the nearest subject, as **captus** in the following sentence:

Orgetorīgis fīlia atque ūnus ē fīliīs captus est: *A daughter and one of the sons of Orgetorix were captured.*

286. PRINCIPAL PARTS IN THE PASSIVE VOICE.—The principal parts of a verb in the passive voice are the present indicative, present infinitive and perfect indicative: **laudor, laudārī, laudātus sum.**
Write the passive parts of the other model verbs and of **iubeō, dūcō** and **iaciō.**

287.   TABLE OF INDICATIVE ENDINGS.

	First Person Singular.	
	ACTIVE.	PASSIVE.
Pres.	-ō	-r
Impf.	-bam	-bar
Fut.	-bō, -am	-bor, -ar
Perf.	-ī	-us sum
Plup.	-eram	-us eram
Fut. Perf.	-erō	-us erō

288.   VOCABULARY

nūper, adv., *recently.*
indicium, -ī, N. (**dīcō**), *information;* **per indicium,** *through an informer.*

TRANSLATE

289. 1. Missus erō. 2. Missī eritis. 3. Missī estis. 4. Missī erātis. 5. Ad Galliam missus eram. 6. Pāx cōnfīrmāta erit.

7. Duae legiōnēs conscrīptae erunt.   8. Nūntiātum est.
9. Appellātae sunt.   10. Pīla importāta erant.   11. Ab
hostibus captī erimus.   12. Ā mīlite vīsus eris.   13. Id
Caesarī nūntiātum erat.   14. Ea coniūrātiō Helvētiīs per
indicium est ēnūntiāta.   15. Pater Casticī ā populō Rōmānō amīcus appellātus erat.   16. Inter fīnēs Helvētiōrum
et Allobrogum, quī nūper pācātī erant, Rhodanus fluit.
17. Gallia sub septentriōnibus, ut [1] ante dictum est, posita
est.   18. Caesaris cōpiae prope hostium castra vīsae erant.
19. Agrīs vāstātīs, cīvitās arma trādidit.   20. Iaciet.
21. Vīderat, vīderit.   22. Vidēns.   23. Videndī causā.
24. Parātus ad videnda castra.

290. 1. We have been influenced.   2. The town had
been defended.   3. The boys will have been captured.
4. You have been called friend.   5. You have been called
friends.   6. The fields have been laid waste.[2]   7. I have
been ordered [3] to report the victory.   8. They will have
been led across the bridge.   9. Stones and javelins had
been thrown [4] from [5] the wall.   10. He persuaded the
sailors to transport the booty.

LESSON XXXVI

Comparison of Adjectives.—Declension of Comparatives.

291. DEGREES OF COMPARISON.—Adjectives in Latin
as in English have three degrees: positive, comparative
and superlative.   Most adjectives in Latin are compared by changing the ending: long-**us**, long-**ior**, long-
issimus, *long, long-er, long-est.*

---

[1] **Ut** with the indicative generally means *as.*   [2] **vāstō.**   [3] **iubeō.**
[4] What gender?   See 285.   [5] **dē.**

292. The comparative is formed by adding **-ior** for the masculine and feminine, and **-ius** for the neuter, to the base of the positive; the superlative, by adding **-issimus, -a, -um.**

BASE.	POSITIVE.	COMPARATIVE.	SUPERLATIVE.
long-	{ longus / -a, -um }	longior, -ius	longissimus, -a, -um
grav-	gravis, -e	gravior, -ius	gravissimus, -a, -um
potent-	potēns	potentior, -ius	potentissimus, -a, -um

293. Positives in **-er** form the superlative by adding **-rimus** to the nominative of the positive.

BASE.	POSITIVE.	COMPARATIVE.	SUPERLATIVE.
ācr-	ācer, ācris, ācre	ācrior, -ius	ācerrimus, -a, -um
liber-	līber, -era, -erum	līberior, -ius	līberrimus, -a, -um

294. Six positives in **-lis** form the superlative by adding **-limus** to the base of the positive. They are **facilis,** *easy,* **difficilis,** *difficult,* **similis,** *like,* **dissimilis,** *unlike,* **gracilis,** *slender,* **humilis,** *low.*

BASE.	POSITIVE.	COMPARATIVE.	SUPERLATIVE.
facil-	facilis, -e	facilior, -ius	facillimus, -a, -um

Compare **fortis, dēnsus, lātus, miser, vēlōx.**

295. DECLENSION OF COMPARATIVES.—The comparative of an adjective belongs to the third declension. Learn the declension of the model comparative **longior** in Appendix (13).

Decline **longius bellum, longior via.**

296. The comparative is usually translated by *more* or *-er*, but sometimes by *too* or *rather;* the superlative by *most* or *-est*, but sometimes by *very;* **longior, -ius,** *longer, too long, rather long;* **longissimus, -a, -um,** *longest, very long.*

297.   V.OCABULARY

āgmen, āgminis, N. (agō), *army* (on the march), *line* (of troops).
novissimum āgmen, *rear* (of an army), *rear guard.*
prīmum āgmen, *front* (of an army), *van.*
cohors, cohortis, F., *cohort* (tenth of a legion).
fīrmus, -a, -um, *strong, firm.*
ferāx, -ācis, adj., *fertile.*
nōbilis, -e, *famous, noble, well-born.*

  impendeō (in + **pendeō**), **-ēre,** ——, ——, *overhang.*
  circumdūcō (**circum** + **dūcō,** 83), *lead around.*

TRANSLATE

298. 1. Lātius flūmen. 2. Lātiōris flūminis. 3. Altiōrēs rīpae. 4. Graviōribus tēlīs. 5. Per dēnsiōrēs silvās. 6. In dēnsissimās silvās. 7. Ā novissimō āgmine. 8. Inter novissimum hostium āgmen et nostrum prīmum (āgmen). 9. Per trēs potentissimōs āc fīrmissimōs populōs. 10. Helvētiī parātiōrēs ad bellum gerendum erunt. 11. Hōrum omnium fortissimī sunt Belgae. 12. Apud Helvētiōs nōbilissimus fuit Orgetorīx. 13. Iter est facilius. 14. Iter erat nōn difficillimum. 15. Agrī sunt lātissimī et ferācissimī. 16. Pūblius Cōnsidius perītissimus habēbātur.[1] 17. Mōns altissimus impendēbat. 18. Helvētiī lēgātōs [2] nōbilissi-

---

[1] *was considered.*   [2] *as ambassadors,* in apposition with **nōbilissimōs.**

mōs ¹ cīvitātis mittunt. 19. Ūnā ex parte Helvētia flūmine Rhēnō, lātissimō atque altissimō, continētur. 20.
Cohortēs longiōre itinere circumductae sunt. 21. Cohorti-
bus decem ad mare relictīs, dē tertiā vigiliā ad hostēs contendit.

299. 1. With a stronger guard. 2. Across a broader
river. 3. Into a more fertile field. 4. Of the highest
mountain. 5. The sword is too heavy. 6. I have seen
the rear guard. 7. The footmen will be very swift. 8.
The children of the most famous (men) of the tribe had
been sent (as) hostages. 9. The chief feared that the
children would be killed.

LESSON XXXVII

Comparison of Adjectives (continued).—The Abla-
tive after a Comparative.

300. The following adjectives are compared irregu-
larly:

Positive.	Comparative.	Superlative.
bonus, -a, -um, *good*	melior, melius	optimus, -a, -um
malus, -a, -um, *bad*	pēior, pēius	pessimus, -a, -um
māgnus, -a, -um, *great, large*	māior, māius	māximus, -a, -um
parvus, -a, -um, *small, little*	minor, minus	minimus, -a, -um
multus, -a, -um, *much*	——, plūs	plūrimus, -a, -um
multī, -ae, -a, *many*	plūrēs, plūra	plūrimī, -ae, -a

Learn the declension of **plūs** in the Appendix (14).

---

¹ Used as a noun, object of **mittunt.**

301.

vetus, *old*	vetustior	veterrimus
senex, *old*	senior (māior nātū [1])	māximus nātū [1]
iuvenis, *young*	iūnior (minor nātū)	minimus nātū
dīves, *rich*	dītior	dītissimus (dīvitissimus)

Learn the declension of **vetus** in the Appendix (14).

302.   MODEL SENTENCE

Helvētia est minor $\left\{\begin{array}{c} \text{quam Aquītānia} \\ \text{or} \\ \text{Aquītāniā} \end{array}\right.$ $\left.\begin{array}{c} \\ \\ \end{array}\right\}$ *Helvetia is smaller than Aquitania.*

In this sentence notice that comparison is expressed with the conjunction **quam,** *than,* both nouns being in the same case, or without **quam,** the second noun then being in the ablative.

303. RULE XXII.—*When two persons or things are compared, the name of the second is put in the ablative if* **quam,** *meaning* than, *is omitted.*

NOTE.—**Quam** may be omitted when the name of the first of the two persons or things is in the nominative or accusative case.

304.   VOCABULARY

fortūna, -ae, F., *fortune, lot.*   hiems, hiemis, F., *winter.*

carrus, -ī, M., carrum, -ī, N.,   brevis, -e, *short.*
    cart.   dīves, dīvitis, *rich.*

---

[1] nātū, an abl. of the fourth declension, meaning *by birth;* sometimes omitted.

3

iūmentum, -ī, N., *beast of*   māiōrēs, -um, M., pl. adj. used
  burden.   as noun, *elders, ancestors.*
continēns, -entis, F., *conti-*
  nent.
quam, conj. and adv., *than, as ;* with superlatives, *as—as*
  possible.[1]
    nāvigō, -āre, -āvī, -ātum, *sail.*
    coëmō (con + emō), -ëmere, -ēmī, -ēmptum, *buy up.*
    discō, discere, didicī, ——, *learn.*
    impōnō (in + pōnō, 166), *place on, mount on.*
    redūcō (re + dūcō, 83), *lead back.*

TRANSLATE

305. 1. Minima altitūdō flūminis. 2. Plūrēs Germānī
Rhēnum trāductī[2] sunt. 3. Omnēs māiōrēs ad imperātōrem
vēnērunt. 4. Helvētiī ā patribus māiōribusque suīs didi-
cerant. 5. Caesar quattuor legiōnēs in māiōra castra
edūxit. 6. Auxilia prō minōribus castrīs cōnstituit. 7. Apud
Helvētiōs nōbilissimus et dītissimus fuit Orgetorīx. 8. Gallī
plūrimās nāvēs, quibus in Britanniam nāvigant. 9. Difficultās nāvigandī. 10. Quam plūrimae cīvitātēs. 11. Sēmentēs
quam māximās faciunt. 12. Helvētiī iūmentōrum et carrōrum quam māximum numerum coëmunt. 13. Caesar in
equōs suōs mīlitēs imposuit, ut praesidium quam amīcissi-
mum habēret. 14. Noctēs in Britanniā breviōrēs esse quam
in continentī vidēbāmus. 15. Hieme diēs[3] sunt breviōrēs
noctibus. 16. Fortūna Sēquanōrum miserior est quam
(fortūna) reliquōrum Gallōrum.

306. 1. Peace is better than war. 2. These ships are
broader than the Roman ships. 3. We have a sword
heavier than a spear. 4. The Helvetians burned as many
towns (as possible). 5. Very many beasts (of burden)

---

[1] For example, quam māximus, *as large as possible, the largest possible.*
[2] Depends on trā- (= trāns) in the verb.   [3] *days.*

have been seen near the river. 6. The cart is too large.
7. The-rest-of the ships are ready to sail (for sailing).

Carrus et Iūmenta

LESSON XXXVIII

Comparison of Adjectives (concluded).—The Ablative of Degree of Difference.—The Dative with Adjectives.

307. Some comparatives and superlatives have no positive, but are referred to corresponding adverbs or prepositions.

	COMPARATIVE.	SUPERLATIVE.
cis, citrā, *on this side,*	**citerior,** *hither,*	**citimus,** *hithermost.*
in, intrā, *in, within,*	**interior,** *inner,*	**intimus,** *inmost.*
prae, prō, *before,*	**prior,** *former,*	**prīmus,** *first.*
ūltrā, *beyond,*	**ūlterior,** *farther,*	**ūltimus,** *farthest.*

308. The following positives are rare except as nouns:

POSITIVE.	COMPARATIVE.	SUPERLATIVE.
(exterus)	**exterior,** *outer,*	**extrēmus (extimus),** *extreme, farthest.*
(īnferus)	**īnferior,** *lower,*	**īnfimus (īmus),** *lowest.*
(posterus)	**posterior,** *latter,*	**postrēmus (postumus),** *last.*
(superus)	**superior,** *higher,*	**suprēmus (summus),** *highest, greatest.*

309. Adjectives in **-eus, -ius** and **-uus** (except **-quus**) are compared by means of **magis** (*more*) and **māximē** (*most*): **idōneus,** *suitable,* **magis idōneus,** *more suitable,* **māximē idōneus,** *most suitable.*

NOTE.—Many adjectives in Latin as in English cannot be compared.

310.   VOCABULARY

pēs, pedis, M., *foot.*   **turris, -is,** F., *tower.*

profectiō, -ōnis, F., *depar-*   **apertus, -a, -um,** *open, ex-*
ture, retreat.   *posed.*

311.   MODEL SENTENCES

1. **Gladius est quattuor pedibus brevior pīlō:** *The sword is four feet shorter (shorter by four feet) than the javelin.*
2. **Iter est multō facilius:** *The way is much easier (easier by much).*

How much shorter is the sword? Is the way easier? The ablatives **pedibus** and **multō,** used in answering these questions, denote the *degree of difference.* The ablative of degree of difference usually answers the question *By how much?*

312. RULE XXIII.—*The ablative is used with comparatives to denote the degree of difference.*

313.   MODEL SENTENCES

1. **Helvētiī sunt proximī Germānīs:** *The Helvetians are next to the Germans.*
2. **Locus esti dōneus castrīs:** *The place is suitable for a camp.*
3. **Puer est similis patrī:** *The boy is like (his) father.*

Notice that after **proximī, idōneus** and **similis** the noun towards which the quality is directed is in the dative. This construction is called the *dative with adjectives*.

314. RULE XXIV.—*The dative is used with adjectives implying* nearness, fitness, likeness, *etc.*

TRANSLATE

315. 1. Interior Gallia. 2. Ē locō superiōre. 3. Ex īnferiōre locō. 4. Ad īnferiōrem partem Rhēnī. 5. In ulteriōre Galliā. 6. Ūltimae nātiōnēs. 7. Ab extrēmīs Galliae fīnibus. 8. In proximum collem. 9. Cum proximīs cīvitātibus. 10. Multō fortior mīles. 11. Multō minor pars āgminis. 12. Profectiō erat similis fugae. 13. Extrēmum oppidum Allobrogum proximumque Helvētiōrum fīnibus est Genāva. 14. Locīs superiōribus occupātīs,[1] itinere cōpiās prohibent. 15. Summus[2] mōns ā Labiēnō tenēbātur. 16. Collis īnfimus[2] erat apertus. 17. Ad extrēmās[2] fossās castella cōnstituit. 18. Turrēs decem pedibus quam mūrus altiōrēs sunt. 19. Monet ut omnēs suspīciōnēs vītet. 20. Puerī Hispāniam esse proximam Galliae didicērunt.

316. 1. The farthest parts of the town. 2. A mountain is very near the town. 3. The lowest (part of the) tower. 4. On the top (of the) hill were many animals. 5. The soldier is like his friend. 6. The bank is a foot higher than the river. 7. He heard that the men were suitable for the work. 8. They hear (that) the towers are very high. 9. Messala has many horses and carts (Express in two ways).

---

[1] See 279.   [2] **Summus** sometimes means *the highest part of, the top of;* **īnfimus**, *the lowest part of, the bottom of;* **extrēmus**, *the end of.*

LESSON XXXIX—REVIEW

Caesar, I . 2 (begun)

317. 1. How is the perfect participle used? 2. What is an ablative absolute? 3. What is a compound tense? 4. How is the comparative degree regularly formed? 5. The superlative? 6. The superlative of adjectives in -er and -lis? 7. Name the six adjectives having -limus in the superlative? 8. Compare **bonus, malus, māgnus, parvus, multus.** 9. What case is used after a comparative? 10. With what adjectives is the dative used? 11. Write a synopsis of **iungō** in the active, third singular. 12. Of **accūsō** in the passive, third plural.

318.   Review Vocabulary

fortūna	māiōrēs	ferāx	circumdūcō
inopia	pēs	nōbilis	indūcō
carrus	profectiō	nūper	redūcō
indicium	turris	quam	coëmō
iūmentum	apertus	accūsō	discō
paucī	fīrmus	exspectō	dispōnō
praesidium	idōneus	impendeō	impōnō
āgmen	invītus	permoveō	iungō
cohors	brevis	addūcō	trādō
hiems	dīves		

319.   Review Sentences

1. Equitēs, auxilī causā ā cīvitāte missī, ad Caesarem vēnērunt. 2. Labiēnus monte occupātō nostrōs exspectābat. 3. Ea coniūrātiō est Helvētiīs per indicium ēnūntiāta. 4. Inter fīnēs Helvētiōrum et Allobrogum, quī nūper pācātī erant, Rhodanus īnfluit. 5. Pūblius Cōnsidius

perītissimus habēbātur. 6. Mōns altissimus impendēbat.
7. Sēmentēs quam māximās faciunt. 8. Caesar auxilia
prō castrīs minōribus cōnstituit. 9. Helvētiī iūmentōrum
et carrōrum quam māximum numerum coëmunt. 10. Fortūna Sēquanōrum miserior est quam reliquōrum. 11. Summus mōns ā Labiēnō tenēbātur. 12. Locīs superiōribus
occupātīs, itinere cōpiās prohibent. 13. Eō opere perfectō,
Caesar praesidia disposuit. 14. Convocātīs prīncipibus,
Caesar eōs accūsat. 15. Extrēmum oppidum Allobrogum
proximumque Helvētiōrum fīnibus est Genāva.

320. HISTORICAL NOTE.—During the year 58 B.C.
Caesar conducted two campaigns, one against a Gallic
tribe, the Helvetii, another against Ariovistus, a German
king. The account of the Helvetian campaign, Chapters 2 to 29 of the first book of the "Commentaries,"
is given in this book.

**321. CAESAR, I. 2 (BEGUN): THE HELVETIANS AND
THE PLANS OF ORGETORIX.**

Apud Helvētiōs longē [1] nōbilissimus fuit et dītissimus Orgetorīx. Is, M.[2] Messālā et M. Pīsōne cōnsulibus,
rēgnī cupiditāte inductus coniūrātiōnem nōbilitātis fēcit,
et cīvitātī persuāsit ut dē fīnibus suīs cum omnibus cōpiīs
exīrent [3]: perfacile esse,[4] cum [5] virtūte [6] omnibus [7] prae- 5
stārent,[8] tōtīus Galliae imperiō potīrī.[9]

NOTES AND VOCABULARY

[1] **longē**, adv., *far, by far*.
[2] **M.**, abbreviation of **Mārcus**, a Roman name.
[3] **exīrent** (impf. subjunctive of **exeō**), *go out*.
[4] (dīxit) **perfacile esse**, *he said it was very easy*,
[5] **cum**, conj., *since* (followed by the subjunctive, 465).
[6] See 144. [7] **praestārent** governs the dative.
[8] **praestō (prae + stō), -stāre, -stitī, -stitum**, (*stand before*), *excel*.
[9] **potīrī**, *to secure;* governs the ablative.

LESSON XL

Adverbs: Their Formation and Comparison.—Use of Adverbs.

322. FORMATION OF ADVERBS.—Adverbs are derived chiefly from adjectives.

(a) Some are derived from adjectives of the first and second declension by adding **-ē** to the base: **lātus,** *wide,* **lātē,** *widely.*

(b) Some are derived from adjectives of the third declension by adding **-ter** (-iter) to the base: **gravis,** *heavy,* **graviter,** *heavily,* **prūdēns,**[1] *prudent,* **prūdenter,** *prudently.*

323. COMPARISON OF ADVERBS.—Adverbs are compared thus: the comparative is the neuter comparative of the adjective (292); the superlative is the superlative of the adjective with final **-us** changed to **-ē.**

POSITIVE.	COMPARATIVE.	SUPERLATIVE.
lātē, *widely*	**lātius**	**lātissimē**
līberē, *freely*	**līberius**	**līberrimē**
facile, *easily*	**facilius**	**facillimē**
graviter, *heavily, severely*	**gravius**	**gravissimē**
bene, *well*	**melius**	**optimē**
male, *ill*	**pēius**	**pessimē**
———	**magis** (*more*)	**māximē** (*most*)
multum, *much*	**plūs**	**plūrimum**
parum, *little*	**minus**	**minimē**
diū, *long* (in time)	**diūtius**	**ditissimē**
prope, *near*	**propius**	**proximē**
saepe, *often*	**saepius**	**saepissimē**

[1] Bases in **-t** (**prūdent-**) drop this letter before the ending **-ter.**

324. In the expressions **fortiter pūgnat, magis idō-neus, minus facile,** notice that an adverb modifies the verb **pūgnat,** the adjective **idōneus** and the adverb **facile.**

325. RULE XXV.—*An adverb may modify a verb, adjective or another adverb.*

326. VOCABULARY

Bibracte, -is, N., *Bibracte* (a town of the Haedui).
plēbs, plēbis, F., *the common people.*
acceptus, -a, -um, *pleasing, popular with.*
cōpiōsus (cōpia), -a, -um, *well-supplied, wealthy.*
audāx, -ācis, adj., *bold.*

conlocō (con + locō), -āre, -āvi, -ātum, *place, station.*
permittō (per + mittō), (*let go*), *intrust, allow, permit.*

TRANSLATE

327. 1. Minimē saepe. 2. Belgae ā prōvinciā longissimē absunt. 3. Continenter bellum gerunt. 4. Orgetorīx facilius eīs persuāsit. 5. Minus lātē. 6. Minus facile. 7. Orgetorīx māximē plēbī acceptus erat. 8. Nostrī cum Helvētiīs proelium cupidius committunt. 9. Au-dācius pūgnant. 10. Caesar graviter prīncipēs accūsat. 11. Multō grāvius. 12. Liscus dīcit līberius atque au-dācius. 13. Ā Bibracte, oppidō Haeduōrum longē māx-imō et cōpiōsissimō, Caesar aberat. 14. In summō iugō suās legiōnēs, quās in Galliā citeriōre proximē[1] cōnscrīp-serat, et omnia auxilia conlocāvit. 15. Diū atque ācriter pūgnāvērunt. 16. Suīs[2] imperāvit[3] nē tēla iacerent. 17. Huic permīsit,[3] utī in hīs locīs legiōnem conlocāret. 18. Conlocārī. 19. Conlocāns. 20. Conlocandī. 21. Con-locandus.[4]

328. 1. The soldiers will not defend the town (any)

---

[1] *last.* [2] Supply **mīlitibus,** indirect object. [3] See 206. [4] See 241.

longer. 2. The lieutenant came more quickly than the messenger. 3. The town was captured [1] very easily. 4. The enemy boldly threw their javelins. 5. We shall send the messengers as quickly [2] (as possible). 6. He commands [3] his (men) to do the same (thing). 7. Those who were popular with the common people had come together for the purpose of buying grain.

LESSON XLI

The Fourth Declension.—Caesar, I. 2 (continued).

329. GENITIVE SINGULAR.—The fourth declension includes all nouns whose genitive singular ends in -ūs.

330. GENDER.—Most nouns of the fourth declension are masculine. **Domus,** *house,* **manus,** *hand,* **Īdus** (pl.), *Ides,* and a few others are feminine. **Cornū,** *horn,* **genū,** *knee,* and **verū,** *a spit,* are neuter.

331. MODEL NOUNS

	SINGULAR.	PLURAL.	ENDINGS.	
	Manus, F., *hand.*	Base: **man-.**		
N.	manus	manūs	-us	-ūs
G.	manūs	manuum	-ūs	-uum
D.	manuī (manū)	manibus	-uī (-ū)	-ibus
Ac.	manum	manūs	-um	-ūs
Ab.	manū	manibus	-ū	-ibus
	Cornū, N., *horn.*	Base: **corn-.**		
N.	cornū	cornua	-ū	-ua
G.	cornūs	cornuum	-ūs	-uum
D.	cornū	cornibus	-ū	-ibus
Ac.	cornū	cornua	-ū	-ua
Ab.	cornū	cornibus	-ū	-ibus

[1] **expūgnō.** [2] **quam** + superlative ; see 304. [3] **imperō** + **ut.**

332. Special Endings.—**Domus** (*house*) has **domō** or **domū** in the ablative singular, **domī** in the locative (*at home*), **domōs** or **domūs** in the accusative plural. **Artūs**, *limbs*, **portus**, *harbor*, and dissyllables in **-cus** have **-ubus** or **-ibus** in the dative and ablative plural.

333.   VOCABULARY

cōnspectus, -ūs, m., *sight.*
cornū, -ūs, n., *horn, wing* (*of an army*).
cultus, -ūs, m., *civilization.*
domus, -ūs, f., *house, home.*
equitātus -ūs, m. (equus), *cavalry.*
exercitus, -ūs, m., *army.*
impetus, -ūs, m., *attack.*

lacus, -ūs, m., *lake.*
manus, -ūs, f., *hand.*
occāsus, -ūs, m., *falling, setting.*
prīncipātus -ūs (prīnceps), m. *leadership.*
senātus, -ūs, m., *senate.*
dexter, -tra, -trum, *right.*

sustineō (sub + teneō), -tinēre, -tinuī, -tentum, *withstand, endure.*

Decline together **īdem exercitus** and **hīc altior lacus.**

Translate

334. 1. Ā cultū prōvinciae absunt. 2. Germānī cultum Gallōrum laudāvērunt. 3. Aquītānia spectat inter occāsum sōlis et septentriōnēs. 4. Tertiā ex parte Helvētia lacū Lemannō continētur. 5. Ā senātū populī Rōmānī[1] amīcus appellātus erat. 6. Dumnorīx prīncipātum in cīvitāte obtinēbat. 7. Meō exercitū rēgnum conciliābō. 8. In cōnspectū exercitūs nostrī[2] agrī Haeduōrum vāstābantur. 9. Dumnorīx māgnum numerum equitātūs habet. 10. Caesar equitātum, quī sustinēret hostium impetum, mīsit.

---

[1] **populī Rōmānī** modifies **senātū.**   [2] **nostrī** modifies **exercitūs.**

11. Hostēs diūtius nostrōrum impetūs nōn sustinuērunt.
12. Oppidum et [1] nātūrā locī et [1] manū mūnītum erat.
13. Auctōritās Dīviciācī erat māgna domī atque in reliquā
Galliā.   14. In dextrō cornū duae legiōnēs conlocābuntur.

335. 1. In the lakes. 2. By the attacks. 3. To the
senate. 4. For the armies. 5. Of the hand. 6. Of the
hands. 7. The height of the houses. 8. The animals have
very long horns. 9. The army was sent under the yoke.
10. A sword is in the lieutenant's right hand. 11. They say
that a sword is in his hand.

336. Caesar, I. 2 (continued) : The Boundaries
of Helvetia

Id [1] hōc [2] facilius eīs [1] persuāsit, quod undique locī
nātūrā Helvētiī continentur: ūnā ex parte flūmine Rhēnō
lātissimō atque altissimō, quī agrum Helvētium ā Germānīs dīvidit; alterā ex parte monte Iūrā altissimō, quī
5 est inter Sēquanōs et Helvētiōs; tertiā [3] lacū Lemannō
et flūmine Rhodanō, quī prōvinciam nostram ab Helvētiīs
dīvidit.

NOTES AND VOCABULARY

[1] See 193, 18.   [2] **hīc,** *on this account,* abl. of cause.   [3] Supply **ex parte.**

[1] **et—et,** *both—and.*

Cornū

LESSON XLII

The Fifth Declension. — Idioms. — Stems of Nouns and Adjectives.

337. GENITIVE SINGULAR.—The fifth declension includes all nouns whose genitive singular ends in -ĕī.

338. GENDER.—Nouns of the fifth declension are feminine except **diēs**, *day*, which is always masculine in the plural and generally so in the singular.

339. MODEL NOUNS

Dies, M., *day.*		**Rēs,**[1] F., *thing.*		ENDINGS.	
N.	diēs	diēs	rēs	rēs	-ēs	-ēs
G.	diēī	diērum	reī	rērum	-ēī	-ērum
D.	diēī	diēbus	reī	rēbus	-ēī	-ēbus
Ac.	diem	diēs	rem	rēs	-em	-ēs
Ab.	diē	diēbus	rē	rēbus	-ē	-ēbus

NOTE.—e is short in the genitive and dative singular endings, when a consonant precedes: **fidĕī, rĕī, spĕī.**

340. **Diēs** and **rēs** are the only words having all the plural cases. **Aciēs, seriēs, speciēs, spēs** and a few other words have the nominative and accusative plural.

341. VOCABULARY

testis, -is, M. or F., *witness.*
aciēs, -ēī, F., *(edge), line, rank, army.*

spēs, -eī, F., *hope.*
secundus, -a, -um, *second.*
vīgintī, (indeclinable adj.), *twenty.*

---

[1] **Res** should usually be translated by a more definite word than *thing.* The context will suggest a better word, as *fact, circumstance, undertaking, agreement, affair, event,* etc.

diēs, -ēī, M., *day.*   aegrē, aegrius, aegerrimē,
rēs, reī, F., *thing.*[1]   *with difficulty.*

comparō (con + parō), -āre, -āvī, -ātum, *prepare, arrange, procure.*

cōnficiō (con + faciō), -ficere, -fēcī, -fectum, *accomplish, carry out.*

Synonyms: **aciēs**, *army in battle array;* **āgmen**, *army on the march;* **exercitus**, *army, a trained force.*

TRANSLATE

342. 1. Ob eam rem.   2. Ad eās rēs cōnficiendās.[2]   3. Hīs rēbus adductī sunt.   4. Ēius reī populus Rōmānus est testis.   5. Is diēs.   6. Caesar ūnō diē id fēcit, quod Helvētiī diēbus vīgintī aegerrimē cōnfēcerant.   7. Omnibus rēbus ad profectiōnem comparātīs[3] diem dīcunt.[4]   8. Tōtā aciē.   9. Prīma ac[5] secunda aciēs.   10. Ad prīmam nostram aciem.   11. In superiōre aciē.   12. Crassus tertiam aciem mīsit.   13. Helvētiī eā spē dēiectī sunt.[6]   14. Dumnorīx summam in spem rēgnī obtinendī[2] vēnit.[7]   15. Omnēs rēs ad bellum Helvēticum comparātae erant.

343. 1. A journey of twenty days.   2. This legion marched four days.[8]   3. The third line (of battle) is longer than the second.   4. The whole line of the enemy was captured (taken).   5. We have great hope[7] of victory.   6. The Helvetians are induced by the scarcity of everything.[9]   7. More men will be sent to carry out these plans. (Express in two ways.)   8. It is said (that) the Germans are witnesses of this fact.

---

[1] See note on page 125.   [2] See 241.   [3] See 279.   [4] *appoint.*
[5] **ac = atque.**   [6] *were disappointed.*   [8] Accusative. What case in English?   [7] **veniō in spem** (*I come into hope*) = *I have hope* (see 344).
[9] Write : *of all things.*

344. IDIOMS —Every language has constructions or expressions peculiar to itself, called *idioms*. Thus, in English we say, *How do you do?* in French, *Comment vous portez-vous?* (*How do you carry yourself?*) Latin has many idioms. For example, it says **equus est Caesarī** (*a horse is to Caesar*) for *Caesar has a horse* (115); **iter faciunt** (*they make a march*) for *they march* (250); **Messālā cōnsule** (*Messala consul*) for *in the consulship of Messala* (277); **novissimum āgmen** (*the newest line*) for *the rear* (297); **in spem venit** (*he comes into hope*) for *he has hope* or *he hopes* (342, 14).

A Latin idiom, of course, must not be translated literally; that is, word for word.

---

345. STEMS OF NOUNS AND ADJECTIVES.[1]—1. The term *base* (22) has been used of nouns and adjectives, to indicate that part of a word which is the same in all the cases (except the nominative of some words of the third declension).

The term *stem* is given to a form which is found by dropping from the genitive plural **-rum** in the first, second and fifth declensions, and **-um** in the third and fourth. It therefore differs from the base of all declined words except some of third declension.

The last letter of the stem is called its *characteristic*, and may be **ā** in the first declension, **o** in the second, **i** or a consonant in the third, **u** in the fourth and **ē** in the fifth.

---

[1] Section 345 should be read and used for reference.

2.

NOMINATIVE.	BASE.	STEM.	CHARACTER-ISTIC.
porta	port-	portā	ā
amīcus	amīc-	amīco- [1]	o [1]
māgnus, -a, -um	māgn-	māgno- (māgnā-)	o (ā)
legiō	legiōn-	legiōn-	n
tempus	tempor-	tempor- (tempos- [2])	r (s)
hostis	host-	hosti-	i
manus	man-	manu-	u
diēs	di-	diē-	ē

3. The declension may be distinguished by the characteristic vowel of the stem as well as by the genitive singular (13). The first, therefore, may be called the ā-declension, the second the o-, the third the i- and consonant, the fourth the u-, the fifth the ē- declension.

4. The stems of the *third declension* may be classified as follows:

I. Consonant stems, including—
   1. Liquid stems (in l, m, n, r): cōnsul-, hiem-, legiōn-, mercātōr-.
   2. Sibilant stems (in r for s): tempor-.
   3. Mute stems (in b, p, d, t, c, g): plēb-, prīncip-, ped-, mīlit-, pāc-, rēg-.

II. i-stems, including—
   1. Nouns in -is or -ēs (with the same number of

---

[1] Final o of the stem is short.
[2] Final s of the stem becomes r between two vowels.

syllables in nominative and genitive singular): **hostis, nūbēs**, with stems **hosti-, nūbi-**.

2. Neuter nouns in -e, -al, -ar: **mare, animal, calcar**, with stems **mari-, animāli-, calcāri-**.

III. Mixed stems (consonant in sing. and i- in plur.), including—

1. Most nouns in -ns or -rs: **cliēns, cohors**, with stems **client-** (clienti-), **cohort-** (cohorti-).

2. Most monosyllables in -s or -x (following a consonant): **pars, arx**, with stems **part-** (parti-), **arc-** (arci-).

5. *Third declension adjectives* of two or three endings (209) have i-stems. Those of one ending have consonant stems in the singular and (with exceptions) i-stems in the plural. Comparatives have consonant stems (295).

Nominative.	Base.	Stem.	Characteristic.
ācer	**ācr-**	**ācri-**	i
fortis	**fort-**	**forti-**	i
potēns	**potent-**	**potent-** (potenti-)	t (i)
longior	**longiōr-**	**longiōr-**	r

LESSON XLIII

Tho Future Active Participle.—The Futuro Active Infinitive.—The Reflexive Pronoun *suī*.

346. THE FUTURE ACTIVE PARTICIPLE.—The future active participle is formed by adding **-ūrus** to the supine stem (273).

> laudātūrus, -a, -um, *about to praise.*
> vīsūrus, -a, -um, *about to see.*

9

rēctūrus, -a, -um, *about to rule.*
captūrus, -a, -um, *about to take.*
audītūrus, -a, -um, *about to hear.*
futūrus, -a, -um, *about to be.*

347.   ENDINGS OF THE PARTICIPLES

ACTIVE.   PASSIVE.

Pres.	-ns (237)	
Fut.	-ūrus	-ndus (Gerundive, 241)
Perf.		-us (274)

Write and translate all the participles of **dō, iubeō, iaciō** and **mūniō.**

348. THE FUTURE ACTIVE INFINITIVE.—The future active infinitive is formed by combining **esse** with the future participle.

laudātūrus esse, *to be about to praise,—will praise.*
vīsūrus esse,   *to be about to see,—will see.*
rēctūrus esse,   *to be about to rule,—will rule.*
captūrus esse,   *to be about to take,—will take.*
audītūrus esse, *to be about to hear,—will hear.*
futūrus esse,   *to be about to be,—will be.*

349. When a subject of the future active infinitive is used, the participial form (**-ūrus, -a, -um**) agrees with the subject in gender, number and case.

1. **Lēgātus dīcit Caesarem mīlitēs laudātūrum esse:** *The lieutenant says that Caesar will praise the soldiers.*

2. **Lēgātus dīcit mīlitēs Caesarem audītūrōs esse:** *The lieutenant says that the soldiers will hear Caesar.*

350.   THE REFLEXIVE PRONOUN

SING. OR PLUR.   M., F. OR N.

N. ——
G. **suī,**   *of himself, herself, itself, themselves.*
D. **sibi,**   *to* or *for*   "   "   "   "
Ac. **sē (sēsē),**   "   "   "   "
Ab. **sē (sēsē),** *from*, etc., "   "   "   "

351. (*a*) **Suī,** a personal pronoun of the third person, is called the *reflexive* pronoun because it refers to the subject of the principal verb for its meaning.

1. **Mīles dīxit sē ventūrum esse:** *The soldier said that he* (*himself*) *would come.*

If **eum** had been used instead of **sē,** the soldier would have meant that some other man would come.   Compare this distinction with that between the possessive pronoun **suus** and the genitive **ēius** (191).

2. **Mīlitēs sē ventūrōs esse dīxērunt:** *The soldiers said that they would come.*

(*b*) The reduplicated form **sēsē** is sometimes used for emphasis in the accusative and ablative.   **Sēcum** is used instead of **cum sē, cum** being an enclitic (7, *c*).

352.   VOCABULARY

biennium, -ī, N. (**annus**), *two years' time, two years.*
suī, refl. pron., *of himself, herself, itself, themselves.*
praeterquam, adv., *except, besides.*

> **exīstimō, -āre, -āvī, -ātum,** *believe, think, estimate.*
> **combūrō (con + ūrō), -ūrere, -ussī, -ūstum,** *burn up, consume.*

recipiō (re + capiō), -cipere, -cēpī, -ceptum, *take back, receive;* with **sē**, *retreat, return, withdraw.*
suscipiō (sub + capiō), -cipere, -cēpī, -ceptum, *take up;* with **sibi**, *take upon one's self, undertake.*

TRANSLATE

353. 1. Caesar Dīviciācum ad sē vocārī iubet. 2. Allobrogēs fugā sē ad Caesarem recipiunt. 3. Helvētiī sēsē Allobrogibus vel persuāsūrōs [1] vel coāctūrōs [1] exīstimābant. 4. Frūmentum omne, praeterquam (id) quod sēcum portātūrī erant, combūrunt. 5. Orgetorīx sē suīs cōpiīs suōque exercitū rēgna conciliātūrum [1] cōnfīrmat.[2] 6. Helvētiī sē angustōs fīnēs habēre dīcunt. 7. Helvētiī suīs fīnibus eōs prohibent. 8. Helvētiī ad eās rēs cōnficiendās biennium sibi satis esse dūxērunt.[3] 9. Orgetorīx sibi lēgātiōnem ad cīvitātēs suscēpit.[4] 10. Is suae cīvitātis imperium obtentūrus erat. 11. Gallī inter sē [5] differunt. 12. Dumnorīx perficit utī obsidēs inter sēsē [5] dent.

354. 1. The Romans are about to fortify the camp. 2. The enemy have retreated to the nearest towns. 3. The daughter of the horseman says (that) she will call the lieutenant. 4. The Germans did not bring grain with them. 5. The Romans think that the Belgae are conspiring against [6] them. 6. Having burned up [7] all the grain, the Helvetians were ready to wage war. 7. The Helvetians persuaded their neighbors to burn up all the grain.

---

[1] Supply **esse**, which is often omitted.   [2] *declares.*   [3] **Dūcō** sometimes means *think.*   [4] **sibi** is an indirect object, with the compound verb **suscēpit** (379).   [5] **inter sē** in 11 = *from each other;* in 12 = *to each other.*   [6] **contrā** + the accusative.   [7] See 278.

LESSON XLIV

Deponent and Semi-Deponent Verbs.—The Ablative with *ūtor*, etc.

355. DEPONENT VERBS.—Deponent verbs are passive in form but active in meaning.[1] They are conjugated like the passive of other verbs, except that they have the *active* form of the future infinitive. They have also the two active participles, and the gerund and supine (411).

MODEL VERBS

356.   PRINCIPAL PARTS (286)

CONJ	PRES. IND.	PRES. INF.	PERF. IND.	
I	hortor	hortārī	hortātus sum	*urge, exhort, encourage.*
II	vereor	verērī	veritus sum	*fear.*
III	sequor	sequī	secūtus sum	*follow.*
IV	potior	potīrī	potītus sum	*get possession of, secure.*

These verbs are conjugated in the Appendix (36).

357. SEMI-DEPONENT VERBS.—Four verbs have the active form in the present system, but the passive in the perfect system,[2] with the active meaning throughout. They are, therefore, called *semi-deponent* verbs. These verbs are:

---

[1] Deponent verbs are so called because they have "laid aside" (**dēpōnō**) their active form and passive meaning.

[2] The perfect system includes the perfect, pluperfect and future perfect tenses.

audeō, audēre, ausus sum, *dare.*
gaudeo, gaudēre, gāvīsus sum, *rejoice.*
soleō, solēre, solitus sum, *be accustomed, be used.*
fīdō, fīdere, fīsus sum, *trust.*

358.   VOCABULARY

iūs, iūris, N., *right, justice.*
urbs, urbis, F., *city.*
cum, conj., *when, while, since, although.*

arbitror, -ārī, -ātus sum, *think, suppose.*
cōnor, -ārī, -ātus sum, *attempt.*
incitō, -āre, -āvī, -ātum, *urge on, rouse.*
vagor, -ārī, -ātus sum, *roam about.*
exsequor (ex + sequor, 356), *follow out;* with iūs, *enforce.*
morior, morī, mortuus sum, *die.*
proficīscor, proficīscī, profectus sum, *depart, set out.*
ūtor, ūtī, ūsus sum, *use.*
orior, orīrī, ortus sum, *rise, begin.*

359.   MODEL SENTENCES

1. **Mīlitēs gladiīs ūtēbantur:** *The soldiers were using their swords.*
2. **Caesar oppidō potītus est:** *Caesar got possession of the town.*

In these sentences notice that the verbs govern the ablative rather than the accusative.

360. RULE XXVI.—*The ablative is used with the deponents* ūtor, fruor, fungor, potior, vēscor *and their compounds.*

NOTE.—**Potior** sometimes takes the genitive. See 380, 10.

TRANSLATE

361. 1. Belgae ab extrēmīs Galliae fīnibus oriuntur. 2. Perfacile est tōtīus Galliae imperiō potīrī. 3. Fīēbat[1] ut Helvētiī minus lātē vagārentur.[2] 4. Helvētiī sē angustōs fīnēs habēre arbitrābantur. 5. Ea ad proficīscendum pertinent. 6. Orgetorīx Dumnorīgī persuāsit ut idem cōnārētur. 7. Cum cīvitās ob eam rem incitāta armīs iūs suum exsequī[3] cōnārētur,[4] Orgetorīx mortuus est. 8. Helvētiī sē ad eam rem parātōs esse arbitrātī sunt. 9. Helvētiī persuādent fīnitimīs ut eōdem cōnsiliō ūtantur. 10. Helvētiī persuādent fīnitimīs ut cum eīs proficīscantur. 11. Helvētiī persuādent fīnitimīs ut eōdem ūsī[5] cōnsiliō cum eīs proficīscantur. 12. Allobrogēs per suōs fīnēs Helvētiōs īre[6] nōn passī sunt. 13. Dīcitur[7] eōs[8] per prōvinciam nostram iter facere cōnārī. 14. Caesar ab urbe proficīscitur. 15. Hortātus[9] suōs proelium commīsit.

362. 1. The cavalry will set out from[10] the city. 2. Our forces are attempting to get possession of the camp. 3. The horsemen roamed about as widely (as possible).[11] 4. The consul thought he would be[12] ready in ten days. 5. Many brave soldiers died on the march. 6. They feared that the army would get possession of the city. 7. They thought that the army would get possession of the city. 8. Having got possession of the city, they attempted to fortify it.

---

[1] From **fīō** (390). **Fīēbat** here means *the result was.* [2] A subjunctive of *result;* translate like the indicative. [3] A complementary infinitive. [4] A subjunctive of *time* (370). [5] Perfect participle agreeing with the subject of **proficīscantur.** See 278, Note. [6] *to go.* [7] *It is said.* [8] Subject of **cōnārī.** [9] See 278, Note. [10] **ex.** [11] See 304. [12] Future infinitive (348).

LESSON XLV—REVIEW

363. 1. How are adverbs formed? 2. How are adverbs compared? 3. What is the gender of nouns of the fourth and fifth declensions? 4. Decline **aciēs, cornū, domus** and **exercitus.** 5. What is an *idiom?* 6. How is the *stem* of a noun found? 7. How are the participles formed? 8. How is the future active infinitive formed? 9. What is a deponent verb?

364.　　　Review　Vocabulary

biennium	manus	aegrē	arbitror
iūs	occāsus	cum (conj.)	cōnor
plēbs	prīncipātus	praeterquam	hortor
testis	senātus	comparō	vagor
urbs	aciēs	conlocō	vereor
cōnspectus	diēs	exīstimō	morior
cornū	rēs	incitō	patior
cultus	spēs	sustineō	proficīscor
domus	suī	combūrō	sequor
equitātus	acceptus	cōnficiō	exsequor
exercitus	audāx	permittō	ūtor
impetus	cōpiōsus	recipiō	orior
lacus	dexter	suscipiō	potior

Mention English words derived from any of the above.

365.　　　Review　Sentences

1. Orgetorīx māximē plēbī acceptus erat. 2. Nostrī cum Helvētiīs proelium cupidius committunt. 3. Ā Bibracte, oppidō Haeduōrum longē māximō et cōpiōsissimō, Caesar aberat. 4. In summō iugō suās legiōnēs, quās in Galliā citeriōre proximē cōnscrīpserat, et omnia auxilia conlocāvit.

5. Oppidum et nātūrā locī et manū mūnītum erat. 6. Caesar equitātum, quī impetum hostium sustinēret, mīsit. 7. Helvētiī aliud iter habēbant nūllum. 8. Caesar ūnō diē id fēcit, quod Helvētiī diēbus vīgintī aegerrimē cōnfēcerant. 9. Helvētiī sēsē Allobrogibus vel persuāsūrōs vel coāctūrōs exīstimābant. 10. Frūmentum, praeterquam quod sēcum portātūrī erant, combūrunt. 11. Helvētiī ad eās rēs cōnficiendās biennium sibi satis esse dūxērunt. 12. Orgetorīx sibi lēgātiōnem ad cīvitātēs suscēpit. 13. Dumnorīx perficit utī [1] obsidēs inter sēsē dent. 13. Orgetorīx sē suīs cōpiīs suōque exercitū rēgna conciliātūrum cōnfīrmat. 14. Perfacile est tōtīus Galliae imperiō potīrī. 15. Helvētiī persuādent fīnitimīs utī eōdem ūsī cōnsiliō cum eīs prōficīscantur.

Translate in review the first chapter of Caesar, and the second as far as **Hīs rēbus,** page 222.

LESSON XLVI

The Perfect and Pluperfect Subjunctive.—Review of the Subjunctive.—*Cum* denoting Time.

366. PERFECT AND PLUPERFECT SUBJUNCTIVE ACTIVE. —The perfect subjunctive active is formed by adding the tense-sign **-eri-** [2] to the perfect stem; the pluperfect, by adding the tense-sign **-isse-**. The perfect is translated by *may have* ——, or like the perfect indicative; the pluperfect by *should have* ——, *would have* ——, or like the pluperfect indicative.

---

[1] The conjunction **utī** (= **ut**) may be distinguished from **ūtī,** the infinitive of **ūtor,** by the difference in the quantity of the first letter.

[2] Notice that the tense-sign of the perfect subjunctive active is the same as that of the future perfect indicative.

MODEL VERBS: ACTIVE VOICE

PERFECT SUBJUNCTIVE.	PLUPERFECT SUBJUNCTIVE.
laudāverim	laudāvissem
laudāveris	laudāvissēs
laudāverit	laudāvisset
laudāverimus	laudāvissēmus
laudāveritis	laudāvissētis
laudāverint	laudāvissent
monuerim, etc.	monuissem, etc.
rēxerim, etc.	rēxissem, etc.
cēperim, etc.	cēpissem, etc.
audīverim, etc.	audīvissem, etc.
fuerim, etc.	fuissem, etc.

Contractions (265): **laudārim, laudārit**, etc.; **laudāssem, laudāssēs**, etc.; **audierim**, etc.; **audīssem**, etc.

367. PERFECT AND PLUPERFECT SUBJUNCTIVE PASSIVE.—The perfect and pluperfect subjunctive passive are compound tenses. The perfect combines the perfect participle with **sim**; the pluperfect with **essem**. The perfect is translated by *may have been* ———, or like the perfect indicative; the pluperfect, by *should have been* ———, *would have been* ———, or like the pluperfect indicative.

MODEL VERBS: PASSIVE VOICE

PERFECT SUBJUNCTIVE.	PLUPERFECT SUBJUNCTIVE.
laudātus sim, etc.	laudātus essem, etc.
monitus sim, etc.	monitus essem, etc.
rēctus sim, etc.	rēctus essem, etc.
captus sim, etc.	captus essem, etc.
audītus sim, etc.	audītus essem, etc.

Conjugate the perfect and pluperfect subjunctive of dō, videō, hortor, vereor, sequor and potior.

368. TABLE OF SUBJUNCTIVE ENDINGS

ACTIVE.	PASSIVE.
Pres. -em, -am	-er, -ar
Impf. -rem	-rer
Perf. -erim	-us sim
Plup. -issem	-us essem

369. MODEL SENTENCES

1. **Cum esset Caesar in citeriōre Galliā, Belgās contrā populum Rōmānum coniūrāre cōgnōvit**: *When Caesar was in hither Gaul, he learned that the Belgians were conspiring against the Roman people.*
2. **Cum nox fīnem oppūgnandī fēcisset, Iccius nūntium ad Caesarem mīsit**: *When night had (made) put an end to the attack, Iccius sent a message to Caesar.*

In these sentences **cum** with **esset,** an imperfect, and with **fuisset,** a pluperfect subjunctive, is used not only to state the time, but also to *describe* the circumstances or situation under which Caesar learned of the conspiracy and Iccius sent a message.

370. RULE XXVII.—**Cum** *meaning* when, *with the imperfect or pluperfect, takes the subjunctive to describe the circumstances under which something occurs.*

NOTE.—**Cum** may be followed by any tense of the indicative to denote time (a date) only and not to describe the situation:—**Illō diē cum Helvētiī convēnērunt**: *On that day when the Helvetians assembled.*

371.   VOCABULARY

impedīmentum, -ī, N., *hin-*   magistrātus, -ūs, M., (*magis-*
drance; pl. *baggage, baggage-*   *tracy*), *magistrate.*
train.   dubius, -a, -um, *doubtful.*
mulier, -is, F., *woman.*   quīn, conj., *that, but that.*
adventus, -ūs, M., *arrival, approach.*

   mātūrō, -āre, -āvī, -ātum, *hasten.*
   pareō, parēre, paruī, paritum, *obey, submit.*
   accēdō (ad + cēdō), -cēdere, -cessī, -cessum, *approach,*
   advance.
   cōnscīscō, -scīscere, -scīvī, -scītum, *resolve;* with sibi
   mortem, *commit suicide.*
   prēndō, prēndere, prēndī, prēnsum, *seize, grasp.*

NOTE.—The conjunction quīn is followed by the subjunctive, after negative expressions of doubt or hindrance.
See 372, 4.

TRANSLATE

372. 1. Caesarī cum id nūntiātum esset, mātūrat ab urbe[1]
proficīscī. 2. Haec cum Dīviciācus flēns ā Caesare peteret,
Caesar ēius dextram (manum) prēndit. 3. Cum cīvitās
suum iūs exsequī cōnārētur multitūdinemque hominum
ex agrīs magistrātūs cōgerent, Orgetorīx mortuus est.
4. Nōn est dubium[2] quīn Orgetorīx sibi mortem cōnscīverit.
5. Diū cum esset pūgnātum,[3] impedīmentīs castrīsque
nostrī potītī sunt. 6. Cum Caesar ad oppidum accessisset
castraque ibi pōneret, puerī mulierēsque pācem ab Rōmānīs
petiērunt.[4] 7. Cum Helvētiī eum in itinere convēnissent[5]
et flentēs pācem petīssent atque Caesar eōs suum adventum
exspectāre iussisset, paruērunt. 8. Magistrātus eōs hor-

---

[1] **Urbs** generally refers to Rome.   [2] **Nōn est dubium**, *there is no*
doubt.   [3] **esset pūgnātum,** *fighting had gone on.*   [4] See 265.
[5] **Conveniō** when used with an object means *meet.*

tātur ut populī Rōmānī amīcitiam sequantur. 9. Parēre.
10. Accēdens. 11. Mātūrandō. 12. Incitandae plēbis causā.

373. 1. When the Belgians were conspiring, Caesar was
in the province. 2. When the Helvetians had burned their
towns,[1] they set out from their country. 3. When the arrival of Labienus had been learned, the Gauls retreated to
the mountain. 4. When he had learned these (things),
Caesar ordered the legions and cavalry to be called back.
5. When the lieutenants were approaching the town, the
magistrates met them on the road. 6. He says (that)
he will come. 7. We shall use the smallest trumpets.
8. Gaul is much larger than Helvetia.

LESSON XLVII

Compounds of *sum.*—The Dative with Compounds.

374. **Sum** is compounded with certain prepositions,
as follows:

absum, *be away, be absent*
adsum, *be near, be present*
dēsum, *be wanting, fail*
īnsum, *be in*
intersum, *be between, be
    among. be engaged in*

obsum, *be against, hinder*
praesum, *be at the head of, be in
    command of*
prōsum, *be useful, benefit*
subsum, *be under*
supersum, *be over, remain,
    survive*

375. These compounds are conjugated like **sum.**
Prōsum has -d- before -e- of the simple verb: **prō-sum,
prōd-es, prōd-est, prōd-eram, prōd-erō, prōd-esse.**

Learn from the Appendix (38) the conjugation of
possum (**potis,** *able;* **sum**), **posse, potuī,** *be able, can.*

376.   MODEL SENTENCES

1. **Puer pīlum iacere potest:** *The boy can (is able to) throw a javelin.*
2. **Puer pīlum iacere poterat:** *The boy could (was able to) throw a javelin.*
3. **Dumnorīx apud Sēquanōs plūrimum poterat:** *Dumnorix was most powerful (influential) among the Sequani.*

Possum is generally used with a complementary infinitive (as in sentences 1 and 2). The present tense (1) is best translated *can*, the imperfect (2) *could*.

Plūrimum possum (3) has the meaning *be most powerful, have great influence.*

377.   VOCABULARY

adolēscentia, -ae, F., *youth.*

praestō (prae + stō, *stand*), -stāre, -stitī, -stitum, (*stand before*), *excel, furnish.*

spērō, -āre, -āvī, -ātum, *hope.*

coepī, *began, have begun.*[1]

occurrō (ob + currō, *run*), -currere, -currī, -cursum, *meet, come upon.*

praeficiō (prae + faciō), -ficere, -fēcī, -fectum, *put in command.*

possum, posse, potuī, *be able, can.*

378.   MODEL SENTENCES

1. **Helvētiī omnibus praestant:** *The Helvetians excel all.*
2. **Dumnorīx equitātuī praeerat:** *Dumnorix was in command of the cavalry.*
3. **Equitēs hostibus occurrēbant:** *The cavalry met the enemy.*

---

[1] **Coepī** is used only in the perfect system. Verbs that lack some of their forms are called *defective* verbs. See Appendix (43).

Notice that the datives in these sentences are used with verbs compounded with prepositions.

379. RULE XXVIII.—*The dative is used with some verbs compounded with* **ad, ante, con, dē, in, inter, ob, post, prae, prō, sub, super.**

TRANSLATE

380. 1. Aberant, aderunt. 2. Sīgnum portāre possum. 3. Oppidum expūgnāre poterimus. 4. Mōns suberat. 5. Biennium¹ supererat. 6. Caesar quam māximīs potest itineribus² in Galliam contendit. 7. Quam celerrimē³ potuit. 8. Fīnitimīs bellum īnferre⁴ possunt. 9. Nōn est dubium quīn tōtīus Galliae plūrimum Helvētiī possint. 10. Tōtīus Galliae⁵ sēsē potīrī posse spērant. 11. Castella commūnit, ut prohibēre hostēs possit. 12. Helvētiī Sēquanīs persuādēre nōn poterant. 13. Haeduī, cum sē suaque⁶ ab eīs dēfendere nōn possent, lēgātōs ad Caesarem mittunt. 14. Omnēs, quī aderant, auxilium ā Caesare petere coepērunt. 15. Eī mūnītiōnī, quam fēcerat, Labiēnum lēgātum praefēcit. 16. Cum Dīviciācus plūrimum domī atque in reliquā Galliā posset, Dumnorīx minimum propter adolēscentiam potuit. 17. Caesar dīcit sē Labiēnum praefectūrum esse. 18. Hīs rēbus cōgnitīs, Caesar spērāvit Ariovistum fīnem iniūriīs factūrum (esse).

381. 1. We can excel. 2. You will be able to see the house. 3. They had begun to retreat to the baggage-train. 4. We shall be able to get possession of the whole province.

---

¹ Nominative.   ² A form of **possum** may be used with **quam** and a superlative (304) : **quam māximīs potest itineribus,** (*by the greatest possible marches*), *by forced marches;* that is, by covering more than the usual daily distance.   ³ *As quickly as.*   ⁴ **īnferre (in + ferō),** *bring upon, make (war) upon.*   ⁵ **Potior** sometimes governs the genitive instead of the ablative (360).   ⁶ **sua,** *their property.*   How is **suaque** accented ?

5. I have not been able to persuade our friends. 6. Labienus had been put-in-command-of the fortification. 7. Galba is-in-command-of the army. 8. He will excel all the
rest in valor. 9. The magistrates collected [1] an army to
attack [2] the legions.

LESSON XLVIII

**The Numeral *mīlle*.—The Genitive of the Whole.—
The Accusative of Space and Time.**

382. Mīlle, *thousand*, may be either an adjective or
a noun. As an adjective it is not declined: mīlle
hominēs. As a noun it has the nominative and accusative singular mīlle, and the plural cases: mīlia (mīllia),
mīlium, mīlibus, mīlia, mīlibus. As a noun it is followed by a genitive plural (384).

383.   VOCABULARY

solum, -ī, N., *soil*.

lātitūdo, -dinis, F. (lātus),
  breadth.

longitūdō, -dinis, F. (longus),
  length.

passus, -ūs, M., *pace* (about
  five feet).[3]

mīlle passuum, pl. mīlia passuum, *mile*.

nihil (indecl.), N., *nothing*.

trēs, tria, *three*.

eō (is), adv., *thither, there*.

ad or circiter, adv., with numbers, *about*.

praeter, prep. with acc., *except,
  beyond*.

dēmōnstrō, -āre, -āvī, -ātum, *point out, explain*.

pateō, patēre, patuī, ———, *extend*.

intermittō (inter + mittō, 101), *stop, discontinue*.

---

[1] cōgō.   [2] See 199.

[3] By **passus** the Romans meant the distance between two successive posi-
tions of the *same* foot, which is therefore longer than the English pace.

Note.—**Trēs** is declined like the plural of **fortis**: Nom.
trēs, tria, gen. **trium, trium,** dat. abl. **tribus, tribus,** acc.
trēs (trīs), tria.

384. Models

1. **Pars mīlitum:** *Part of the soldiers.*
2. **Decem mīlia passuum:** *Ten thousand (of) paces, ten miles.*
3. **Minus timōris:** *Less (of) fear.*
4. **Ūnus fīliōrum:** *One of the sons.*
5. **Hōrum omnium fortissimī sunt Belgae:** *The bravest of all these are the Belgians.*

In the above expressions the genitive denotes the
whole, which is modified by a word denoting a *part.*
The genitive so used is called the *genitive of the whole.*
The word denoting a part may be a noun, pronoun
(chiefly interrogative or indefinite), adjective (especially numeral or superlative) or adverb (of quantity,
degree or place).

385. Rule XXIX.—*The genitive may denote the
whole, depending upon a word denoting a part.*

386. Model Sentences

1. **Ab castrīs oppidum aberat mīlia passuum octō:** *A town
   was eight miles away from the camp.*
2. **Rēgnum multōs annōs obtinuerat:** *He had held the royal
   power many years.*

How far away was the town? How long had he
held the power? The answers to these questions require the accusatives **mīlia** and **annōs,** the former denoting *extent of space,* the latter *duration of time.* Compare the accusative of time with the ablative of time

10

(158). The former denotes time *how long*, the latter *time when* or *within which*.

387. RULE XXX.—*The accusative is used to denote extent of space and duration of time.*

TRANSLATE

388. 1. Multitūdō Germānōrum Rhēnum ¹ trādūcēbātur. 2. Orgetorīx ad ² hominum mīlia decem coēgit. 3. Nūllam partem noctis iter intermissum est. 4. Eō ³ diē hostēs sequitur et mīlia passuum tria ab eōrum castrīs castra pōnit. 5. Quod mōns suberat circiter mīlle passuum, eō ⁴ sē recipere coepērunt. 6. Caesar mīlia passuum decem mūrum in longitūdinem perdūcit. 7. Allobrogēs dēmōnstrant sibi ⁵ praeter agrī solum nihil esse reliquī.⁶ 8. Fīnēs Helvētiōrum in longitūdinem mīlia passuum CCXL ⁷ (ducenta quadrāgintā), in lātitūdinem CLXXX ⁷ (centum octōgintā) patēbant. 9. Circiter mīlia hominum CXXX ⁷ (centum trīgintā) superfuērunt. 10. Circiter hominum mīlia VI ⁷ (sex) ēius pāgī, quī Verbigēnus appellātur, ad Rhēnum fīnēsque Germānōrum contendērunt. 11. Verentur ut ⁸ habeam satis praesidī.⁹

389. 1. A great number of horses. 2. The largest of all the rivers. 3. The army marched (for) three days. 4. Caesar fought with ¹⁰ the Gauls (for) eight years. 5. The hill was a thousand feet high. 6. The lake extends a mile in breadth. 7. The forest extended ten miles. 8. The length of the camp will not be much greater than the breadth. 9. When they had built (made) as many ships as possible, they were ready to sail.

---

¹ **Rhēnum** depends upon **trā-** in the verb.   ² See 383.   ³ Agrees with **diē**.   ⁴ Adverb ; see 383.   ⁵ See 115.   ⁶ Genitive of the whole with **nihil**, *nothing left.*   ⁷ Modifies **milia.**   ⁸ What does **ut** mean here ? See 206.   ⁹ Accent ? See 56.   ¹⁰ Use a preposition.

LESSON XLIX

The Verb *fīō.*—The Ablative of Cause.—Caesar, I. 2 (concluded).

390. THE PASSIVE OF **faciō**—Except in forms compounded with prepositions (**adficiō, cōnficiō**, etc.), **faciō** is not used in the passive of the present system (245). This system is supplied by the irregular verb **fīō, fierī, factus sum,** *be made, be done, happen, result.* Learn from the Appendix (39) the conjugation of this verb, except the imperative and the perfect and future infinitive. Notice that -i- is long except in **fit** and before **-er-**.

391. **Certior,** the comparative of **certus,** *certain, sure,* is used as a predicate adjective in the idioms **faciō certiōrem,** *I inform* (*make more sure*), and **fīō certior,** *I am informed* (*made more sure*).

1. **Lēgātus Caesarem certiōrem facit montem ab hostibus tenērī:** *A lieutenant informs Caesar that the mountain is held by the enemy.*

2. **Caesar ā lēgātō certior fit montem tenērī:** *Caesar is informed by a lieutenant that the mountain is held.*

Notice (1) that **certior** agrees with the name of the person informed; (2) that the information is expressed by an infinitive clause, just as after a verb of saying (232).

392. MODEL SENTENCE

Spē victōriae fortius pūgnāvērunt: *They fought more bravely because of the hope of victory.*

The ablative **spē** answers the question *Why?* and is called an *ablative of cause.*

NOTE.—Cause is frequently expressed by a *phrase* consisting of **dē** or **ex** with an ablative, or of **propter** or **ob** with an accusative. **Quā dē causā reliquōs Gallōs praecēdunt; propter timōrem; ob eam rem.**

393. RULE XXXI.—*The ablative may be used to denote cause.*

394.   VOCABULARY

dolor, -ōris, M., (*pain*), dis-   **fidēs, -eī,** F., (*faith*), *pledge,*
tress.   *protection.*
ōrātiō, ōnis, F., *speech, argument.* **certus,** *certain, sure.*

   adficiō (ad + ficiō), -ficere, -fēcī, -fectum, *affect;* in passive, *suffer.*
   fīō, fierī, factus sum, *be made, be done, happen, result.*

395. 1. Impetus ā legiōne fīet. 2. Caesar pontem fierī iubet. 3. Helvētiī dē ēius adventū certiōrēs factī sunt. 4. Galba certior factus est montēs ā māximā multitūdine tenērī. 5. Litterīs Labiēnī Caesar certior fīēbat omnēs Belgās contrā populum Rōmānum coniūrāre. 6. Haeduī Caesarem certiōrem faciunt sēsē nōn facile ab oppidīs hostēs prohibēre. 7. Hīs rēbus fīēbat ut minus lātē vagārentur. 8. Factum est multīs dē causīs ut hostēs impetum sustinēre nōn possent. 9. Hāc ōrātiōne adductī inter sē fidem dant. 10. Id eā dē causā faciēbat. 11. Auxilī causā.[1] 12. Quā[2] ex parte hominēs[3] bellandī cupidī māgnō dolōre adficiēbantur.[4] 13. Labiēnus nostrōs exspectābat, ut undique ūnō tempore in hostēs impetus fieret. 14. Lūcium Pīsōnem lēgātum eōdem proeliō (interfēcerant), quō Cassium interfēcerant.

---

[1] *for the sake.*   [2] A relative pronoun at the beginning of a sentence is often best translated *and* + a demonstrative : **Quā ex parte** (= **Et ex eā parte**), *and for that reason.*   [3] Not the subject, but an appositive, *being men.*   [4] **māgnō dolōre adficiēbantur,** *were greatly distressed.*

396. 1. We shall be informed of [1] the arrival of our friends.   2. They will inform the leader (that) the road is narrow.   3. (Because of) Caesar's arrival the soldiers were fighting more bravely.   4. Having given [2] a pledge to each other, the kings joined their forces.   5. The army will remain there for-the-sake of grain.   6. The Germans had lived for many years across the Rhine.   7. When we had seen part of the forest, we were informed that it was [3] ten miles long.

397. CAESAR, I. 2 (CONCLUDED) : THE EXTENT OF HELVETIA.

Hīs rēbus fīēbat ut et minus lātē vagārentur et minus facile fīnitimīs [1] bellum īnferre possent; quā ex parte hominēs bellandī [2] cupidī māgnō dolōre adficiēbantur. Prō [3] multitūdine autem [4] hominum et prō glōriā [5] bellī atque fortitūdinis, angustōs sē fīnēs habēre arbitrāban-   5 tur, quī in longitūdinem mīlia passuum CCXL, in lātitūdinem CLXXX patēbant.

NOTES

[1] See 379.   [2] See 213.   [3] *considering.*   [4] **autem,** conj., *then again, furthermore.*   [5] **glōria, -ae,** F., *fame (in),* or *reputation (for).*

LESSON L

The Subjunctive of Result.—The Historical Present. The Sequence of Tenses.

398.   VOCABULARY

dolus, -ī, M., *deceit, trickery.*   **amplius,** comp. adv., *more.*
servitūs, -tūtis, F., *slavery.*   **paene,** adv., *almost.*

---

[1] **dē.**   [2] See 279.   [3] Translate by a present form.

THE FIRST YEAR OF LATIN

perpaucī, -ae, -a, *very few*. tam, adv., *so* (with adj. and
plēnus, -a, -um, *full*. adv.).
tantus, -a, -um, *so great, such*.

dēbeō, -ēre, -uī, -itum, (*owe*), *ought*.
mereor, -ērī, -itus sum, *deserve*.
accidō (ad + cadō, *fall*), -cidere, -cidī, ——, *happen, occur*.
cōnsuēscō, -suēscere, -suēvī, -suētum, *become accustomed*; in perf., *be accustomed*.
īnstituō (in + statuō), -stituere, -stituī, -stitūtum, (*put in place*), *train*.
perficiō (250), *accomplish, bring about, cause*.

399. RESULT CLAUSES.—We have seen that the subjunctive is used in purpose clauses (199) and in some temporal clauses (370). It is also used to express *result* or *consequence* with **ut**, as in the following:—

1. **Mōns altissimus impendēbat, ut perpaucī prohibēre possent:** *A very high mountain was overhanging, so that very few could hinder.*
2. **Mōns est tam altus ut nōn facile ascendere possīmus:** *The mountain is so high that we cannot easily climb* (*it*).
3. **Fīēbat ut minus lātē vagārentur.** (395, 7.)
4. **Dumnorīx perficit ut obsidēs dent:** *Dumnorix brings* (*it*) *about that they give hostages.*

(*a*) In each of these complex sentences the subordinate clause is called a *result* clause, or a *consecutive* (consequence) clause. In sentences 1 and 2 the result clause is adverbial (186); in 3 and 4 it is a noun-clause (186), being the subject of **fit** and the object of **perficit**.

(*b*) Negative result is expressed by **ut nōn**, as in sentence 2. How is negative purpose expressed?

(*c*) There is often in the principal clause a correlative

word meaning *so, such, so great,* as **ita, sīc, tam, tālis, tantus.** Notice **tam** in sentence 2. A word of this meaning may be understood, as in sentence 1.

(*d*) A noun-clause with **ut** may be the subject of a verb meaning (*it*) *happens,* (*it*) *follows;* or the object of a verb meaning *accomplish, cause.*

400. RULE XXXII.—*The subjunctive is used with* **ut** *or* **ut nōn** *to express result.*

401. COMPARISON OF PURPOSE AND RESULT.—A purpose clause expresses the *aim* of the action of the principal clause. It always implies some one's will: *He ran to win (that he might win) the prize.* (The purpose of running.)

A result clause expresses a *fact* resulting from the principal statement: *He ran so swiftly that he won the prize.* (The result of running.)

402. THE HISTORICAL PRESENT.—The present tense is frequently used to state or describe a *past* event more vividly. It is then called the *historical present,* and is generally to be translated by the English past: **Helvētiī sua oppida incendunt:** *The Helvetians burned their towns.*

403. SEQUENCE OF TENSES.—Tenses are either primary or secondary. The primary tenses are the present, future and future perfect. The secondary are the imperfect, perfect and pluperfect.

The historical present (402) may be used as a secondary tense, and the present perfect (translated by *have,* 175) as a primary.

404.   MODEL SENTENCES

PRES.   **Veniō ut videam:** *I am coming to see (that I*
                  may see).
PRES. PERF.   **Vēnī ut videam:** *I have come to see.*
FUT.   **Veniam ut videam:** *I shall come to see.*
FUT. PERF.   **Vēnerō ut videam:** *I shall have come to see.*
IMPF.   **Veniēbam ut vidērem:** *I was coming to see*
                  (that I might see).
HIST. PERF.   **Vēnī ut vidērem:** *I came to see.*
PLUP.   **Vēneram ut vidērem:** *I had come to see.*

In these complex sentences notice that a primary
tense in the principal clause is followed by the present
in the subordinate, and that a secondary tense is followed by the imperfect.

405. RULE XXXIII.—*In complex sentences primary*
tenses follow primary, and secondary follow secondary.

This is called the rule for the *sequence* of tenses (**sequor,**
follow).

TRANSLATE

406. 1. Tanta est altitūdō flūminis ut āgmen trānsīre [1]
nōn possit. 2. Eādem nocte accidit ut esset lūna plēna.
3. Nostrī nāvēs [2] hostium sīc expūgnāvērunt ut perpaucae
ad terram pervenīrent. 4. Ita ā patribus māiōribusque
nostrīs didicimus ut magis virtūte contendāmus quam dolō.
5. Ita Helvētiī ā māiōribus suīs īnstitūtī sunt utī obsidēs [2]
accipere, nōn dare, cōnsuērint. 6. Ita dē populō Rōmānō
meritī sumus ut paene in cōnspectū exercitūs [3] nostrī agrī
vāstārī, līberī in servitūtem abdūcī, oppida expūgnārī nōn
dēbuerint. 7. Ita diēs [4] circiter quīndecim [5] iter fēcērunt

---

[1] *to cross.*   [2] Accusative.   [3] The Roman army.
[4] See 387.   [5] **quīndecim = quīnque + decem.**

utī inter novissimum hostium āgmen et nostrum prīmum
nōn amplius quīnīs¹ aut sēnīs mīlibus² passuum interesset.   8. Nōn abest suspīciō quīn Orgetorīx coniūrātiōnem
fēcerit.

407. 1. It happens that the river is deep.   2. The javelin is so heavy that it cannot easily be thrown.   3. So great
was their valor that they always conquered.   4. There is
no doubt that he is the bravest of the boys.   5. Very few
soldiers used trickery.³   6. They had been advised to
come⁴ as quickly as possible.   7. The consul will praise
the deserving.⁵   8. We ought not to devastate the fields.
9. Having devastated the fields, they carried off the children into slavery.

LESSON LI—REVIEW

Caesar, I. 3 (begun)

408. 1. Review the conjugation of the subjunctive
mood (368).   2. Conjugate fīō and **possum.**   3. Decline
mīlle and **trēs.**   4. With what parts of speech is the
genitive of the whole used?   5. With what compound
verbs is the dative used?   6. By what cases is time
expressed, and what is the difference in meaning?
7. What is the rule for **cum** (*when*)?   8. What is the difference between a purpose clause and a result clause?
9. What is the historical present?   10. What is the
rule for the sequence of tenses?

---

¹ **quīnī, -ae, -a,** *five* (each); **sēnī, -ae, -a,** *six* (each); distributive numeral
adjectives, denoting here how many miles each day.   ² See 303.
³ What case (360)?   ⁴ What mood and tense (405)?
⁵ Pres. participle, used as noun.

409. Review Vocabulary

adolēscentia	nihil	propter	adficiō
dolus	certus	autem	coepī
dolor	dubius	quīn	cōnscīscō
impedīmentum	perpaucī	dēmōnstrō	cōnsuēsco
solum	plēnus	mātūrō	fīō
lātitūdō	tantus	praestō	īnstituō
longitūdō	mīlle	spērō	intermittō
mulier	trēs	dēbeō	occurrō
ōrātiō	amplius	mereor	possum
servitūs	circiter	pareō	praeficiō
adventus	eō (adv.)	pateō	prēndō
magistrātus	paene	accēdō	
passus	tam	accidō	
fidēs	praeter		

Mention some English words derived from these Latin words.

Translate in review sections 372, 380, 388, 395, 406.

410. CAESAR, I. 3 (BEGUN): THE HELVETIANS PREPARE TO LEAVE THEIR COUNTRY

Hīs rēbus adductī et auctōritāte Orgetorīgis permōtī cōnstituērunt ea quae ad proficīscendum pertinērent comparāre,[1] iūmentōrum et carrōrum quam māximum numerum coëmere,[1] sēmentēs quam māximās facere,[1]
5 ut in itinere cōpia frūmentī suppeteret, cum proximīs cīvitātibus pācem et amīcitiam cōnfīrmāre.[1] Ad eās rēs cōnficiendās biennium sibi satis esse dūxērunt; in[2] tertium annum profectiōnem lēge cōnfīrmant.[3]

NOTES

[1] See 230. [2] *for*. [3] *fix*, historical present.

LESSON LII

The Supine and its Uses. — Expressions of Purpose.—Caesar, I. 3 (continued).

411. THE SUPINE.—The supine has been given as the fourth of the principal parts of verbs (17). It is a verbal noun having two forms, an accusative in -um and an ablative in -ū.

412. The supine in -um is used—

(1) With verbs of *motion*, to express purpose. **Oppūgnātum patriam nostram veniunt:** *They come to attack our country.*

(2) With **īrī,**[1] to form the future passive infinitive: **laudātum īrī,** *to be about to be praised.* This infinitive seldom occurs.

413. The supine in -ū is used chiefly as an ablative of specification (144) with adjectives meaning *easy, good, strange* or the opposite. Caesar uses only **factū. Difficile factū est.** *It is hard to do (with respect to the doing).*

414. PURPOSE.—In Latin prose four forms of the verb are used to express purpose:

(1) The subjunctive with **ut, nē, quī, quō**[2] (199).
(2) The gerund, } with **ad** or **causā** (240, 242).
(3) The gerundive, }
(4) The supine (412).

Mittunt Orgetorīgem { ut (or quī) pācem cōnfīrmet.
ad pācem cōnfīrmandam.
pācis cōnfīrmandae causā.
pācem cōnfīrmātum.

---

[1] Present passive infinitive of **eō,** *go* (435).   [2] **quō** (= **ut eō**), with comparatives.

415.   VOCABULARY

perfacilis, -e (per + facilis), *very easy.*
propinquus, -a, -um (prope), *near;* plur. as noun, *relatives.*
quō (= ut eō), conj. with comparatives, (*that thereby*), *that, in order that.*

  frūmentor, -ārī, -ātus sum (frūmentum), *gather grain.*
  grātulor, -ārī, -ātus sum, *congratulate.*
  populor, -ārī, -ātus sum, *ravage, devastate.*
  probō, -āre, -āvī, -ātum, *show, prove.*
  rogō, -āre, -āvī, -ātum, *ask, ask for.*
  nūbō, nūbere, nūpsī, nūptum, (*veil one's self*), *marry;*
    conlocō (——) nūptum, *give in marriage.*
  queror, querī, questus sum, *complain.*

TRANSLATE

416. 1. Perfacile factū. 2. Est perfacile factū. 3. Id [1]
perfacile factū esse probat. 4. Perfacile factū esse illīs probat cōnāta [2] perficere.[1] 5. Haeduī lēgātōs mittunt rogātum
auxilium. 6. Dumnorīx suās propinquās nūptum conlocāvit. 7. Prīncipēs cīvitātum ad Caesarem grātulātum convēnērunt. 8. Haeduī veniēbant questum quod Harūdēs
fīnēs eōrum populārentur. 9. Ūna legiō frūmentātum
missa erat. 10. Māgna pars equitātūs frūmentandī causā
missa est. 11. Castra mūnīre coepērunt, quō facilius
hostium impetūs sustinēre possent. 12. Castra movērī iubet, quō facilius hostibus timōris det suspīciōnem. 13. Ad
haec cōgnōscenda Labiēnum esse idōneum arbitrābātur.

417. 1. I shall send men to [3] ask for aid. 2. The boy's
friends came to [4] congratulate him. 3. He built (made)
forts that [5] he might defend the place with a smaller number

---

[1] Subject of **esse**.   [2] Object of **perficere**.   [3] Use a relative.
    [4] Use **ut**.   [5] Use **quō**.

of soldiers.   4. We shall be ready to ² sail.   5. You thought three ships would be ¹ enough to ² transport the animals. 6. The mountain was so high that we could not climb it in one day.

418. CAESAR, I. 3 (CONTINUED): ORGETORIX CONSPIRES WITH CASTICUS AND DUMNORIX

Ad eās rēs cōnficiendās Orgetorīx dēligitur.³ Is sibi ⁴ lēgātiōnem ad cīvitātēs suscēpit. In eō itinere persuādet Casticō, Catamantāloedis fīliō,⁵ Sēquanō,⁵ cūius pater rēgnum in Sēquanīs multōs annōs⁶ obtinuerat et ā senātū populī Rōmānī amīcus⁷ appellātus erat, ut rēg-   5 num in cīvitāte suā occupāret,⁸ quod pater ante ¹ habuerat; itemque² Dumnorīgī⁰ Haeduō, frātrī Dīviciācī, quī eō tempore prīncipātum in cīvitāte obtinēbat āc māximē plēbī acceptus erat, ut idem cōnārētur persuādet, eīque fīliam suam in mātrimōnium dat.   10

NOTES AND VOCABULARY
¹ **ante,** adv., *before.*
² **item,** adv., *in the same way, also.*
³ **dēligō** (**dē** + **legō**), **-ligere, -lēgī, -lēctum,** *choose, select.* See 402.
⁴ See 379.   ⁵ See 135.   ⁶ See 387.   ⁷ See 95.   ⁸ See 206.   ⁰ With **persuādet,** line 9.

LESSON LIII

The Perfect Infinitive.—Review of the Infinitive.— The Perfect and Supine Systems.—Caesar, I. 3 (concluded).

419. THE PERFECT INFINITIVE.—The perfect active infinitive is formed by adding **-isse** to the perfect stem; the perfect passive, by combining **-esse** with the perfect participle.

¹ See 348.   ² Use **ad,**

ACTIVE.	PASSIVE.
laudāvisse, *to have praised.*	laudātus (-a, -um) esse, *to have been praised.*
monuisse, *to have advised.*	monitus (-a, -um) esse, *to have been advised.*
rēxisse, *to have ruled.*	rēctus (-a, -um) esse, *to have been ruled.*
cēpisse, *to have taken.*	captus (-a, -um) esse, *to have been taken.*
audīvisse, *to have heard.*	audītus (-a, -um) esse, *to have been heard.*

NOTE.—The -v- of the perfect stem may be dropped and the vowels contracted: **laudāsse, audīsse.** See 265.

420.   TABLE OF INFINITIVE ENDINGS

	ACTIVE.	PASSIVE.
Pres.	-re (228)	-rī (-ī)
Perf.	-isse	-us esse
Fut.	-ūrus esse (348)	-um īrī (412)

Write all the infinitives of **dō, videō, vincō.** Review the uses of the infinitive (230–232).

421.   TENSES OF THE INFINITIVE

I. The present infinitive denotes the *same* time as the principal verb:

1. **Dīcit sē laudāre:** *He says that he praises (is praising).*
2. **Dīxit sē laudāre:** *He said that he praised (was praising).*

II. The perfect infinitive denotes time *before* that of the principal verb:

1. **Dīcit sē laudāvisse**: *He says that he praised (has praised).*
2. **Dīxit sē laudāvisse**: *He said that he had praised.*

III. The future infinitive denotes time *after* that of the principal verb:

1. **Dīcit sē laudātūrum esse**: *He says that he will praise.*
2. **Dīxit sē laudātūrum esse**: *He said that he would praise.*

422. VOCABULARY

taceō, -ēre, -uī, -itum, *be silent, keep silent.*
cōnsīdō (con + sīdo), -sīdere, -sēdī, -sessum, *(sit down), encamp.*
largior, -īrī, -ītus sum, *give lavishly, bribe.*
reperiō, reperīre, repperī, repertum, *find out, discover.*

TRANSLATE

423. 1. Nūntiāmus oppidum esse mūnītum. 2. Respondērunt pācem cōnfirmātam esse. 3. Dīxērunt sē ā patribus didicisse. 4. Dīvicō respondit Helvētiōs ā suīs māiōribus īnstitūtōs esse. 5. Liscus dīcit sē ob eam causam tacuisse. 6. Dīxistī hostēs sub monte cōnsēdisse. 7. Caesar certior factus est trēs partēs[1] cōpiārum Helvētiōs id flūmen[2] trādūxisse. 8. Caesar reperit Dumnorīgem facultātēs ad largiendum māgnās[3] comparāsse. 9. Reperiēbat initium fugae equitum factum esse ā Dumnorīge. 10. Cōnsidius dīcit id sē ā Gallicīs armīs cōgnōvisse. 11. Cōgnōvit montem ā suīs tenērī et Helvētiōs castra mōvisse. 12. Persuāsit eīs ut auxilium rogārent. 13. Cum cōnsēdissent, imperātor eam legiōnem laudāvit quae fuerat fortissima.

---

[1] Object of **-dūxisse,** erned by **trā- (trāns-).** [2] " Secondary object " of **trādūxisse,** governed by **trā- (trāns-).** [3] Agrees with **facultātēs.**

424. 1. They are moving the tower.[1] 2. He discovers that they are moving the tower. 3. He discovers that the tower is being moved. 4. He discovered that the tower had been moved. 5. We heard that they had been in Gallia. 6. The lieutenant says he will report the victory. 7. I reported that the soldiers would fortify the town. 8. I reported that the soldiers had fortified the town.

425. THE PERFECT SYSTEM.—The perfect system includes all forms of the verb derived from the perfect stem. The forms are all active. For **laudō** they are:

	INDICATIVE.	SUBJUNCTIVE.	INFINITIVE.
Perfect.	**laudāv-ī**	**laudāv-erim**	**laudāv-isse**
Pluperf.	**laudāv-eram**	**laudāv-issem**	
Fut. Perf.	**laudāv-erō**		

426. THE SUPINE SYSTEM.—The supine system includes all forms of the verb derived from the supine stem. The forms are all passive, except the future active infinitive, future active participle and the supine. For **laudō** the system is:

	INDICATIVE.	SUBJUNCTIVE.
Perfect.	**laudāt-us sum**	**laudāt-us sim**
Pluperf.	**laudāt-us eram**	**laudāt-us essem**
Fut. Perf.	**laudāt-us erō**	
	INFINITIVE.	PARTICIPLE.
Future.	{ **laudāt-ūrus esse** { **laudāt-um īrī**	**laudāt-ūrus**
Perfect.	**laudāt-us esse**	**laudāt-us**
	SUPINE.	
	laudāt-um	

---

[1] See 310.

427. CAESAR, 1. 3 (CONCLUDED): THE ARGUMENT OF ORGETORIX

Perfacile factū esse illīs [2] probat cōnāta perficere, proptereā quod ipse suae cīvitātis imperium obtentūrus [3] esset: nōn esse [4] dubium quīn [5] tōtīus Galliae [6] plūrimum Helvētiī possent; sē suīs cōpiīs suōque exercitū illīs rēgna conciliātūrum [7] cōnfīrmat.   Hāc ōrātiōne adductī inter 5 sē fidem et iūsiūrandum [1] dant, et rēgnō occupātō [8] per trēs [9] potentissimōs ac fīrmissimōs populōs tōtīus Galliae [10] sēsē potīrī posse spērant.

NOTES

[1] **iūsiūrandum** (**iūs** + **iūrandum**), iūrisiūrandī, N., *oath* (a compound noun).   [2] See 63.   [3] See 346.   [4] See 232.   [5] See 371, Note.   [6] See 385.   [7] See 348.   [8] See 279.   [9] The Helvetii, Haedui and Sequani.   [10] See 360, note.

Gallic Soldier

LESSON LIV

**Impersonal Verbs.—Noun-Clauses.—Caesar, I. 4
(begun).**

428. IMPERSONAL VERBS.—An *impersonal* verb is
one that has no personal subject, and hence is used in
the third person singular only. It is often introduced
in English by the expletive *it: it rains, it happens*. In
Latin, impersonal verbs include (besides a few others)—

1. Verbs taking a phrase or a clause as their subject.
Accidit ut esset lūna plēna: *It happened that there was full
moon.*

2. Intransitive verbs used in the third singular passive:
Pūgnātur: *There is fighting (fighting goes on).*

Impersonal verbs are found in the indicative, subjunctive, and present and perfect infinitive.

429. Among the verbs used impersonally are:

accēdit, accēdere, accessit, *it is added.*

accidit, accidere, accidit, *it happens.*

fit, fierī, factum est, *it happens, it results.*

licet, licēre, licuit (licitum est), *it is allowed.*

oportet, oportēre, oportuit, *it is necessary.*

pūgnātur, pūgnārī, pūgnātum est, *there is fighting.*

430. NOUN-CLAUSES.—A noun-clause (186) may be
the subject or object of a verb, an appositive or a predicate nominative (or accusative). It may be expressed
in the following ways—

1. By an indicative, introduced by the conjunction
quod *(that, the fact that)*.

Accēdēbat quod flūmen erat lātum: *There was added the
fact that the river was broad.*

2. By a subjunctive introduced by **ut, nē, quīn**, etc., or an interrogative word (Review 206; 371, Note; 399).

Fīēbat ut flūmen esset lātum: *It happened that the river was broad.*

3. By an infinitive with a subject-accusative (231).

Dīcit flūmen esse lātum: *He says that the river is broad.*

431.   VOCABULARY

poena, -ae, F., *punishment.*   **mōs, mōris,** M., *custom.*
īgnis, īgnis, M., *fire.*   **ascēnsus, -ūs,** M., *ascent.*

cremō, -āre, -āvī, -ātum, *burn;* with **īgnī,** *burn to death.*

TRANSLATE

432. 1. Poenam sequī oportet.   2. Poenam sequī oportēbat ut īgnī cremārētur.[1]   3. Frūmentum mīlitibus dare oportēbit.   4. Renūntiātum est ascēnsum montis facilem esse.   5. Diū atque ācriter pūgnātum est.   6. Ab horā septimā ad vesperum pūgnātum erat.   7. Helvētiīs [2] est in animō iter facere.   8. Lēgātī dīcunt sibi [2] esse in animō sine ūllō maleficiō iter per prōvinciam facere.   9. Id [3] eīs facere licet.   10. Lēgātī rogant ut id sibi facere liceat.   11. Mōre [4] Caesaris.   12. Mōribus Helvētiōrum.   13. Caesar dīcit sē mōre populī Rōmānī nōn posse iter dare.   14. Accēdēbat [5] quod Gallī Rōmānōs oppida occupāre cōnārī exīstimābant.   15. Verētur nē hōc faciās.   16. Verētur ut hōc faciās.

433. 1. It is necessary (for) the traders to come to Gaul.   2. It happened that the sailors were about to make [6] a conspiracy.   3. We think (that) he was not burned to

---

[1] ut—cremārētur, in apposition with **poenam**.   [2] See 115.
[3] Object of **facere**.   [4] *According to the custom.*   [5] *It was*
added = there was an additional reason.   [6] See 346.

death. 4. There is no doubt that the ascent of the mountain is easy. 5. He ordered [1] them to do this. 6. He persuaded them to do this. 7. Having brought up carts and pack-animals they were ready to set out.[2]

434. CAESAR, I. 4 (BEGUN): THE CONSPIRACY IS DISCOVERED

Ea rēs est Helvētiīs per indicium ēnūntiāta. Mōribus suīs Orgetorīgem ex vinculīs [1] causam [2] dīcere coēgērunt. Damnātum [3] poenam sequī oportēbat ut īgnī cremārētur.

NOTES AND VOCABULARY

[1] **vinculum, –ī,** N., *chain;* **ex vinculīs,** *in chains.*

[2] **causam dīcere,** *to plead (his) cause, stand trial.*

[3] **damnō, -āre, -āvi, -ātum,** *condemn;* **damnātum** (agreeing with **eum,** the supplied object of **sequī**) has a conditional force, *if condemned.*

Gallic Weapons

LESSON LV

The Verb *eō.* — **The Ablative of Accompaniment.** — **Caesar, I. 4 (concluded).**

435. IRREGULAR VERBS.—Sum, eō, fcrō, fīō, volō and their compounds are called *irregular* verbs. Review **sum** and **fīō** (Appendix, 37 and 39). Learn from the

---

[1] **iubeō.** See 233.   [2] **proficīscor.** See 239.

Appendix (40) the conjugation of **eō, īre, īvī, itum**, *go.*
Stems: **ī-, īv-, it-.**

436. The passive of **eō** is used only impersonally; for the use of **īrī**, see 412, 2. The compounds **ad-eō** and **trāns-eō** may be transitive in meaning, and therefore may be conjugated in the passive: **adeor, adīris, adītur, adīmur, adīminī, adeuntur,** etc.

437. VOCABULARY

vadum, -ī, N., *ford;* **vadō,** *by fording.*

Nōricus, -a, -um, *Norican.*
nōndum, adv., *not yet.*

> **eō, īre, īvī, itum,** *go.*
> **exeō (ex + eō),** *go out.*
> **subeō (sub + eō),** *go under, undergo.*
> **trānseō (trāns + eō),** *go across, cross.*

438. MODEL SENTENCES

1. **Helvētiī cum omnibus cōpiīs exiērunt:** *The Helvetians went out with all their forces.*

2. **Ad castra Caesaris omnibus cōpiīs vēnērunt:** *They came to Caesar's camp with all their forces.*

3. **Caesar cum equitibus centum pervēnit:** *Caesar arrived with a hundred horsemen.*

In these sentences the ablatives with **cum** denote *accompaniment,* answering the question *With whom?* or *With what?* **Cum** is sometimes omitted with military expressions (sentence 2), unless a numeral is used (sentence 3).

439. RULE XXXIV.—*The ablative with* **cum** *is used to denote accompaniment.*

TRANSLATE

440. 1. Cum Germānīs contendunt. 2. Caesar cum quīnque legiōnibus īre contendit.[1] 3. Bōiī in agrum Nōricum trānsierant. 4. Rhodanus nōnnūllīs locīs vadō trānsītur. 5. Helvētiī id, quod cōnstituerant, facere cōnantur, ut ē fīnibus suīs exeant.[2] 6. Parātī ad omnia perīcula subeunda erant. 7. Helvētiī Caesare invītō[3] trānsīre nōn cōnābuntur. 8. Dē tertiā vigiliā cum legiōnibus tribus ē castrīs profectus, ad eam partem Helvētiōrum pervēnit, quae nōndum flūmen trānsierat. 9. Hīc pāgus, cum domō[4] exīsset, Cassium cōnsulem interfēcerat. 10. Ariovistus dīxit sē sine exercitū in Galliam venīre nōn audēre.[5]

441. 1. They are going to the forest. 2. They are giving hostages to the king.[6] 3. Ariovistus will come with a large army. 4. Ariovistus says he will come with a large army. 5. It is easy to cross the river by fording. 6. We urged[7] the sailors to go[8] with Cassius. 7. The sailor's friends congratulated him (as he was) going[9] to the ship.

442. Review chapters 2 and 3, pages 221–223.

CAESAR, I. 4 (CONCLUDED): THE DEATH OF ORGETORIX

Diē[5] cōnstitūtā causae dictiōnis[2] Orgetorīx ad iūdicium omnem suam familiam, ad[6] hominum mīlia decem, undique coēgit, et omnēs clientēs[1] obaerātōsque suōs, quōrum māgnum numerum habēbat, eōdem[3] 5 condūxit; per eōs nē[7] causam dīceret sē ēripuit.[4]

Cum cīvitās ob eam rem incitāta armīs iūs suum exsequī cōnārētur, multitūdinemque hominum ex agrīs magistrātūs cōgerent, Orgetorīx mortuus est; neque

---

[1] *endeavors.* [2] See 430. [3] See 279. [4] See 332. [5] See 357.
[6] Is the word for *king* to be in the same case here as the word for *forest* in sentence 1? [7] **hortor.** [8] See 206. [9] Present participle.

abest suspīciō, ut [8] Helvētiī arbitrantur, quīn ipse sibi
mortem cōnscīverit.   10

[1] cliēns, -entis, M., *vassal, client.*
[2] dictiō, -ōnis, F., *a speaking;* dictiōnis causae, (*for* [*of*] *the pleading
of the case*), *for the trial.*
[3] eōdem (īdem), adv., *to the same place.*
[4] ēripiō (ē + rapiō), -ripere, -ripuī, -reptum, *snatch away ;* with sē, etc.
—nē, *save one's self from* —.

[5] See 159.   [6] Adverb (383).   [7] See 199.   [8] *as*, with the indicative.

LESSON LVI

**Tho Verb *ferō.* — Expressions of Place.—The Abla-
tive of Separation.—Caesar, I. 5 (begun).**

443. Learn from the Appendix (41) the conjugation,
active and passive (except the imperative), of **ferō,
ferre, tulī, lātum,** *bear, carry.* Stems: **fer-, tul-, lāt-.**
Translate each form.

444.   **VOCABULARY**

cibāria, -ōrum, N., *food;* with **molita,** *meal.*
reditiō, -ōnis, F. (**redeō**), *return.*
rūs, rūris, N., *country* (as opposed to the city).

> **cōnferō (con + ferō),** *bring together*; with **sē,** (*betake
> one's self*), *flee.*
> **efferō (ex + ferō), efferre, extulī, ēlātum,** *carry out,
> carry away.*
> **īnferō (in + ferō),** *bring in,* make or *bring* ―― *upon.*
> **molō, -ere, -uī, -itum,** *grind.*
> **redeō (red + eō,** 435), *go back, return.*
> **tollō, tollere, sustulī, sublātum,** (*raise*), *take away.*

445.   MODEL SENTENCES

1. **Aquītānia ad Hispāniam pertinet** (272).
2. **Rōmam vēnit:** *He came to Rome.*
3. **Domum iērunt:** *They went home.*

4. **Aquītānia ā Garumnā flūmine pertinet** (272).
5. **Rōmā profectus est:** *He departed from Rome.*
6. **Hīs itineribus domō exiērunt:** *By these roads they went forth from home.*

7. **Ea cīvitās est in Prōvinciā:** *That tribe is in the Province.*
8. **Caesar Rōmae**[1] **nōn remānsit:** *Caesar did not remain at Rome.*
9. **Domī**[1] **remānsērunt:** *They remained at home.*

(*a*) In sentence 1 the place *to* which is expressed by the accusative case with the preposition **ad.** But the preposition is omitted with the names of towns, small islands, **domus** and **rūs,** as in 2 and 3.

(*b*) In sentence 4 the place *from* which is expressed by the ablative with the preposition **ā.** But the preposition is omitted with the names of towns, small islands, **domus** and **rūs,** as in 5 and 6.

(*c*) In sentence 7 the place *where* (*in, on* or *at* which) is expressed by the ablative with **in.** But the locative case[9] is used instead of the ablative in the *singular* of names of towns of the first, second and sometimes third declension, and in **domī,** *at home,* **rūrī,** *in the country,* and a few other words. The ending of the locative is **-ae** for the first declension, and **-ī** for the second and third. See sentences 8 and 9.

---

[1] Locative case. See 445, *c.*

446. RULE XXXV.—*Place* to *which is expressed by the accusative with* **ad** *or* **in**; *place* from *which, by the ablative with* **ab, dē** *or* **ex**; *place* where, *by the ablative, generally with* **in**, *or by the locative.*

447. MODEL SENTENCES

1. **Belgae ā cultū prōvinciae absunt** (261).
2. **Helvētiōs itinere prohibuit:** *He kept the Helvetians from marching.*

In these sentences the ablatives denote *separation.* This use of the ablative is found with verbs (or kindred adjectives) meaning *keep away, deprive, free, be absent, be without, need.* After verbs meaning *free, deprive* or *need*, a preposition is regularly not used. After verbs compounded with **ab, dē** or **ex**, one of these prepositions is repeated with the ablative.

448. RULE XXXVI.—*The ablative, with or without a preposition, is used to express separation.*

NOTE.—The first use of the ablative was to express separation. Observe the derivation of the word *ablative,* from **ab,** *from,* and the supine stem of **ferō,** *bear.*

TRANSLATE

449. 1. Tēla cōnferuntur. 2. Helvētiī impedīmenta in ūnum locum contulērunt. 3. Haeduī frūmentum nōn cōnferent, quod [1] dēbent. 4. Hostēs ad impedīmenta sē contulērunt. 5. Eī, quī flūmen trānsierant, suīs [2] auxilium ferre nōn potuērunt. 6. Domum reditiōnis spēs sub-

---

[1] Pronoun.   [2] Indirect object.

lāta est. 7. Fīnitimīs [1] bellum īnferunt. 8. Ea pars cīvitātis Helvētiae calamitātem populō [1] Rōmānō intulerat. 9. Mīles molita cibaria sibi [2] domō [3] effert. 10. Molita cibaria sibi mīlitēs [4] domō efferre iubent. 11. Caesar Bibracte [5] īvit. 12. Eōrum, quī domum rediērunt, erat numerus mīlium [6] centum et decem. 13. Dīviācus plūrimum domī et in reliquā Galliā potuit. 14. Mīlitēs ā proeliō continēbantur. 15. Caesar Galliam omnem ab Ariovistī iniūriā dēfendere potest.

450. 1. I shall go to Germany. 2. I shall go to Geneva. 3. We shall go home. 4. He went out of the camp. 5. He went from Geneva. 6. They live at Geneva.[7] 7. They lived in Germany. 8. They will live in the country. 9. The hope of return will be taken away. 10. A disaster had been brought upon the Roman people. 11. The soldiers were assisting (carrying aid to) their [8] (comrades). 12. Grain was brought together by the Haedui. 13. They will grind the grain and carry it from home with them.

451. CAESAR, CHAPTER I. 5 (BEGUN): THE HELVETII CONTINUE THEIR PREPARATIONS

Post ēius mortem nihilō [7] minus Helvētiī id quod cōnstituerant facere cōnantur, ut [8] ē fīnibus suīs exeant. Ubi iam [9] sē ad eam rem parātōs esse arbitrātī sunt, oppida sua omnia, numerō [10] ad duodecim,[5] vīcōs ad 5 quadringentōs,[6] reliqua prīvāta [4] aedificia [1] incendunt; frūmentum omne, praeter quod sēcum portātūrī erant, combūrunt, ut—domum reditiōnis spē [11] sublātā—parātiōrēs ad omnia perīcula subeunda essent ; trium

---

[1] See 379.   [2] *for himself.*   [3] See 332.   [4] Subject of
efferre.   [5] See 326.   [6] Predicate genitive.   [7] See
Introduction (10).   [8] Indirect object.

mēnsium [2] molita cibāria sibi quemque [3] domō efferre
iubent.   10

NOTES AND VOCABULARY

[1] aedificium, -ī, N., *building.*   [2] mēnsis,-is, M., *month.*   [3] quemque, acc. of indefinite pronoun, *each one.*   [4] prīvātus, -a, -um, *private.*
[6] duodecim = duo + decem.   [6] quadringentī, -ae, -a, *four hundred.*
[7] nihilō, abl. as adv., *none* (*by nothing*); nihilō minus, *nevertheless.*

[8] See 430.   [9] *at length.*   [10] See 144.   [11] See 279.

LESSON LVII—REVIEW

452.   CAESAR, I. 5 (CONCLUDED)

1. What are the uses of the supine? 2. Mention
four ways of expressing purpose. 3. What are the infinitive endings? 4. How are the tenses of the infinitive used? 5. What is an impersonal verb? 6. Name
some verbs used impersonally. 7. How may a noun-
clause be expressed? 8. How is place expressed?
9. Accompaniment? 10. Separation? Conjugate **eō**
and **ferō.**

453.   Review Vocabulary

poena	reditiō	populor	largior
aedificium	ascēnsus	probō	reperiō
cibāria	prīvātus	rogō	eō
iūsiūrandum	propinquus	licet	exeō
vadum	perfacilis	oportet	redeō
vinculum	quō (conj.)	taceō	subeō
cliēns	item	cōnsīdō	trānseō
dictiō	nōndum	ēripiō	ferō
īgnis	cremō	molō	cōnferō
mēnsis	frūmentor	queror	efferō
mōs	grātulor	tollō	īnferō

Mention some English derivatives.

454. Translate in review the sentences of 416, 423, 432, 440 and 449.

455. CAESAR, CHAPTER I . 5 (CONCLUDED) : THE ALLIES OF THE HELVETII

Persuādent Rauracīs et Tulingīs et Latobrīgīs fīnitimīs utī eōdem ūsī⁵ cōnsiliō, oppidīs ⁶ suīs vīcīsque exūstīs,⁴ ūnā ² cum eīs proficīscantur ; Bōiōsque,⁷ quī trāns Rhenum incoluerant et in agrum Nōricum trānsi-
5 erant Nōrēiamque oppūgnārant, receptōs ad sē sociōs ¹ sibi adscīscunt.³

NOTES AND VOCABULARY

¹ **socius, –i,** M., *ally.*
² **ūnā (ūnus),** adv., *together.*
³ **adscīscō, –scīscere, –scīvī, –scītum,** *attach, unite.*
⁴ **exūrō (ex + ūrō), –ūrere, –ussī, –ūstum,** *burn up.*

⁵ See 353. ⁶ See 279. ⁷ **Bōiōs—adscīscunt,** *having received into their number the Boii, who,* etc., *they unite with them as allies.*

LESSON LVIII

Numeral Adjectives.—Clauses of Characteristic.— Caesar, I. 6 (begun).

456. CLASSES OF NUMERALS.—There are three classes of numeral adjectives: *cardinal,* denoting how many; *ordinal,* denoting which one of a series; *distributive,* denoting how many at a time.

CARDINAL.	ORDINAL.	DISTRIBUTIVE.
ūnus, *one,*	**prīmus,** *first,*	**singulī,** *one by one, one each.*
duo, *two,*	**secundus,** *second,*	**bīnī,** *two each.*
trēs, *three,*	**tertius,** *third,*	**ternī,** *three each.*
quattuor, *four,*	**quārtus,** *fourth,*	**quaternī,** *four each.*

CARDINAL.	ORDINAL.	DISTRIBUTIVE.
quīnque, *five*,	quīntus, *fifth*,	quīnī, *five each.*
sex, *six*,	sextus, *sixth*,	sēnī, *six each.*
septem, *seven*,	septimus, *seventh*,	septēnī, *seven each.*
octō, *eight*,	octāvus, *eighth*,	octōnī, *eight each.*
novem, *nine*,	nōnus, *ninth*,	novēnī, *nine each.*
decem, *ten*,	decimus, *tenth*,	dēnī, *ten each.*

Other numerals are given in the Appendix (17).

457. DECLENSION OF NUMERALS.—Ordinals are declined like the singular of **māgnus**; distributives, like the plural of **māgnus**. The only cardinals declined are **ūnus** (177), **duo**, **trēs** (383), the hundreds above **centum** and the plural of **mīlle** (382). Learn the declension of **duo** in the Appendix (14).

458.   **VOCABULARY**

famēs, famis, F., *hunger.*
tempestās, -tātis, F., *(season),*
    weather, storm.
nōnāgintā, *ninety.*

quīngentī, -ae, -a, *five hundred.*
quā, rel. adv., *by which, where.*
vix, adv., *with difficulty, scarcely.*

tolerō, -āre, -āvī, -ātum, *endure;* with **famem,** *keep from starving.*

459. CLAUSES OF CHARACTERISTIC.—A clause beginning with a relative pronoun, adjective or adverb is a relative clause. A relative clause which describes or characterizes an antecedent is called a clause of *description* or *characteristic.* The verb in such a clause is in the subjunctive when the antecedent is incomplete in itself, or when the clause states what *kind* of person or thing the antecedent is. A common use of the clause of characteristic is after such phrases as **est quī, sunt quī.**

1. **Sunt multī quī dīcant:** *There are many who say.*
2. **Erant itinera duo quibus itineribus** [1] **Helvētiī domō exīre possent:** *There were two roads by which the Helvetians could go from home.*

Sentence 1 means: There are many *of the kind that say*, not many *who actually say.* The latter would require the indicative **quī dīcunt.** So sentence 2 tells what *kind* of roads there were.

TRANSLATE

460. 1. Quīnque diēs. 2. Quīntus diēs. 3. Diē septimō 4. Quattuor pāgī. 5. Ad numerum quattuor mīlium. 6. Ab quīngentīs equitibus. 7. Mīlitēs decimae legiōnis. 8. Nōn amplius quīnīs aut sēnīs mīlibus [2] passuum. 9. Cum duābus legiōnibus. 10. Erat ūnum iter quā [3] vix singulī carrī dūcerentur. 11. Diem dīcunt [4] quā [5] diē ad rīpam Rhodanī omnēs conveniant. 12. Domī nihil erat, quō [6] famem tolerārent. 13. Tempestās idōnea ad nāvigandum. 14. Accidit ut essent māgnae tempestātēs. 15. Secūtae sunt tempestātēs, quae nostrōs in castrīs continērent. 16. Eōrum, quī arma ferre possent, fuit numerus mīlium [7] nōnāgintā duōrum.

461. 1. A hundred men. 2. Two hundred men, two hundred ships, two hundred animals. 3. Of two roads. 4. Of three houses. 5. Of one sword. 6. On the sixth day. 7. In the eighth month. 8. In the ninth year. 9. There

---

[1] The antecedent of a relative is sometimes repeated in the relative clause.
[2] See 303. [3] Rel. adv. [4] *appoint.* [5] Rel. adj.
[6] Rel. pron. [7] Predicate genitive.

is no ship in which the soldiers can cross. 10. There are some [1] who say (that) the road will be too [2] narrow. 11. The seventh legion was five miles away.[3] 12. Caesar was informed that the legion was five miles away. 13. When they were two miles away, they saw the enemy's line (of battle).

462. CAESAR, I. 6 (BEGUN): THE TWO ROADS FROM HELVETIA

Erant omnīnō [2] itinera duo quibus itineribus domō exīre possent [4]: ūnum per Sēquanōs, angustum et diffi-

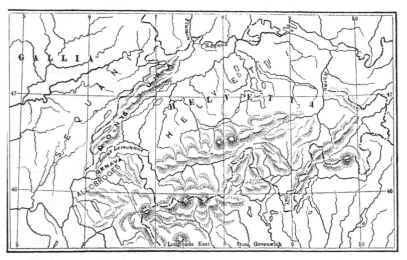

MAP OF HELVETIA

cile, inter montem Iūram et flūmen Rhodanum, vix quā singulī carrī dūcerentur; mōns autem [3] altissimus impendēbat, ut facile perpaucī prohibēre possent: alterum 5

---

[1] **nōnnūllī.**   [2] See 296.   [3] **absum.**

per prōvinciam nostram, multō ⁵ facilius atque expedītius,¹ proptereā quod inter fīnēs Helvētiōrum et Allobrogum, quī nūper pācātī erant, Rhodanus fluit, isque
nōn nūllīs locīs ⁶ vadō trānsītur. Extrēmum oppidum
10 Allobrogum est proximumque Helvētiōrum fīnibus ⁷
Genāva.⁸

NOTES AND VOCABULARY

¹ **expedītus, -a, -um,** *free from obstacles, easy.*
² **omnīnō (omnis),** adv., *in all, altogether.*
³ **autem,** conj., *besides.* **Autem** never stands first, but usually second in
the sentence.

⁴ See 459.   ⁵ See 311.   ⁶ See 446.   ⁷ See 313.   ⁸ Note
the Latin order. In English we should say *Geneva is,* etc.

LESSON LIX

**The Genitive and Ablative of Description.—Causal
Clauses.—Caesar, I. 6 (concluded).**

463.   MODELS

1. **Vir māgnae auctōritātis:** *A man of great influence.*
2. **Fossa trium pedum:** *A ditch of three feet.*
3. **Vir bonō animō:** *A man well disposed,* or *of good dis-
position.*
4. **Bōiī erant magnā virtūte:** *The Boii were (men) of great
valor.*

In these illustrations the genitive or ablative is used
to *describe.* The two cases are generally used in this
way without any distinction, except that *size, weight*
and *number* are expressed by the genitive only. Either
case must be modified by an adjective. These constructions are called the genitive and ablative of
description (quality or *characteristic).*

464. RULE XXXVII.—*The genitive or ablative, with an adjective in agreement, is used to describe a noun.*

465. CAUSAL CLAUSES.—Clauses that express cause or reason are called *causal* clauses. They are adverbial and may begin with these words:

1. **quod** or **quoniam** (**quia, quandō**), *because, since.* The verb is in the indicative, or, *if the reason is quoted,* the subjunctive.

Helvētiī reliquōs Gallōs virtūte praecēdunt, quod cum Germānīs contendunt (261).

2. **cum,** *since, because.* The verb is in the subjunctive:

Hīs cum persuādēre nōn possent, lēgātōs ad Dumnorīgem mittunt: *Since they could not persuade them, they sent ambassadors to Dumnorix.*

NOTE.—**Cum** often denotes both cause and time, as in the last sentence.

466. Vis, F., *force,* pl. *strength,* is declined thus: Sing. —**vīs, vīs, vī, vim, vī**; pl.—**vīrēs, vīrium, vīribus, vīrēs, vīribus.**

TRANSLATE

467. 1. Aciēs legiōnum quattuor. 2. Dumnorīx erat summā audāciā. 3. Hominēs erunt inimīcō animō. 4. Perfacile est tōtīus Galliae [1] potīrī, cum Helvētiī virtūte omnibus [2] praestent. 5. Haeduī, cum sē ab eīs dēfendere nōn possent, lēgātōs ad Caesarem mīsērunt. 6. Iter per prōvinciam faciēmus, proptereā quod aliud iter habēmus nūllum. 7. Allobrogibus persuādēbunt, quod sunt nōndum bonō animō in populum Rōmānum. 8. Exīstimant sē Allobrogibus persuāsūrōs esse, quod sint nōndum bonō

---

[1] See 360.   [2] See 379.

12

animō.   9. Caesar dīxit sē Haeduōs dēfēnsūrum, quoniam
Ariovistus bellum eīs intulisset.   10. Vīribus.   11. Vīs
flūminis.   12. Vim facere ¹ cōnantur.   13. Eōs vī cōgent.

468. 1. A journey ² of ten days.   2. Soldiers of better
spirit.³   3. The town was easily taken,⁴ because it was not
fortified.   4. He says the town will easily be taken, because it is not fortified.   5. Since they could not persuade
the Allobroges, they compelled them by force.   6. The
sword is four feet shorter than the spear.   7. The same
day aid was brought to the foot-soldiers, who had fought,
as bravely as they could.⁵

469. CAESAR, I . 6 (CONCLUDED) : THE HELVETII CHOOSE
THE ROAD THROUGH THE ROMAN PROVINCE

Ex eō oppidō pōns ad Helvētiōs pertinet. Allobrogibus sēsē ³ vel persuāsūrōs (quod nōndum bonō animō in
populum Rōmānum vidērentur) ⁴ exīstimābant, vel vī
coāctūrōs ut per suōs fīnēs eōs īre paterentur.⁵ Omnibus
5 rēbus ⁶ ad profectiōnem comparātīs diem dīcunt quā diē
ad rīpam Rhodanī omnēs conveniant. Is diēs erat a.⁷
d. v. Kal.¹ Apr.,² L. Pīsōne A. Gabīniō cōnsulibus.⁸

NOTES AND VOCABULARY

¹ **Kalendae, -ārum,** F., *Calends,* the first day of the Roman month.
² **Aprīlēs, -e,** adj., *of April.*

³ See 350.   ⁴ The passive of **videō** may mean *seem,* as here.
⁵ See 206.   ⁶ See 279.   ⁷ **ante diem quīntum Kalendās Aprīlēs,**
March 28. The Romans did not number the days of the month as we do,
but called the first day the *Calends* (**Kalendae**), the fifth (seventh of Mar.,
May, Jul. and Oct.) the *Nones* (**Nōnae**), and the thirteenth (fifteenth of
Mar., May, Jul. and Oct.) the *Ides* (**Īdūs**).

The days between the Calends and the Nones were reckoned as so many
days each before the Nones ; the days between the Nones and the Ides as

---

¹ *to use.*   ² **iter.**   ³ **animus.**   ⁴ **expūgnō.**   ⁵ **possum.**

so many days each before the Ides ; the days after the Ides as so many days each before the Calends of the next month. But they counted both the day *from* which and the day *to* which they reckoned. Therefore, to determine a date falling before the Calends, add two to the number of days in the current month before subtracting the given ordinal. Thus, in the above date, 31 + 2— 5 = 28.

The phrases **ante diem quintum Kalendās Aprīlēs** is idiomatic, for which we should expect **diē quīntō ante Kal. Apr.**

⁸ See 279. The Roman year was designated by the names of the consuls for that year, as though we were to say "during the administration of Lincoln." The year above referred to was 61 B.C.

LESSON LX

The Dative with Certain Verbs.—Temporal Clauses.
Caesar, I. 7 (begun).

470. The dative of indirect object (61) is used as follows:—

1. With transitive verbs in connection with the direct object (63): **Belgae Gallīs victōriam nūntiant** (62).

2. With verbs compounded with certain prepositions (379): **Helvētiī omnibus praestant** (378).

3. With intransitive verbs. Some verbs which in English are transitive, and therefore take a direct object, are intransitive in Latin and take an indirect. object. These verbs are given in 471:—

1. **Fīnitimīs persuādent:** *They persuade the neighbors.*

2. **Allobrogibus imperāvit, ut eīs frūmentum darent:** *He ordered the Allobroges to give them grain.*

471. RULE XXXVIII.—*The dative of the indirect object is used with verbs meaning* favor, help, please, trust, command, obey, serve, resist, believe, persuade, envy threaten, pardon, spare.

NOTE.—In the passive construction these verbs are impersonal (428), and the dative is retained:—**Fīnitimīs persuādētur** : *The neighbors are persuaded (it is persuaded to,* etc.). See 206, *b.*

472. TEMPORAL CLAUSES.—Temporal[1] clauses (clauses expressing *t me*) begin with these words—

1. **cum,** *when.* Review 369.

2. **postquam,** *after,* **ubi, ut, simul (atque),** *when, as soon as.* Indicative mood.

Ubi diēs vēnit, lēgātī revertērunt : *When the day came, the ambassadors returned.*

3. **dum,** *while.* Indicative historical present.

Dum haec geruntur, lēgātus pervēnit : *While these things were going on, the lieutenant arrived.*

4. **dum, donec, quoad,** *as long as.* Indicative mood.

5. **dum, donec, quoad,** *until.* Indicative, to denote an actual event; subjunctive, to denote an expected event.

Caesar Genāvae manēbit, dum mīlitēs conveniant : *Caesar will stay at Geneva, until the soldiers assemble.*

6. **antequam, priusquam,** *before.* Mood the same as in 5.

473.   **VOCABULARY**

paucī, -ae, -a, *few.*   postquam, conj., *after.*
praecipuē, adv., *especially.*   priusquam, conj., *before.*
dum, conj., *while, as long as, until.*

moror, -ārī, -ātus sum, *tarry, wait.*
indulgeō, -dulgēre, -dulsī, -dultum, *favor.*
nōscō, nōscere, nōvī, nōtum, *know.*
resistō, -sistere, -stitī, ——, *withstand, resist.*

---

[1] From **tempus.**

TRANSLATE

474. 1. Prōvinciae tōtī quam māximum numerum mīlitum imperat.[1] 2. Prīma aciēs hostibus resistet. 3. Decimae legiōnī Caesar indulsit praecipuē. 4. Ariovistus eīs, quōs vīcit, imperābit. 5. Postquam id vīdit, cōpiās suās Caesar in proximum collem dūxit. 6. Nōn exspectāre statuit, dum in prōvinciam Helvētiī pervenīrent. 7. Dum paucōs diēs[2] frūmentī causā morātur, dē Germānīs certior factus est. 8. Priusquam dē Dumnorīge statueret, Diviciācum ad sē vocat. 9. Priusquam mīlitēs laudō, pauca dē virtūte dīcam. 10. Ipse, quoad potuit, fortissimē restitit. 11. Cum hostibus resistere nōn possent, ad montem sē recēpērunt. 12. Hostēs nōtīs omnibus vadīs, ubi nostrōs ad flūmen euntēs vīderant, celeriter impetum fēcērunt.

475. 1. We shall remain until you return.[3] 2. While they tarried a few hours, they were informed of [4] the battle. 3. After the Helvetians formed (made) the conspiracy, they emigrated.[5] 4. Before they emigrated, Orgetorix died. 5. Caesar sent a lieutenant to levy two legions. 6. There are many who say that the first line cannot withstand the enemy. 7. He thinks that the general will favor the sixth legion.

476. Review Chapters 4, 5 and 6, page 223.

CAESAR, I. 7 (BEGUN): CAESAR GOES TO GENEVA.
THE HELVETII SEND AMBASSADORS

Caesarī cum id nūntiātum esset eōs[1] per prōvinciam nostram iter facere cōnārī, mātūrat[2] ab urbe[3] proficīscī, et quam māximīs potest itineribus in Galliam ūlteriōrem contendit et ad[4] Genāvam pervenit. Prō-

---

[1] *levies* (*upon*).   [2] See 387.   [3] *revertor.*   [4] *dē.*   [5] *exeō domō.*

5 vinciae tōtī quam māximum potest mīlitum numerum
imperat (erat omnīnō in Galliā ūlteriōre legiō ūna), pontem quī erat ad Genāvam iubet rescindī.

Ubi dē ēius adventū Helvētiī certiōrēs factī sunt,
lēgātōs ad eum mittunt nōbilissimōs cīvitātis, cūius
10 lēgātiōnis Nammēius et Verudoctius prīncipem ⁵ locum
obtinēbant,⁶ quī dīcerent ⁷ ' sibi esse ⁹ in animō sine ūllō
maleficiō iter per prōvinciam facere, proptereā quod
aliud iter habērent nūllum; rogāre ut ēius voluntāte
id sibi facere liceat.'

NOTES

¹ See 430.   ² See 402.   ³ What city?   ⁴ **Ad** with the
meaning *towards, near to*, may be used with the names of towns (446).
⁶ Adjective.   ⁶ See 122.   ⁷ See 199.   ⁸ See 115.   ⁹ What
is the subject ?

LESSON LXI

**The Periphrastic Conjugations.—The Dative of the
Agent.—Caesar, I. 7 (continued).**

477. ACTIVE   PERIPHRASTIC.¹ — The *future   active
participle* may be used with forms of **sum,** to express
future or intended action:

laudātūrus (-a, -um) sum, *I am about to praise, am going to
praise.*

This is called the *active periphrastic* conjugation, and
is found in the indicative, subjunctive, and present and
perfect infinitive.   Write a synopsis of **laudō** in this conjugation.

¹ A '' periphrastic '' form is a form consisting of more than one word.
The compound tenses of the passive voice (283) are therefore periphrastic,
but the word is limited to the above use.

478. PASSIVE PERIPHRASTIC.— The *gerundive* may be used with forms of **sum,** to express action which is necessary or ought to take place.

laudandus (-a, -um) sum, *I am to be praised, have to be praised, must be praised.*

This is called the *passive periphrastic* conjugation, and is found in the same forms as the active periphrastic. Write a synopsis of **moneō** in this conjugation.

479. DATIVE OF AGENT.—The agent or doer of the action expressed by a passive periphrastic form is denoted by the dative instead of the ablative (104).

1. **Caesarī omnia ūnō tempore erant agenda:** *Everything had to be done by Caesar at one time.*

2. **Statuit sibi Rhēnum esse trānseundum:** *He decided that he ought to cross the Rhine* (literally, *that the Rhine ought to be crossed by him*).

480. RULE XXXIX.—*The dative of the agent is used with the passive periphrastic conjugation.*

481. Some verbs have the passive periphrastic used impersonally: **Caesar exspectandum esse sibi statuit:** *Caesar decided that he ought to wait (waiting must be by him).*

482.   VOCABULARY

putō, -āre, -āvī, -ātum, *think, suppose.*
concēdō (con + cēdō), -cēdere, -cessī, -cessum, *yield, make a concession.*
īnstruō, -struere, -strūxī, -strūctum, *build, draw up* (troops).

TRANSLATE

483. 1. Sīgnum dandum est.   2. Sīgnum datūrī sumus.
3. Aciēs īnstruenda erit.   4. Aciem est īnstrūctūrus.
5. Mīlitēs revocandī erant.   6. Mīlitēs revocātūrus sum.
7. Frūmentum portātūrī sunt.   8. Frūmentum mīlitibus
portandum erat.   9. Oportet [1] frūmentum darī mīlitibus.
10. Orgetorīx suae cīvitātis imperium obtentūrus est.
11. Orgetorīgī imperium obtinendum est.   12. Dīcit Orgetorīgem imperium esse obtenturum.   13. Caesar concessūrus
erat.   14. Caesar concēdendum (esse sibi) nōn putābat.
15. Timēbam nē Orgetorīx imperium obtentūrus esset.
16. Timeō ut frūmentum comportātum sit.   17. Sine causā
timendum (esse sibi) nōn putat.   18. Locus erat idōneus
ad aciem īnstruendam.

484. 1. The lieutenant is about to advise the merchants.
2. The lieutenant must advise the merchants.[2]   3. We are
about to praise the sailor.   4. The sailor must be praised.
5. The boy is going[3] to announce the victory.   6. The victory had to be announced by the boy.   7. Peace must be
made.   8. They were about to make peace.   9. They must
send a letter to their friends.[2]   10. Caesar himself is going[3]
to command the legions.   11. He thinks that Caesar is
going to command the legions.[4]   12. When the lines had
been drawn up, the signal was given.

485. CAESAR, I. 7 (CONTINUED): CAESAR DISTRUSTS THE
HELVETII

Caesar, quod memoriā tenēbat L.[4] Cassium cōnsulem
occīsum[2] exercitumque ēius ab Helvētiīs pulsum[3] et sub
iugum missum[5] concēdendum nōn putābat; neque ho-

---

[1] See 428.   [2] Change this sentence to the passive construction before
translating.   Why?   See 478.   [5] See 477.   [4] See 471.

mines inimīcō animō,⁶ datā facultāte ⁷ per prōvinciam itineris faciendī temperātūrōs ¹ ab iniūriā ⁸ et maleficiō 5 existimābat.

NOTES AND VOCABULARY

¹ temperō, –āre, –āvī, –ātum, *refrain*.

² occīdō (ob + caedō), –cīdere, –cīdī, –cīsum, *kill*.

³ pellō, pellere, pepulī, pulsum, (*strike, drive*), *defeat*.

⁴ Lūcium. What kind of clause begins with this word ?   ⁶ Supply esse with occīsum, pulsum and missum.   ⁶ See 464.   ⁷ See 277. ⁸ See 448.

LESSON LXII

The Verbs *volō* and *nōlō*.—Conditional Sentences.— Caesar, I. 7 (concluded).

486. Learn from the Appendix (42) the conjugation of the irregular verbs **volō, velle, voluī,** *wish, be willing,* and **nōlō, nōlle, nōluī,** *not wish, be unwilling.* Notice that the irregular forms are chiefly the present indicative, present and imperfect subjunctive, and present infinitive.¹

487. These verbs may take a complementary infinitive (230, 2), or an infinitive with subject-accusative (231, 2).

1. **Venīre voluit:** *He wished to come.*
2. **Germānōs in Galliā esse nōluērunt:** *They did not wish the Germans to be in Gaul.*

488. CONDITIONAL SENTENCES. — Conditional sentences are complex sentences of which one clause expresses a condition, and the other a conclusion: *If he tries, he will succeed.* *If he tries* is the condition; *he will*

¹ Mālō (= magis + volō), *wish rather, prefer,* is given in the Appendix.

succeed, the conclusion. In Latin the condition generally begins with the conjunction **sī,** *if.*

489. The condition may be of the following kinds:

I. Present con-
dition.
1. Stated as a fact. Present indicative. *If he is coming, it is well:* **Sī
venit, bene est.**
2. Contrary to fact. Imperfect subjunctive. *If he were coming, it would
be well:* **Sī venīret, bene esset.**

II. Past condi-
tion.
1. Stated as fact. A past indicative.
If he came, it was well: **Sī vēnit, bene
fuit.**
2. Contrary to fact. Pluperfect subjunctive. *If he had come, it would have
been well:* **Sī vēnisset, bene fuisset.**

III. Future con-
dition.
1. More probable (*shall, will*). Future
or future perfect indicative. *If he
comes (shall come), it will be well:* **Sī
veniet, bene erit.**
2. Less probable (*should, would*).
Present (or perfect) subjunctive.
If he should come, it would be well:
Sī veniat, bene sit.

TRANSLATE

490. 1. Sī volt. 2. Sī voluit. 3. Sī volet. 4. Sī velit.
5. Sī vellet. 6. Sī voluisset. 7. Putat eōs velle. 8. Putat
eōs voluisse. 9. Nōn est dubium quīn voluerit. 10. Nō-
lumus. 11. Nōluerant. 12. Sī nōlītis. 13. Sī nōllētis.
14. Sī nōluissētis. 15. Sunt quī īre nōlint. 16. Sī trānsīre
cōnantur. 17. Sī cōnentur. 18. Sī cōnātī essent. 19. Sī

trānsīre cōnābuntur,[1] eōs prohibēbit. 20. Sī obsidēs ab eīs dentur, cum eīs pācem faciat. 21. Sī proeliō contendere voluisset, vīcisset. 22. Sī facultās dētur,[2] ab maleficiō nōn temperent.

491. 1. To have been willing. 2. I do not think he is unwilling. 3. If the soldiers are brave, they are praised. 4. If the soldier is (shall be)[1] brave, he will be praised. 5. If the soldier should be brave, he would be praised. 6. If the soldier was brave, he was praised. 7. If the soldier were brave,[3] he would be praised. 8. If the soldier had been brave,[4] he would have been praised. 9. The army must not be sent under the yoke.

492. Caesar, I. 7 (concluded): Caesar Postpones his Reply to the Helvetii

Tamen,[3] ut spatium [1] intercēdere [4] posset dum [5] mīlitēs quōs imperāverat convenīrent, lēgātīs respondit diem [6] sē ad dēlīberandum [7] sūmptūrum; sī quid [8] vellent,[9] ad Īdūs.[2] Aprīlēs reverterentur.[10]

[1] **spatium, -ī,** N., *space, space of time.*
[2] **Īdūs, -uum,** F., *Ides.* See 469, 7.
[3] **tamen,** adv., *yet, nevertheless.*
[4] **intercēdō (inter + cēdō),** -cēdere, -cessī, -cessum, *come between, intervene.*
[5] See 472. [6] *time.* [7] See 414. [8] *anything,* indefinite pronoun, object of **vellent.** [9] *should wish.* **Vellent** is in the imperfect subjunctive, not according to 489, I. 2, but because the sentence is quoted. Quoted sentences are explained in 548. [10] *should return.* The passive of **revertō** is deponent in the present system.

---

[1] The English generally uses the *present* in a future more probable condition, though the Latin requires the future. [2] How else can this condition be expressed (279)? [3] Does this mean that he is brave? [4] Does this mean that he was brave?

LESSON LXIII—REVIEW

CAESAR, I. 8 (BEGUN)

493. 1. How are numeral adjectives classified? 2. What numerals are declined? 3. Decline **ūnus** and **duo.** 4. Conjugate **volō** and **nōlō.** 5. Explain the periphrastic conjugations. 6. Give an example of a genitive of description. 7. With what verbs is the dative of indirect object used? 8. By what cases is the agent of an action expressed? 9. Classify causal clauses. 10. Temporal clauses. 11. Conditional sentences. 12. What is a clause of characteristic?

494.   **VOCABULARY**

Kalendac	omnīnō	sī	intercēdō
spatium	praecipuē	moror	nōscō
famēs	tamen	putō	occīdō
tempestās	vix	temperō	pellō
vīs	autem	tolerō	resistō
Īdūs	dum	indulgeō	nōlō
expedītus	postquam	concēdō	volō
paucī	priusquam	īnstruō	

495. Translate in review the sentences of 460, 467, 474, 483, 490.

496. CAESAR, I. 8 (BEGUN): CAESAR CONSTRUCTS FORTIFICATIONS

Intereā [1] eā legiōne [2] quam sēcum [3] habēbat mīlitibusque quī ex prōvinciā convēnerant, ā lacū Lemannō, quī in flūmen Rhodanum īnfluit, ad montem Iūram, quī

fīnēs Sēquanōrum ab Helvētiīs dīvidit, mīlia [4] passuum [5]
decem novem mūrum in altitūdinem pedum [6] sēdecim 5
fossamque perdūcit. Eō opere [7] perfectō praesidia dispōnit, castella commūnit, quō facilius, sī sē invītō [7]
trānsīre cōnārentur,[8] prohibēre posset.

NOTES AND VOCABULARY

[1] intereā (inter + ea), adv., *meanwhile.*

[2] See 74.   [3] See 439.   [4] See 387.   [5] See 385.   [6] See 464.   [7] See 279.
[8] sī —cōnārentur is not a present contrary-to-fact condition (489, I. 2),
but a future less probable. It seems, therefore, that it should be in the
present subjunctive (489, III. 2) rather than the imperfect. For this change,
see the rule for sequence of tenses (405).

LESSON LXIV

**The Interrogative Pronoun *quis.* — Questions and
Answers.—Caesar, I. 8 (concluded).**

497. The interrogative pronoun **quis** is declined thus:

SING.	M. AND F.	N.	
N.	quis	quid,	*who? what?*
G.	cūius	cūius,	*whose?*
D.	cui	cui,	*to, for whom?*
Ac.	quem	quid,	*whom? what?*
Ab.	quō	quō,	*with, from, by whom* or *what?*

The plural is like that of the relative **quī.**

498. The interrogative adjective **quī, quae, quod,**
which? what? is declined like the relative **quī.** For
the interrogative adjective **uter,** see 177.

499. QUESTIONS.—Questions in Latin may be introduced by an interrogative pronoun, interrogative ad-

jective or interrogative adverb, especially **-ne, nŏnne**
or **num**. **Nŏnne** implies the answer *yes;* **num**, the answer *no;* **-ne** is an enclitic attached to the emphatic
word, and implies nothing regarding the answer.

1. **Quis coniūrātiōnem fēcit?** *Who made the conspiracy?*
2. **Quī Helvētius coniūrātiōnem fēcit?** *What Helvetian
   made a conspiracy?*
3. **Ubi coniūrātiōnem fēcit?** *Where did he make a conspiracy?*
4. **Gallusne coniūrātiōnem fēcit?** *Did a Gaul make a conspiracy?*
5. **Nŏnne coniūrātiōnem fēcit?** *Did he not make a conspiracy?*
6. **Num coniūrātiōnem fēcit?** *He did not make a conspiracy,
   did he?*

500. ANSWERS.—A question may be answered by
repeating the verb (with **nōn**, if negative), or by using
the adverbs **certē**, *certainly,* **etiam,** *even so,* **ita,** *so, yes,*
nōn, *no,* **minimē,** *by no means,* etc.

501. DIRECT AND INDIRECT QUESTIONS.—Questions
like those in 499 are *direct;* that is, they are the exact
words of the inquirer. If a question is dependent on a
verb meaning *ask, say, see, tell, wonder,* etc., it is *indirect:
They ask who made the conspiracy.* The verb in a Latin
indirect question is in the subjunctive: **Rogant quis
coniūrātiōnem fēcerit.**

NOTE.—Indirect questions are noun-clauses (430).

502. RULE XL.—*An indirect question has its verb in
the subjunctive.*

503.   VOCABULARY

oculus, -ī, M., *eye.*

iūdicō, -āre, -āvī, -ātum, *decide, judge.*
fluō, fluere, fluxī, fluxum, *flow.*

TRANSLATE

504. 1. Galliane incolitur? 2. Quī incolunt Galliam? 3. Num Rōmānī incolunt Galliam? 4. Quis apud Helvē- tiōs fuit nōbilissimus? 5. Nōnne Helvētiī omnia sua op- pida incendērunt? 6. Ubi est Genāva? 7. Flūmenne trānsīre possumus? 8. Cōnābimur sī[1] trānsīre possīmus.[2] 9. In utram partem[3] Rhodanus fluit? 10. Oculīs in utram partem[3] fluat iūdicārī nōn potest. 11. Quālis erat nātūra montis? 12. Cōgnōvērunt quālis esset nātūra mon- tis. 13. Num Caesar recentium iniūriārum memoriam dēponere potuit? 14. Quās in partēs hostēs iter faciunt? 15. Praemīsit explōrātōrēs quī vidērent quās in partēs iter facerent.

505. 1. Did the Helvetians go through the province? 2. (By) which road will they go? 3. What does the lieu- tenant wish to do? 4. He has not said what he wishes to do. 5. How[4] deep is the river? 6. What mountain is between the Sequani and the Helvetii? 7. He asks what mountain is between the Sequani and the Helvetii. 8. If the men had gone in another direction,[5] they would have been informed[6] of the danger.

---

[1] (*to see*) *if.*   [2] **sī—possīmus**, an indirect question, not a condition.
[3] *direction.*   [4] **quam.**   [5] **pars.**   [6] See 391.

506. CAESAR, I. 8 (CONCLUDED): THE HELVETII FAIL TO CROSS THE RHONE

Ubi ea diēs quam cōnstituerat cum lēgātīs vēnit, et lēgātī ad eum revertērunt, negat sē mōre[1] et exemplō populī Rōmānī posse iter ūllī per prōvinciam dare; et, sī vim facere cōnentur, prohibitūrum[2] ostendit. Hel-
5 vētiī, eā spē[3] dēiectī,[4] nāvibus[5] iūnctīs ratibusque complūribus factīs, aliī vadīs[6] Rhodanī, quā minima altitūdō flūminis erat, nōn numquam interdiū, saepius noctū, sī perrumpere possent[7] cōnātī, operis mūnītiōne[6] et mīlitum concursū et tēlīs repulsī, hōc cōnātū[3] dēstitērunt.

NOTES AND VOCABULARY

[1] See 432, 11.   [2] Supply sē esse.   [3] See 448.   [4] eā—dēiectī, *disappointed in this hope.*   [5] See 279.   [6] See 74.   [7] See 502.

exemplum, -ī, N., *precedent, (example).*
ratis, -is, F., *raft.*
complūrēs, -a or **-ia,** gen. **-ium,** adj., *a great many, very many.*
cōnātus, -ūs, M. (**cōnor**), *attempt.*

concursus, -ūs, M. (**currō,** *run*), *charge, onset.*
interdiū, adv., *by day.*
noctū, adv., *by night.*
numquam, adv., *never.*

negō, -āre, -āvī, -ātum, *say — not, refuse.*
dēiciō (dē + iaciō), dēicere, dēiēcī, dēiectum, *throw down, cast down.*
dēsistō, -sistere, -stitī, -stitum, *cease, desist from.*
ostendō, -tendere, -tendī, -tentum, *show, declare.*
perrumpō (per + rumpō), -rumpere, -rūpī, -ruptum, *break through, force a passage.*
repellō (re + pellō), repellere, reppulī, repulsum, *drive back, repel.*

LESSON LXV

Personal Pronouns.—Indefinite Pronouns.—Review of Pronouns.

507. PERSONAL PRONOUNS.—The personal pronouns are **ego,** *I,* of the first person, and **tū,** *thou, you,* of the second person. For the third person, as already learned, the demonstratives or the reflexive suī are used. Learn the declension of **ego** and **tū** (Appendix, 18).

508. Use of ego and tū.—The nominatives **ego, tū, nōs** and **vōs** are seldom used, except for emphasis. The genitives **nostrum** and **vestrum** are used only after words implying a part: **Quis vestrum ībit?** *Who of you will go?*

509. Indefinite Pronouns.—The indefinite pronouns are so called because they do not refer to any definite person or thing. They are **quis** (**quī**) and its compounds.

1. **quis,** *any* (*one*), *anything.*
2. **aliquis,** *some* (*one*), *some thing.*
3. **quispiam,** *any* (*one*) *at all.*
4. **quisquam,** *any* (*one*) *at all* (chiefly in negative sentences).
5. **quīlibet,** *any* (*one*) *you please.*
6. **quīvīs,** *any* (*one*) *you will.*
7. **quisque,** *each* (*one*), *every* (*one*).
8. **quīdam,** *a certain* (*one*).

510. Declension of Indefinite Pronouns.—**Quis** as a pronoun is declined like the interrogative **quis** (497); as an adjective, like the relative **quī** (182). Only the pronominal part of the compounds is declined. **Aliquis** has **aliqua** instead of **aliquae** in the nominative feminine singular and in the neuter plural. **Quidam** has **n** instead of **m** before **d** in **quendam, quandam, quōrundam, quārundam.** **Quisquam** has **c** for **d** in the neuter: **quicquam.**

511. Classes of Pronouns.—Pronouns have been classified as follows:—

13

1. Personal and reflexive: **ego, tū, suī.**
2. Possessive: **meus, tuus, suus, noster, vester.**
3. Demonstrative: **hīc, iste, ille, is, īdem.**
4. Intensive: **ipse.**
5. Relative: **quī.**
6. Interrogative: **quis.**
7. Indefinite: **quis,** etc.

TRANSLATE

512. 1. Ego vōs laudō. 2. Nōs tē laudāmus. 3. Vōs eum laudātis. 4. Tū eōs laudās. 5. Persuāsitne tibi? 6. Mihi persuādēbant. 7. Dīcit tē īre sēcum.[1] 8. Nōnne īs mēcum?[1] 9. Quis nostrum īre volt? 10. Hī virī īre nōlunt. 11. Puerī mihi[2] vocandī sunt. 12. Sī nōbīs persuādēbit, bene erit. 13. Ipsī ad Rhēnum ībant. 14. Ab ipsīus[3] castrīs. 15. Caesar iīsdem ducibus ūsus est quī nūntiī[4] vēnerant. 16. Priusquam[5] Caesar quicquam cōnārētur, Dīviciācum ad sē vocārī iubet. 17. Sī quid volent, revertentur. 18. Quīdam ex mīlitibus[6] decimae legiōnis. 19. Quisque sibi frūmentum domō extulit. 20. Nōn sine aliquā spē.

513. 1. Caesar sent a certain man (as) scout. 2. I am going[7] to see the same ships. 3. Was your brother praised by his friends? 4. Our house is very[8] large. 5. Some friends have come to see[11] us. 6. My father has given me[9] a letter. 7. If anyone is[10] able to cross the river, he will be praised. 8. Every one waited until he heard the signal.

---

[1] **Cum** is an enclitic with the ablative of the personal, reflexive and relative pronouns. [2] See 480. [3] See 257. [4] Predicate nominative. [5] See 472. [6] **ex mīlitibus = mīlitum.** [7] See 477. [8] How is this to be expressed in Latin (296)? [9] What case? [10] What tense is to be used in Latin? [11] See 414.

LESSON LXVI

The Objective Genitive.—Review of the Genitive.—
Caesar, I. 9 (begun).

514.   VOCABULARY

contumēlia, -ae, F., *disgrace,*
insult.
fortūna, -ae, F., *chance, for-*
tune; pl. *property.*
deus, -ī, M., *god* (App. 10).
incommodum, -ī, N., *disad-*
vantage, misfortune.

dubitātiō, -ōnis, F., (*doubt*),
hesitation.
prōditiō, -ōnis, F., *treason.*
cōnscius, -a, -um, *knowing;*
with **sibi,** *conscious.*
prīstinus, -a, -um, *former,*
early.

commoveō (con + moveō), (*put in motion*), *stir, alarm.*
miseret, miserēre, miseruit, *it distresses, excites pity in.*
oblīvīscor, oblīvīscī, oblītus sum, *forget.*
reminīscor, reminīscī, *recall* (*to mind*), *remember.*
interest, interesse, interfuit, *it interests, concerns.*

515. OBJECTIVE GENITIVE.—The genitive is sometimes used to denote the object of an action or feeling
(expressed or implied), and is then called the objective
genitive. It is used with:—

1. Nouns: **Cupiditās victōriae,** *the desire of victory.*

2. Adjectives (review 213): **Cupidus victōriae,** *desirous of victory.*

3. Verbs: denoting *memory, interest, feeling, acquitting, condemning,* etc.[1]

(*a*) **Reminīscitur virtūtis Helvētiōrum:** *He recalls the valor
of the Helvetians.*

(*b*) **Caesaris interest:** *It concerns Caesar.*

---

[1] See also 360.

(c) **Eōrum nōs miseret:** *We pity them.* (*It excites pity of them in us.*)

(d) **Prōditiōnis accūsātus est:** *He was charged with treason.*

NOTE.—With verbs of *memory*, an object denoting things may be in the accusative.

516. RULE XLI.—*The objective genitive is used with nouns and adjectives denoting* desire, memory, knowledge, *etc.*, *and with verbs of* memory, interest, feeling, acquitting, condemning, *etc.*

517. REVIEW OF THE GENITIVE.—The Genitive is used chiefly as follows:—

1. Genitive of possession (47): **tēla mīlitum.**
2. Genitive of description (464): **mīles māgnae virtūtis.**
3. Genitive of the whole (385): **pars mīlitum.** Used with certain nouns, pronouns, adjectives, adverbs.
4. Objective genitive (515): **Mīlitum interest.** Used with certain nouns, adjectives, verbs.

Since the genitive is so frequently used to modify nouns, it may be called the *adjective* case.

518. PREDICATE GENITIVE.—A genitive denoting possession, description or the whole may be used to complete the predicate:—**Gladius est mīlitis:** *The sword is the soldier's.*

TRANSLATE

519. 1. Māgna pars eōrum. 2. Sociī eōrum. 3. Fortūnae sociōrum. 4. Memoriā patrum nostrōrum. 5. Cōnsiliō deōrum. 6. Oppidum ūlteriōris prōvinciae. 7. Multitūdō equitum. 8. Ōrātiōne Caesaris. 9. Imperium Gallōrum. 10. Frāter Dīviciācī. 11. Satis causae. 12. In exercitū Crassī. 13. Spēs fugae. 14. Āgmen hostium. 15. Duo mīlia passuum. 16. Inopia omnium rērum. 17. Minus dubitātiōnis. 18. Cupidus rērum novārum.[1] 19. Helvētiī ēius adventū commōtī sunt. 20. Alicūius iniūriae nōn (sibi) cōnscius fuit. 21. Veteris contumēliae oblīvīscī volō. 22. Reminīscimur veteris incommodī populī Rōmānī et prīstinae virtūtis Helvētiōrum. 23. Intererat [2] populī Rōmānī Gallōs pācārī.

520. 1. They had been accused of treason. 2. It will interest all the citizens. 3. Do you remember the general's hesitation? 4. Did they forget their former friends? 5. The hill was not of great height. 6. He [3] pitied the children who had been sent (as) hostages. 7. If each (man) fights [4] bravely, we shall conquer. 8. Who was the bravest of the sailors?

521. CAESAR, I. 9 (BEGUN): THE WAY THROUGH THE SEQUANIAN TERRITORY

Relinquēbātur ūna per Sēquanōs via, quā Sēquanīs invītīs propter angustiās īre nōn poterant. Hīs cum suā sponte[1] persuādēre nōn possent, lēgātōs ad Dumnorīgem Haeduum mittunt, ut eō dēprecātōre [2] ā Sēquanīs impetrārent. Dumnorīx grātiā [3] et largītiōne [4] 5 apud Sēquanōs plūrimum poterat et Helvētiīs erat amīcus, quod ex eā cīvitāte Orgetorīgis fīliam in mātrimōnium dūxerat.

VOCABULARY

[1] **sponte** (abl. sing. of **spōns**), F., *of one's own accord, voluntarily.*
[2] **dēprecātor, -ōris,** M., *mediator.* See 279.
[3] **grātia, -ae,** F., *favor, good-will, influence.* See 393.
[4] **largītiō, -ōnis,** F., *(a giving freely), bribery.*

---

[1] *new things = revolution.* [2] What is the subject? [3] What case must be used in Latin? See **nōs** in 515, *c.* [4] What tense in Latin?

LESSON LXVII

The Datives of Purpose and of Reference.—Review
of the Dative.—Caesar I. 9 (concluded).

522.   VOCABULARY

mandō, -āre, -āvī, ātum, (*put in hand*), *intrust;* with sē
fugae, *betake himself to.*
renūntiō (re + nūntiō, 38), *bring back word, report.*
studeō, -ēre, -uī, ——, *be eager, desire* (with dative).
dēligō (dē + legō), -ligere, -lēgī, -lēctum, *choose, select.*
satisfaciō (satis + faciō, 250), *give satisfaction, make amends,*
apologize.

523.   MODEL SENTENCES

1. **Castrīs locum dēlēgit:** *He selected a place for a camp.*
2. **Vōbīs praesidiō relīctī sunt:** *They have been left as (for)*
   a guard to you.
3. **Mīlitēs erant sibi impedīmentō:** *The soldiers were a hin-*
   drance to themselves.[1]

Castrīs and praesidiō (sentences 1 and 2) are datives
for which some thing is or is done, and are called datives
of *purpose.*   Impedīmentō (sentence 3) may be called
a dative of *result.*   Vōbīs and sibi (sentences 2 and 3)
denote the person to whom something is of interest,
and are called datives of *reference.*   The dative of reference is often used with the dative of purpose or result,
as in sentences 2 and 3.

524. RULE XLII.—*A noun in the dative may denote
the purpose or result of an action.*

---

[1] Being in close array.

525. RULE XLIII.—*A noun in the dative may denote the object to which something is of interest.* (Dative of reference.)

526. REVIEW OF THE DATIVE.—The dative is used chiefly as follows:

1. Dative of indirect object, with—

   (a) Transitive verbs (63): **Tuba puerō dabitur.**
   (b) Certain intransitive (471): **Ariovistus Germānīs imperāvit.**
   (c) Certain compounds (379): **Equitātuī Dumnorīx praeerat.**

2. Dative of the possessor (115): **Tuba est mihi.**
3. Dative of the agent (480): **Tibi sīgnum dandum est.**
4. Dative with certain adjectives (313): **Puer est similis patrī.**
5. Dative of purpose or result (524).
6. Dative of reference (525).

TRANSLATE

527. 1. Hīs Caesar ita respondit. 2. Reliquī sēsē fugae mandārunt.[1] 3. Vēnit Belgīs auxiliō. 4. Novīs rēbus studēbant. 5. Novissimīs [2] praesidiō erant. 6. Dīviciācus fuit amīcissimus Caesarī. 7. Cui legiōnī Caesar praecipuē indulsit? 8. Helvētiīs est in animō. 9. Caesarī renūntiātur Helvētiīs esse in animō per agrum Sēquanōrum iter facere. 10. Liscus summō magistrātuī praeerat.[3] 11. Locus idōneus castrīs tibi dēligendus est. 12. Caesar dīcit sibi nūllam cum hīs amicitiam esse posse. 13. Sī vōs Haeduīs dē [4] iniūriīs, quās ipsīs sociīsque eōrum intulistis, satisfaciētis, ego vōbīscum pācem faciam.

---

[1] See 265.　　[2] **Novissimīs = novissimō āgminī.**　　[3] *held.*　　[4] *for.*

528. 1. The Belgae are next to the Celts. 2. The Allobroges made amends to the Haedui. 3. They had inflicted injuries upon the Haedui. 4. Caesar persuaded the Allobroges to make amends. 5. We are about to select a leader. 6. You can be a help (aid) to your brother. 7. The boys have many rafts, in order that they may cross [1] the river. 8. It happened that the boys had many rafts.

529. CAESAR, I. 9 (CONCLUDED): THE AGREEMENT BETWEEN THE SEQUANI AND THE HELVETII

Cupiditāte rēgnī adductus novis rēbus studēbat et quam plūrimās cīvitātēs suō beneficiō [1] habēre obstrictās [2] volēbat. Itaque rem suscipit et ā Sēquanīs impetrat ut per fīnēs suōs Helvētiōs īre patiantur, obsidēsque utī
5 inter sēsē dent perficit: Sēquanī nē itinere Helvētiōs prohibeant; Helvētiī ut sine maleficiō et iniūriā trānseant.

VOCABULARY

[1] **beneficium -ī,** N. (bene + faciō), (*well-doing*), *favor, kindness.*
[2] **obstringo** (ob + stringō), **-stringere, -strinxī, -strictum,** *bind, lay under obligation.*

---

[1] *go across.*

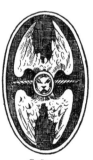

Scūtum
(Shield)

LESSON LXVIII

Two Accusatives.—Review of the Accusative and
Ablative.—Caesar, I. 10 (begun).

530. VOCABULARY

portōrium, -ī, N., *tax, toll, duty.*
nēmō, dat. nēminī, M. and F. (nē + homō), *no one.*
flāgitō, -āre, -āvī, -ātum, *demand urgently.*
doceō, -ēre, -uī, doctum, *teach.*
liceor, licērī, licitus sum, *bid.*
cōnsūmō (con + sūmō, 245), *consume, waste, destroy.*
redimō (red + emō, *buy*), -imere, -ēmī, -ēmptum, *buy
back, buy up.*

531. MODEL SENTENCES

1. **Celtās Gallōs appellāmus:** *We call the Celts Gauls.*
2. **Dīcimus Celtās esse Gallōs:** *We say that the Celts are
Gauls.*

In these sentences **Gallōs** completes the predicate,
and is called a *predicate accusative.* If the sentences
were **Celtae Gallī appellantur** and **Celtae sunt Gallī,**
how would the case of **Gallī** be explained? Review 105.

532. RULE XLIV.—*A predicate accusative may be
used after the active of the verbs* make, name, choose, call,
etc. (together with a direct object); and after the infinitive
esse.[1]

---

[1] Or any other verb which in the *indicative* may have a predicate nominative.

533.   MODEL SENTENCES

1. **Nōs litterās docuit:** *He taught us (our) letters.*
2. **Cōpiās pontem trādūxit:** *He led the troops over the bridge.*

Here **nōs** and **cōpiās** are the direct objects, while **litterās** and **pontem** may be called *secondary* objects.

534. RULE XLV.—*A secondary object in the accusative (together with a direct object) may be used with verbs meaning* ask, demand, teach, conceal; *and after transitive verbs compounded with* **trāns.**

535. REVIEW OF THE ACCUSATIVE.—An accusative may be used chiefly as follows:—

1. Direct object (40): **Puerōs laudat.**
2. Predicate accusative (532).
3. Secondary object (534).
4. Object of a preposition (49): **Trāns pontem.**
5. Subject of an infinitive (233): **Dīcit montem esse altum.**
6. Accusative of place to which (446).
   (*a*) With prepositions (**ad, in**): **Ad montem īvit.**
   (*b*) Without prepositions: **Rōmam īvit.**
7. Accusative of duration of time (387): **Duās hōrās nāvigāvit.**
8. Accusative of extent of space (387): **Duo mīlia passuum nāvigāvit.**

536. REVIEW OF THE ABLATIVE.—The following are the principal uses of the ablative:—

1. Ablative of separation (with or without **ab, dē** or **ex,** 448): **Celtae ā Belgīs differunt.**
2. Ablative of agent (**ab,** 104): **Ab lēgātō laudābātur.**
3. Ablative of comparison (303): **Sōl est māior lūnā.**

4. Ablative of means (74): **Oculīs vīdemus.**
Including ablative with **ūtor,** etc. (360): **Gladiīs ūsī sumus.**
5. Ablative of manner (**cum,** 252): **Māgna cum virtūte contendunt.**
6. Ablative of cause (393): **Grātiā plūrimum poterat.**
7. Ablative of accompaniment (**cum,** 439): **Cum amīcīs īvit.**
8. Ablative of degree of difference (311): **Ūnō pede brevior.**
9. Ablative of description (464): **Puer māgnā grātiā.**
10. Ablative of specification (144): **Virtūte praestant.**
11. Ablative absolute (with a participle, an adjective or another noun, 279): **Hōc prōeliō fāctō.**
12. Ablative of place in which (**in,** 446): **In castris.**[1]
13. Ablative of place from which (446).
    (a) With a preposition (**ab, dē, ex**): **Ex Ītaliā vēnit.**
    (b) Without a preposition: **Rōmā vēnit.**
14. Ablative of time when or within which (159): **Eōdem diē vēnit.**

The ablative may be called the *adverbial* case, for it is most frequently used to modify a verb.

TRANSLATE

537. 1. Per Alpēs. 2. In fīnēs Aquītānōrum. 3. In proximās silvās. 4. Posterō diē. 5. Ex omnī prōvinciā. 6. Cum equitātū Helvētiōrum. 7. Paucī dē nostrīs.[2] 8. Teneō memoriā.[3] 9. Minōre cum perīculō. 10. Causā cōgnitā.[4] 11. Pīlīs missīs.[4] 12. Agrīs populātīs. 13. Hīs cīvitātibus pulsīs.[5] 14. Omnibus fortūnīs sociōrum cōnsūmptīs. 15. Ea cīvitās est in prōvinciā. 16. Ā magi-

---

[1] For the names of towns, small islands, etc., see 446.
[2] **dē nostrīs = nostrōrum.**   [3] See 344.   [4] The exact translation of an ablative absolute cannot be given without the rest of the sentence. Translate these phrases in several ways.   [5] From **pellō.**

strātū accūsābātur.   17. Helvētiī ratibus flūmen trānsībant.   18. Cum eīs ducibus quī iter cōgnōverant.   19. Caesar Haeduōs frūmentum flāgitābat.   20. Nōn longius quīngentīs passibus abest.   21. Nōn longē ab Allobrogum fīnibus absunt.   22. Complūrēs annōs Dumnorīx portōria redēmit, proptereā quod illō licente nēmō contrā ¹ licērī audēbat.²

538. 1. The Helvetians chose Orgetorix (as) leader.   2. Orgetorix was chosen leader.   3. Do you think that Orgetorix will be leader?   4. Having given a pledge,³ Orgetorix became⁴ leader.   5. We asked ⁵ the sailor his name.   6. The boys had been taught their letters ⁶ at home.   7. We shall not go home until you return.

539. Review chapters 7, 8 and 9, pages 224 and 225.

CAESAR, I. 10 (BEGUN): CAESAR LEARNS OF THE PLAN

Caesarī renūntiātur Helvētiīs esse in animō per agrum Sēquanōrum et Haeduōrum iter in Santonum fīnēs facere, quī nōn longē ā Tolōsātium fīnibus absunt, quae cīvitās est in Prōvinciā.   Id⁴ sī fieret, intellegēbat ³
5 māgnō cum perīculō prōvinciae futūrum ⁵ ut hominēs bellicōsōs,¹ populī Rōmānī inimīcōs, locīs patentibus ⁶ māximēque frūmentāriīs ² fīnitimōs ⁷ habēret.

NOTES AND VOCABULARY

¹ bellicōsus, -a, -um (bellum + ōsus), *warlike.*
² frūmentārius, -a, -um (frūmentum + ārius), *abounding in grain.*
³ intellegō (inter + legō), -legere, -lēxī, -lēctum, *perceive, understand.*
⁴ Subject.   ⁵ Supply esse, *it would be.*   ⁶ *in open places.*
⁷ Predicate acc., *have as neighbors.*

---

¹ Adverb.   ² Not from audiō. See 357.   ³ fidēs.   ⁴ fīō.
⁵ rogō.   ⁶ After a passive the accusative is retained.

LESSON LXIX

The Imperative Mood.—Negative Command (Prohibition).—Caesar, I. 10 (concluded).

·

540. THE IMPERATIVE MOOD. — The imperative mood is used to express command or entreaty. It has two tenses in each voice, the *present* and the *future*. The present tense has only the second person, the third being supplied by the subjunctive (562). The future, which is rarely used, has the second and third persons. The forms of the imperative are made by adding to the *present stem* the following:

PERSONAL ENDINGS OF THE IMPERATIVE

		ACTIVE.		PASSIVE.	
		Singular.	*Plural.*	*Singular.*	*Plural.*
Pres.	2.	(Stem)	-te	-re	-minī
Fut.	2.	-tō	-tōte	-tor	
	3.	-tō	-nto	-tor	-ntor

541. Active Imperative of **laudō.**

		SINGULAR.	PLURAL.
Pres.	2.	laudā, *praise thou.*	laudāte, *praise ye.*
Fut.	2.	laudātō, *thou shalt praise.*	laudātōte, *ye shall praise.*
	3.	laudātō, *he shall praise.*	laudanto, *they shall praise.*

542. Passive Imperative of **laudō.**

	SINGULAR.	PLURAL.
Pres. 2.	laudāre, *be thou praised.*	laudāminī, *be ye praised.*
Fut. 2.	laudātor, *thou shalt be praised.*	•
3.	laudātor, *he shall be praised.*	laudantor, *they shall be praised.*

Learn from the Appendix the *present* imperative of **moneō, regō, capiō, audiō;** and of **sum, eō, ferō, fīō** and **nōlō.**

543. NEGATIVE COMMAND.—The *negative* of a command (a prohibition) is usually not expressed by the imperative of the given verb, but by either of the following ways:

1. **Nōlī (nōlīte)** + the present infinitive :—**Nōlī laudāre:** *Do not praise.*

2. **Nē, cavē,**[1] or **cavē nē,** + the present or perfect subjunctive:—**Nē laudāveris:** *Don't praise.* **Cāvē nē laudēs:** *Don't praise (Take care lest you praise).*

TRANSLATE

544. 1. Mitte nūntium. 2. Nōlī mittere nūntium. 3. Persuādēte fīnitimīs. 4. Nōlīte persuādēre fīnitimīs. 5. Cōnāre trānsīre. 6. Nōlī cōnārī trānsīre. 7. Ūtiminī gladiīs. 8. Nōlīte ūtī gladiīs. 9. Venīte. 10. Nē vēnerītis. 11. Iace pīlum. 12. Cavē nē iaciās pīlum. 13. Mo-

---

[1] Imperative of **caveō, cavēre, cāvī, cautum,** *take care, beware.*

nētō, monentō. 14. Monētor, monentor. 15. Audītōte.
16. Reminīsciminī virtūtis Gallōrum. 17. Nōlī timēre sine
causā. 18. Nē oblīvīscāris bonī amīcī. 19. Castra movēte,
nē hostēs in nōs impetum noctū faciant. 20. Ascendite
montem ut videātis quam in partem āgmen iter faciat.[1]
545. 1. Boys,[2] be brave. 2. Throw the javelins, soldiers. 3. Come to the ship, sailor. 4. Friend,[3] go with
me. 5. Choose a man to report[4] the victory. 6. Fight
so bravely that you will conquer.[5] 7. Order a bridge to
be made. 8. Destroy the bridge before[6] the enemy cross.

546. CAESAR, I. 10 (CONCLUDED): CAESAR INCREASES HIS ARMY

Ob eās causās eī mūnītiōnī quam fēcerat Ṫ. Labiēnum lēgātum praeficit; ipse in Ītaliam māgnīs[8] itineribus
contendit duāsque ibi legiōnēs cōnscrībit, et trēs quae
circum Aquilēiam[1] hiemābant ex hībernīs ēdūcit, et, quā
proximum iter in ulteriōrem Galliam per Alpīs erat, cum 5
hīs quīnque legiōnibus īre contendit.

Ibi Ceutronēs[4] et Grāioceli[5] et Caturīgēs[3] locīs superiōribus occupātīs itinere exercitum prohibēre cōnantur.
Complūribus[9] hīs proeliīs pulsīs, ab Ocelō,[2] quod est
citeriōris prōvinciae extrēmum, in fīnēs Vocontiōrum[7] 10
ulteriōris prōvinciae diē septimō pervenit; inde in Allobrogum fīnēs, ab Allobrogibus in Segusiāvōs[6] exercitum
dūcit. Hī sunt extrā prōvinciam trāns Rhodanum
prīmī.

NOTES AND VOCABULARY

[1] **Aquilēia, -ae, F.**, a Roman town at the head of the Adriatic.
[2] **Ocelum, -i, N.**, a town in the Alps.

---

[1] Indirect question, 502.   [2] Vocative case. See 10. Like what other
case is it usually spelled in Latin?   [3] See 57.   [4] Use **quī**. See 199.
[6] What mood and tense? See 399.   [6] **priusquam.**

³ **Caturīgēs, -um, M.**, an Alpine tribe.
⁴ **Ceutronēs, -um, M.**, an Alpine tribe.
⁵ **Grāiocelī, -ōrum, M.**, an Alpine tribe.
⁶ **Segusiāvī, -ōrum, M.**, a tribe west of the Rhone.
⁷ **Vocontiī, -ōrum, M.**, an Alpine tribe.

⁸ *forced.* The ordinary day's march was 15 miles ; a **magnum iter,** 20 or 25 miles.   ⁹ Order : **His pulsīs complūribus proeliīs.** The order in the text is called "interlocked."

LESSON LXX

Indirect Discourse.—Caesar, I. 11 (begun).

547. INDIRECT DISCOURSE.—If we say *The man is brave*, we make a direct statement.   If we say *He knows the man to be brave*, or *He said that the man was brave*, the words following *knows* and *said* form indirect statements.   When a sentence is quoted in dependence on a verb of *saying, thinking, knowing*, etc., the quotation is an indirect statement or indirect discourse.

548.   MOODS IN INDIRECT DISCOURSE

1. **Virum vīdī quī erat fortis :** *I saw the man who was brave.*
2. **Dīcit sē vīdisse virum, quī esset fortis :** *He says that he saw the man who was brave.*

Notice the change of **vīdī**, a principal verb, to **vīdisse**, and of **erat**, a subordinate verb, to **esset**.   It is stated in 231 that after a verb of *saying*, etc., an infinitive with subject-accusative is to be used.   The general rule for the mood, when direct discourse becomes indirect, is the following :

RULE XLVI.—*When direct discourse is made indirect, a principal declarative verb in the indicative becomes infinitive; all subordinate verbs become or remain subjunctive.*

NOTE.—Imperative and most interrogative principal verbs become subjunctive.

549. TENSES IN INDIRECT DISCOURSE.—The tenses of the infinitive are used according to 421; those of the subjunctive, according to the rule for sequence (405).

550. PRONOUNS IN INDIRECT DISCOURSE.—In changing from the first or second person to the third, **ego** and **nōs** become **sē**; **meus** and **noster** become **suus**; **tū** and **vōs** become **ille** or **is**.

1. **Ego meum frātrem vidēbō:** *I shall see my brother.*
Dīcit sē (suum) frātrem vīsūrum esse: *He says he shall see his brother.*
2. **Tū lacūs vidēbis:** *You will see the lakes.*
Dīxī illum lacūs vīsūrum esse: *I said that he would see the lakes.*

551. **VOCABULARY**

colō, -ere, -uī, cultum, *till, cultivate.*
polliceor, pollicērī, pollicitus sum, (*offer*), *promise.*

Write the infinitives of these verbs. Review 420.

TRANSLATE

552. 1. Nōbīs est in animō iter per prōvinciam facere, proptereā quod aliud iter nōn habēmus. 2. Dīxērunt sibi esse in animō iter per prōvinciam facere, proptereā quod aliud iter nōn habērent. 3. Ita nōs dē populō Rōmānō meritī sumus,[1] ut nostrī agrī vāstārī nōn dēbeant. 4. Dīcunt ita sē dē populō Rōmānō meritōs esse, ut suī agrī vāstārī nōn dēbērent. 5. Sī pācem populus Romanus cum

---

[1] Present perfect,

14

Helvētiīs faciet, in aliam partem Galliae ībunt. 6. Putāvit sī pācem populus Rōmānus cum Helvētiīs faceret, eōs in aliam partem Galliae itūrōs. 7. Sī obsidēs ā vōbīs mihi dabuntur, utī ea quae pollicēminī vōs factūrōs intellegam, vōbīscum pācem faciam. 8. Dīcit sī obsidēs ab eīs sibi dentur, utī ea quae polliceantur factūrōs intellegat, sēsē cum eīs pācem factūrum. 9. Postquam Germānī agrōs Gallicōs vīdērunt, colere eōs voluērunt. 10. Dīcēbat postquam Germānī agrōs Gallicōs vīdissent, sē colere eōs voluisse. 11. Ubi est lēgātus prīmae legiōnis? 12. Rogat ubi sit[1] lēgātus prīmae legiōnis.

553. 1. You will conquer, because you are brave. 2. I say that you will conquer, because you are brave. 3. I said you would conquer, because you were brave. 4. I said they had conquered, because they were brave. 5. We are laying waste the fields that the Belgians cultivate. 6. They say they are laying waste the fields that the Belgians cultivate. 7. Are you going home? 8. They asked whether[2] he was going home.

554. CAESAR, I. 11 (BEGUN): THE HAEDUI ASK CAESAR FOR HELP AGAINST THE HELVETII

Helvētiī iam per angustiās et fīnēs Sēquanōrum suās cōpiās trādūxerant, et in Haeduōrum fīnēs pervēnerant eōrumque agrōs populābantur.[1] Haeduī, cum sē suaque ab eīs[2] dēfendere nōn possent, lēgātōs ad Caesarem
5 mittunt rogātum[3] auxilium: ' Ita sē omnī tempore dē populō Rōmānō meritōs esse ut paene in cōnspectū exercitūs nostrī[4] agrī vāstārī, līberī in servitūtem abdūcī, oppida expūgnārī nōn dēbuerint.'

NOTES

[1] Notice the difference in tense.   [2] What kind of ablative?
[3] See 412.   [4] Modifies **exercitūs.**

---

[1] See 502.   [2] **-ne,** enclitic.

LESSON LXXI

Review of the Indicative.—Caesar, I. 11 (concluded).

555. THE INDICATIVE IN PRINCIPAL CLAUSES.—In principal clauses the indicative is used in direct statements of fact and questions of fact: **Mīlitem laudat; Mīlitemne laudat?**

556. THE INDICATIVE IN SUBORDINATE CLAUSES.—The indicative is used chiefly in the following subordinate clauses:—

1. Relative clause, with **quī,** etc. This may be—
    (a) *Determining,* that is, it may indicate what person or thing (not what kind [1] of person or thing): **Pōns, quī erat ad** (*near*) **Genāvam.**
    (b) *Parenthetical,* adding a fact not necessary to the main statement: **Proximī sunt Germānīs, quibuscum bellum gerunt.**

2. Causal clause, with **quod, quia, quoniam, quandō,** when the speaker or writer gives his own reason (465): **Virtūte praecēdunt, quod cum Germānīs contendunt.**

3. Temporal clause, with **ubi, ut, simul, atque, postquam,** and sometimes **cum, dum, quoad, antequam, priusquam** (472): **Ubi sē esse parātōs arbitrātī sunt,** etc.

4. Conditional clause, with **sī;** present or past condition stated as a fact, or future condition more probable (489): **Sī quid voltis, revertiminī.**

5. Concessive clause, with **quamquam** (*although*), etc. (569).

6. Parenthetical clause, or a clause of comparison, with **ut,** *as:* **Gallia sub septentriōnibus, ut ante dictum est, posita est.**

---

[1] This would require the subjunctive of characteristic (459).

557. TENSES OF THE INDICATIVE.—Of the six tenses of the indicative, the present, the imperfect and future represent uncompleted action: **laudō,** *I praise, I am praising, I do praise;* **laudābam,** *I was praising, I praised;* **laudābō,** *I shall praise.* The perfect, pluperfect and future perfect represent completed action: **laudāvī,** *I have praised, I praised;* **laudāveram,** *I had praised;* **laudāverō,** *I shall have praised.*

Which of these are called principal tenses? Which historical? Review 403.

558. **VOCABULARY**

factiō, -ōnis, F., *party, faction.*
conventus -ūs (con + veniō),
  M., *meeting, assembly.*
pūblicus, -a, -um, *of the people, public.*
stīpendiārius, -a, -um, *tributary (tax-paying).*

alter — alter. (178), *one — the other;* plur. *one party — the other.*
nōn sōlum — sed etiam, *not only — but also.*

sublevō (sub + levō), -āre, -āvī, -ātum, *(lighten, raise),* assist.
superō, -āre, -āvī, -ātum, *overcome, conquer.*
poscō, -ere, poposcī, ——, *demand.*
quaerō, -ere, quaesīvī, quaesītum *(seek for),* *inquire, ask.*
subvehō (sub + vehō), -vehere, -vēxī, -vectum, *bring up, convey.*
ulcīscor, ulcīscī, ultus sum, *avenge, punish.*

Write synopses of the indicative of the verbs in this vocabulary. Review 285.

TRANSLATE

559. 1. Caesar nōn sōlum pūblicās sed etiam prīvātās iniūriās ultus est. 2. Eō frūmentō,[1] quod nāvibus[2] sub-

---

[1] See 360.　　　　[2] See 74.

vēxerat, ūtī nōn poterat. 3. Prīncipēs accūsāvit, quod ab eīs nōn sublevābātur. 4. Quaerit ex Liscō sōlō ea quae in conventū dīxerat. 5. Postquam Caesar pervēnit, obsidēs poposcit. 6. Haeduī Ariovistō, quoniam superātī sunt, stīpendiāriī sunt factī. 7. Dum haec in conventū geruntur,[1] Caesarī nūntiātum est equitēs Ariovistī impetum in nostrōs facere. 8. Ubi frūmentum mīlitibus darī oportēre [2] intellēxit, prīncipēs convocāvit. 9. Alterī sē, ut coeperant, in montem recēpērunt, alterī ad impedīmenta sē contulērunt. 10. Cum Caesar in Galliam vēnit, alterius factiōnis prīncipēs erant Haeduī, alterius Sēquanī. 11. Sī alter factiō Gallōs superāverit, alter auxilium Caesarem poscet. 12. Superā, posce, quaere, ulcīscere. 13. Superāns, poscēns, ulcīscēns. 14. Belgās superātūrī sumus. 15. Ultus. 16. In quaerendō. 17. Ad frūmentum subvehendum.

560. CAESAR, I. 11 (CONCLUDED): THE AMBARRI AND THE ALLOBROGES ALSO ASK HELP

Eōdem tempore Haeduī Ambarrī, necessāriī et cōnsanguineī Haeduōrum, Caesarem certiōrem faciunt sēsē dēpopulātīs agrīs nōn facile ab oppidīs vim hostium prohibēre. Item Allobroges, quī trāns Rhodanum vīcōs
5 possessiōnēsque habēbant, fugā sē ad Caesarem recipiunt et dēmōnstrant sibi praeter agrī sōlum nihil esse reliquī. Quibus rēbus adductus Caesar nōn exspectandum [1] sibi [2] statuit dum, omnibus fortūnīs sociōrum cōnsūmptīs, in Santonōs Helvētiī pervenīrent.

NOTES AND VOCABULARY

[1] See 478.   [2] See 480.

Ambarrī, -ōrum, M., allies of the Haedui.
Santonī, -ōrum, M., a Gallic tribe.

---

[1] **Dum,** *while*, takes the historical present (402).   [2] See 428.

possessiō, -ōnis, F., *possession.*
cōnsanguineus -a, -um (sanguis, *blood*), (*related by blood*), *kindred;*
as noun, *kinsman.*
necessārins, -a, -um, *necessary;* as noun, *connection, close friend.*
item, adv., *in like manner, likewise.*
dēpopulor (de + populor, 415), *ravage, lay waste.*

LESSON LXXII

The Subjunctive in Principal Clauses.—Caesar, I. 12 (begun).

561. VARIETIES OF THE SUBJUNCTIVE.—It was stated in section 197 that the subjunctive represents action as *willed, desired* or *possible:*—

1. **Mīlitem laudēmus:** *Let us praise the soldier.*   Act willed.
2. **Frāter veniat:** *May (my) brother come.*   Act desired.
3. **Aliquis dīcat:** *Some one may say.*   Act possible.

The subjunctive of possibility (or potential subjunctive) is not often found except in subordinate clauses. The two other varieties of this mood are best shown in principal clauses (562, 563).

562. THE SUBJUNCTIVE OF WILL.[1]—This always expresses some one's will: *Let us go (It is my will that we go).* It includes chiefly:

(a) The subjunctive of exhortation, used in the *first* person plural, to express exhortation:—**Sīmus fortēs:** *Let us be brave.*

(b) The subjunctive of command, used in the *third* person (chiefly), to express command:—**Castra mūniant:** *Let them fortify the camp.*

---

[1] Sometimes called *volitive* subjunctive (**volō,** *I will*).

(c) The subjunctive of prohibition, with **nē** (**cavē nē,** 543), used in the *second* person, to express negative command:—**Nē eās:** *Do not go.*

563. THE SUBJUNCTIVE OF DESIRE.[1]—This expresses some one's desire (without authority). The adverb **utinam,** *O that! Would that!* sometimes begins the sentence when the verb is in the present tense, and always when it is in the imperfect or pluperfect:— .

1. (**Utinam**) **frāter veniat:** *O that my brother would come* (in the future)!
2. **Utinam frāter venīret:** *O that my brother were coming* (now)!
3. **Utinam frāter vēnisset:** *O that my brother had come* (in the past)!

564. Nē AND nōn.—The negative adverb used with the subjunctives of will and desire (and rarely with the imperative) is **nē;** with all other forms **nōn** is the negative.

1. **Nē eāmus:** *Let us not go.*
2. **Utinam nē īvisset!** *O that he had not gone!*

NOTE.—Conjugate in review the subjunctive of the model and irregular verbs. Review 368.

TRANSLATE

565. 1. Proficīscātur, proficiscāmur, proficīscantur. 2. Mulierēs līberōsque dēfendāmus. 3. Nē oppida incendāmus. 4. Nē dēspērēmus. 5. Sīs amīcus lēgātī. 6. Orgetorīx dēligātur. 7. Casticō persuādeat. 8. Imperium

---

[1] Sometimes called *optative* subjunctive (**optō,** *I desire*).

obtineant. 9. Comparēmus ea quae ad proficīscendum pertinent. 10. Faciāmus sēmentēs quam māximās. 11. Utinam cōnēris. 12. Utinam cōnātī essēmus. 13. Utinam iter esset facile. 14. Utinam auxilium ferrētis. 15. Utinam cōnāta perficere potuisset. 16. Utinam nē Orgetorīx coniūrātiōnem fēcisset. 17. Cōgite Orgetorīgem causam dīcere. 18. Nē coēgeritis Orgetorīgem causam dīcere.

566. 1. May you be praised. 2. Let us not forget [1] the brave men.[2] 3. Let two legions be a guard [3] to the baggage. 4. O that our fields had not been devastated! 5. Ask the general (for) aid.[4] 6. Do not spend-the-winter in Helvetia. 7. Let the merchant go to the camp, that he may inform Caesar about [5] the roads. 8. The merchant says he will go, because he is a friend of the general.

567. CAESAR, I. 12 (BEGUN): THE HELVETII CROSS THE SAÔNE

Flūmen est Arar, quod per fīnēs Haeduōrum et Sēquanōrum in Rhodanum īnfluit, incrēdibilī lēnitāte,[1] ita ut oculīs in utram partem fluat [2] iūdicārī nōn possit.[3] Id Helvētiī ratibus āc lintribus iūnctīs trānsībant. Ubi per
5 explōrātōrēs Caesar certior factus est trēs iam partēs cōpiārum Helvētiōs id flūmen [4] trādūxisse, quārtam ferē partem [5] citrā flūmen Ararim reliquam esse, dē tertiā vigiliā [6] cum legiōnibus tribus ē castrīs profectus, ad eam partem pervēnit quae nōndum flūmen trānsierat.

NOTES AND VOCABULARY

[1] See 464.   [2] See 502.   [3] See 399.   [4] See 534.   [5] See 233.
[6] The night from sunset to sunrise was divided into four watches (**vigiliae**), the third beginning at midnight.

lēnitas, -tātis, F. (**lēnis,** *gentle*), *gentleness, sluggish current* (of a river).

[1] See 514.   [2] See 515.   [3] See 524.   [4] See 534.   [5] **dē.**

linter, lintris, F., *canoe.*
incrēdibilis, -e (in, *not;* crēdō, *I believe*), *incredible, extraordinary.*
citrā, prep. with acc., *this side of.*

Linter

LESSON LXXIII

Concessive Clauses.—Review of the Subjunctive in Subordinate Clauses.—Caesar, I. 12 (concluded).

568.   VOCABULARY

custōs, -tōdis, M., *guard, spy.*
quantus, -a, -um, *how much?*
*how great ? as much as, as
great as.*
aliter (alius), adv., *otherwise.*

cum, concessive conj., *although.*
etsī, conj., *even if, although.*
quamquam, conj., *although.*
tamen, conj., *yet, nevertheless.*

sciō, scīre, scīvī, scītum, *know.*

569. CONCESSIVE CLAUSES.—A subordinate clause beginning with a conjunction meaning *though, although,* is called *concessive.*[1]   The conjunction in Latin may be quamquam, etsī, cum, etc., and the mood may be indicative or subjunctive, as follows:—

(*a*) Indicative, with quamquam:

Quamquam, mīlitēs sunt paucī, tamen fortiter pūgnant:
Although the soldiers are few, yet they are fighting bravely.

---

[1] From concēdō, *I grant* (something).

(*b*) Indicative or subjunctive, with **etsī, etiamsī, tametsī** (according to section 489):

Caesar, etsī in hīs locīs mātūrae sunt hiemēs, tamen in Britanniam īre contendit: *Though the winters are early in these parts, nevertheless Caesar made haste to go to Britain.*

(*c*) Subjunctive, with **cum, quamvīs, etc.:**

Cum ea ita sint, tamen Caesar pācem faciet: *Although these things are so, yet Caesar will make peace.*

570. REVIEW OF THE SUBJUNCTIVE IN SUBORDINATE CLAUSES.—The subjunctive has been shown to be used in the following clauses:

1. Clauses of purpose, with **ut, nē, quī, quō** (199).
2. "   "   result, with **ut, ut nōn** (399).
3. "   "   characteristic, with **quī,** etc. (459).
4. "   "   time, often with **cum, antequam, priusquam, dum, donec, quoad** (472).
5. "   "   cause, with **cum,** and sometimes[1] **quod, quia, quoniam, quandō** (465).
6. "   "   concession, with **cum, quamvīs,** etc. (570).
7. "   "   condition (of certain kinds),[2] with **sī** (489).
8. Noun-clauses, depending on verbs meaning *command, persuade, urge, induce, fear,* etc. (430 and 371, Note).
9. Indirect questions (502).
10. Subordinate clauses of indirect discourse (548).

571. 1. Fīēbat ut omnēs Gallī commovērentur. 2. Intellegō quantō cum perīculō id fēcerim. 3. Dīcit sē intellegere quantō cum perīculō id fēcerit. 4. Dīviciācus verētur nē Caesar oppidīs Haeduōrum potiātur. 5. Dumnorīgī custōdēs pōnit ut quae agat scīre possit. 6. Nōn dubium erat quīn Rōmānī Helvētiōs superāturī essent.[3]

---

[1] When?   [2] What kinds?   [3] See 477.

7. Helvētiī, cum [1] āgmen Caesaris ūnō diē Ararim trānsīsse intellegerent, commōtī sunt. 8. Cum prō Haeduīs bellum suscēperit, quod [2] ab eīs nōn sublevētur, queritur. 9. Cum ab hōrā septimā ad vesperum pūgnātum sit,[3] āversum [4] hostem vidēre nēmō potuit. 10. Caesar, etsī difficultātem faciendī pontis [5] scīret, propter lātitūdinem, rapiditātem altitūdinemque flūminis, tamen aliter nōn trādūcendum [6] exercitum exīstimābat.

572. 1. The Helvetians will join their rafts and canoes. 2. If Caesar should not be informed of their plan, the Helvetians would easily cross the Saône. 3. They joined their rafts in order to [7] cross more easily. 4. Although the Helvetians have joined their rafts, they will not be able to cross before Caesar reaches [8] the river.[9] 5. He urged Dumnorix to be a friend of the Roman people. 6. Caesar had sent horsemen to select a place suitable for the camp. 7. Although the Helvetians had a large army, yet they could not resist the Roman forces.

573. CAESAR, I. 10 (CONCLUDED): THE ROMANS DE-FEAT PART OF THE HELVETII

Eōs impedītōs et inopīnantēs adgressus māgnam partem eōrum concīdit; reliquī sēsē fugae mandārunt atque in proximās silvās abdidērunt. Is pāgus appellābātur Tigurīnus; nam omnis cīvitās Helvētia in quattuor pāgōs dīvīsa est. Hīc pāgus ūnus cum domō exīsset, patrum 5 nostrōrum memoriā L. Cassium cōnsulem interfēcerat et ēius exercitum sub iugum mīserat.

---

[1] **Cum** has been given as an introductory word for three kinds of clauses, with the meanings *when, since, although*. [2] Conjunction.
[3] See 428. [4] *turned away = fleeing*. [5] Over the Rhine. [6] See 478.
[7] How is purpose expressed when there is a comparative in the sentence?
[8] Future perfect of **perveniō**. [9] Use **ad**.

Ita sīve cāsū sīve cōnsiliō deōrum immortālium, quae
pars cīvitātis Helvētiae īnsīgnem calamitātem populō
10 Rōmānō intulerat, ea prīnceps poenās persolvit.   Quā
in rē Caesar nōn sōlum pūblicās sed etiam prīvātās
iniūriās ultus est; quod ēius socerī L. Pīsōnis avum, L.
Pīsōnem lēgātum, Tigurīnī eōdem proeliō quō Cassium
interfēcerant.

VOCABULARY

avus, -ī, M., *grandfather.*
socer, -erī, M., *father-in-law.*
cāsus, -ūs, M. (**cadō**, *fall*), *accident,*
    chance.
immortālis, -e (**mors**), *immortal.*

inopīnāns, -antis, (*not expecting*),
    unaware.
īnsīgnis, -e, (*marked*), *remarkable*
sīve — sīve, conj.,   *either — or,*
    whether — or.

abdō, -dere, -didī, -ditum, *put away, hide.*
adgredior (ad + gradior), -gredī, -gressus, (*go towards*), *attack.*
concīdō (con + caedō), -cīdere, -cīdī, -cīsum, *cut to pieces, kill.*
persolvō (per + solvō), -solvere, -solvī, -solūtum, (*release com-*
    pletely), *pay.*
impediō, -īre, -īvī, -ītum, *entangle, impede.*

THE WAR WITH THE HELVETII

CAESAR, BOOK I, CHAPTERS 1–12.[1]

1. Gallia est omnis dīvīsa in partēs trēs, quārum ūnam incolunt Belgae, aliam Aquītānī, tertiam quī ipsōrum linguā Celtae, nostrā Gallī appellantur. Hī omnēs linguā, īnstitūtīs, lēgibus inter sē differunt. Gallōs ab Aquītānīs Garumna flūmen, ā Belgīs Mātrona et Sēquana dīvidit. Hō- 5
rum omnium fortissimī sunt Belgae, proptereā quod ā cultū atque hūmānitāte prōvinciae longissimē absunt, minimēque ad eōs mercātōrēs saepe commeant atque ea quae ad effēminandōs animōs pertinent important; proximīque sunt Germānīs, quī trāns Rhēnum incolunt, quibuscum conti- 10
nenter bellum gerunt. Quā dē causā Helvētiī quoque reliquōs Gallōs virtūte praecēdunt, quod ferē cotīdiānīs proeliīs cum Germānīs contendunt, cum aut suīs fīnibus eōs prohibent aut ipsī in eōrum fīnibus bellum gerunt. Eōrum ūna pars, quam Gallōs obtinēre dictum est, initium capit ā 15
flūmine Rhodanō; continētur Garumnā flūmine, Ōceanō, fīnibus Belgārum; attingit etiam ab Sēquanīs et Helvētiīs flūmen Rhēnum; vergit ad septentriōnēs. Belgae ab extrēmīs Galliae fīnibus oriuntur; pertinent ad īnferiōrem partem flūminis Rhēnī; spectant in septentriōnem et orien- 20
tem sōlem. Aquītānia ā Garumnā flūmine ad Pȳrēnaeōs montēs et eam partem Ōceanī quae est ad Hispāniam pertinet ; spectat inter occāsum sōlis et septentriōnēs.

2. Apud Helvētiōs longē nōbilissimus fuit et dītissimus Orgetorīx. Is, M. Messālā et M. Pīsōne cōnsulibus, rēgnī

---

[1] All the text of Chapters 1–12 has been given in the preceding lessons, and is here repeated for connected reading in review.

cupiditāte inductus coniūrātiōnem nōbilitātis fēcit, et cīvitātī persuāsit ut dē fīnibus suīs cum omnibus cōpiīs exīrent:
5 perfacile esse, cum virtūte omnibus praestārent, tōtīus Galliae imperiō potīrī. Id hōc facilius eīs persuāsit, quod undique locī nātūrā Helvētiī continentur: ūnā ex parte flūmine Rhēnō lātissimō atque altissimō, quī agrum Helvētium ā Germānīs dīvidit; alterā ex parte monte Iūrā
10 altissimō, quī est inter Sēquanōs et Helvētiōs; tertiā lacū Lemannō et flūmine Rhodanō, quī prōvinciam nostram ab Helvētiīs dīvidit. Hīs rēbus fīēbat ut et minus lātē vagārentur et minus facile fīnitimīs bellum īnferre possent; quā ex parte hominēs bellandī cupidī māgnō dolōre afficiēbantur,
15 Prō multitūdine autem hominum et prō glōriā bellī atque fortitūdinis angustōs sē fīnēs habēre arbitrābantur, quī in longitūdinem mīlia passuum ccxl, in lātitūdinem clxxx patēbant.

3. Hīs rēbus adductī et auctōritāte Orgetorīgis permōtī cōnstituērunt ea quae ad proficīscendum pertinērent comparāre, iūmentōrum et carrōrum quam māximum numerum coëmere, sēmentēs quam māximās facere, ut in itinere cōpia
5 frūmentī suppeteret, cum proximīs cīvitātibus pācem et amīcitiam cōnfīrmāre. Ad eās rēs cōnficiendās biennium sibi satis esse dūxērunt; in tertium annum profectiōnem lēge cōnfīrmant. Ad eās rēs cōnficiendās Orgetorīx dēligitur. Is sibi lēgātiōnem ad cīvitātēs suscēpit. In eō itinere
10 persuādet Casticō, Catamantāloedis fīliō, Sēquanō, cūius pater rēgnum in Sēquanīs multōs annōs obtinuerat et ā senātū populī Rōmānī amīcus appellātus erat, ut rēgnum in cīvitāte suā occupāret, quod pater ante habuerat; itemque Dumnorīgī Haeduō, frātrī Dīviciācī, quī eō tempore
15 prīncipātum in cīvitāte obtinēbat ac māximē plēbī acceptus erat, ut idem cōnārētur persuādet, eīque fīliam suam in mātrimōnium dat. Perfacile factū esse illīs probat cōnāta perficere, proptereā quod ipse suae cīvitātis imperium obtentūrus esset: nōn esse dubium, quīn tōtīus Galliae plū-
20 rimum Helvētiī possent; sē suīs cōpiīs suōque exercitū

illīs rēgna conciliātūrum cōnfīrmat. Hāc ōrātiōne adductī inter sē fidem et iūsiūrandum dant, et rēgnō occupātō per trēs potentissimōs ac fīrmissimōs populōs tōtīus Galliae sēsē potīrī posse spērant.

4. Ea rēs est Helvētiīs per indicium ēnūntiāta. Mōribus suīs Orgetorīgem ex vinculīs causam dīcere coēgērunt: damnātum poenam sequī oportēbat ut īgnī cremārētur. Diē cōnstitūtā causae dictiōnis Orgetorīx ad iūdicium omnem suam familiam, ad hominum mīlia decem, undique 5 coēgit, et omnēs clientēs obaerātōsque suōs, quōrum māgnum numerum habēbat, eōdem condūxit; per eōs, nē causam dīceret, sē ēripuit. Cum cīvitās ob eam rem incitāta armīs iūs suum exsequī cōnārētur, multitūdinemque hominum ex agrīs magistrātūs cōgerent, Orgetorīx mortuus est; 10 neque abest suspīciō, ut Helvētiī arbitrantur, quīn ipse sibi mortem cōnscīverit.

5. Post ēius mortem nihilō minus Helvētiī id quod cōnstituerant facere cōnantur, ut ē fīnibus suīs exeant. Ubi iam sē ad eam rem parātōs esse arbitrātī sunt, oppida sua omnia numerō ad duodecim, vīcōs ad quadringentōs, reliqua prīvāta aedificia incendunt; frūmentum omne, praeter quod 5 sēcum portātūrī erant, combūrunt, ut, domum reditiōnis spē sublātā, parātiōrēs ad omnia perīcula subeunda essent; trium mēnsium molita cibāria sibi quemque domō efferre iubent. Persuādent Rauracīs et Tulingīs et Latobrīgīs, fīnitimīs, utī eōdem ūsī cōnsiliō, oppidīs suīs vīcīsque exūs- 10 tīs, ūnā cum eīs proficīscantur; Bōiōsque, quī trāns Rhēnum incoluerant et in agrum Nōricum trānsierant Nōrēiamque oppūgnārant, receptōs ad sē sociōs sibi adscīscunt.

6. Erant omnīnō itinera duo quibus itineribus domō exīre possent: ūnum per Sēquanōs, angustum et difficile, inter montem Iūram et flūmen Rhodanum, vix quā singulī carrī dūcerentur; mōns autem altissimus impendēbat, ut facile perpaucī prohibēre possent: alterum per prōvinciam nos- 5 tram, multō facilius atque expedītius, proptereā quod inter fīnēs Helvētiōrum et Allobrogum, quī nūper pācātī erant,

Rhodanus fluit, isque nōnnūllīs locīs vadō trānsītur. Extrēmum oppidum. Allobrogum est proximumque Hel-
10 vētiōrum fīnibus Genāva. Ex eō oppidō pōns ad Helvētiōs pertinet. Allobrogibus sēsē vel persuāsūrōs, quod
nōndum bonō animō in populum Rōmānum vidērentur,
exīstimābant, vel vī coāctūrōs ut per suōs fīnēs eōs īre pate-
rentur. Omnibus rēbus ad profectiōnem comparātīs, diem
15 dīcunt quā diē ad rīpam Rhodanī omnēs conveniant. Is
diēs erat a. d. v. Kal. Apr., L. Pīsōne A. Gabīniō cōnsulibus.
7. Caesarī cum id nūntiātum esset, eōs per prōvinciam
nostram iter facere cōnārī, mātūrat ab urbe proficīscī, et
quam māximīs potest itineribus in Galliam ulteriōrem
contendit et ad Genāvam pervenit. Prōvinciae tōtī quam
5 māximum potest mīlitum numerum imperat (erat omnīnō
in Galliā ulteriōre legiō ūna), pontem quī erat ad Genāvam
iubet rescindī. Ubi dē eius adventū Helvētiī certiōrēs factī
sunt, lēgātōs ad eum mittunt nōbilissimōs cīvitātis, cūius
lēgātiōnis Nammēius et Verudoctius prīncipem locum ob-
10 tinēbant, quī dīcerent sibi esse in animō sine ūllō maleficiō
iter per prōvinciam facere, proptereā quod aliud iter habērent nūllum: rogāre ut eius voluntāte id sibi facere liceat.
Caesar, quod memoriā tenēbat L. Cassium cōnsulem occīsum
exercitumque eius ab Helvētiīs pulsum et sub iugum mis-
15 sum, concēdendum nōn putābat; neque hominēs inimīcō
animō, datā facultāte per prōvinciam itineris faciundī, temperātūrōs ab iniūriā et maleficiō exīstimābat. Tamen, ut
spatium intercēdere posset dum mīlitēs quōs imperāverat
convenīrent, lēgātīs respondit diem sē ad dēlīberandum
20 sūmptūrum: sī quid vellent, ad Id. Apr. reverterentur.
8. Intereā eā legiōne quam sēcum habēbat mīlitibusque
quī ex prōvinciā convēnerant, ā lacū Lemannō, quī in flūmen
Rhodanum influit, ad montem Iūram, quī fīnēs Sēquanōrum ab Helvētiīs dīvidit, mīlia passuum decem novem mū-
5 rum in altitūdinem pedum sēdecim fossamque perdūcit.
Eō opere perfectō praesidia dispōnit, castella commūnit,
quō facilius, sī sē invītō trānsīre cōnārentur, prohibēre pos-

sit. Ubi ea diēs quam cōnstituerat cum lēgātīs vēnit, et
lēgātī ad eum revertērunt, negat sē mōre et exemplō populī
Rōmānī posse iter ūllī per prōvinciam dare; et, sī vim facere 10
cōnentur, prohibitūrum ostendit. Helvētiī eā spē dēiectī,
nāvibus iūnctīs ratibusque complūribus factīs, aliī vadīs
Rhodanī, quā minima altitūdō flūminis erat, nōnnumquam
interdiū, saepius noctū, sī perrumpere possent cōnātī, operis
mūnītiōne et mīlitum concursū et tēlīs repulsī hōc cōnātū 15
dēstitērunt.

9. Relinquēbātur ūna per Sēquanōs via, quā Sēquanīs
invītīs propter angustiās īre nōn poterant. Hīs cum suā
sponte persuādēre nōn possent, lēgātōs ad Dumnorīgem
Haeduum mittunt, ut eō dēprecātōre ā Sēquanīs impetrārent. Dumnorīx grātiā et largītiōne apud Sēquanōs plūri- 5
mum poterat, et Helvētiīs erat amīcus quod ex eā cīvitāte
Orgetorīgis fīliam in mātrimōnium dūxerat; et cupiditāte
rēgnī adductus novīs rēbus studēbat, et quam plūrimās
cīvitātēs suō beneficiō habēre obstrictās volēbat. Itaque
rem suscipit et ā Sēquanīs impetrat ut per fīnēs suōs Hel- 10
vētiōs īre patiantur, obsidēsque utī inter sēsē dent perficit:
Sēquanī, nē itinere Helvētiōs prohibeant; Helvētiī, ut sine
maleficiō et iniūriā trānseant.

10. Caesarī renūntiātur Helvētiīs esse in animō per
agrum Sēquanōrum et Haeduōrum iter in Santonum fīnēs
facere, quī nōn longē ā Tolōsātium fīnibus absunt, quae
cīvitās est in prōvinciā. Id sī fieret, intellegēbat māgnō
cum perīculō prōvinciae futūrum ut hominēs bellicōsōs, 5
populī Rōmānī inimīcōs, locīs patentibus māximēque frūmentāriīs fīnitimōs habēret. Ob eās causās eī mūnītiōnī
quam fēcerat T. Labiēnum lēgātum praefēcit; ipse in Ītaliam māgnīs itineribus contendit duāsque ibi legiōnēs
cōnscrībit, et trēs, quae circum Aquilēiam hiemābant, ex 10
hībernīs ēdūcit, et, quā proximum iter in ulteriōrem Galliam
per Alpēs erat, cum hīs quīnque legiōnibus īre contendit.
Ibi Ceutronēs et Grāiocelī et Caturīgēs locīs superiōribus
occupātīs itinere exercitum prohibēre cōnantur. Complūri-

15

15 bus hīs proeliīs pulsīs, ab Ocelō, quod est citeriōris prōvinciae extrēmum, in fīnēs Vocontiōrum ulteriōris prōvinciae
diē septimō pervenit; inde in Allobrogum fīnēs, ab Allobrogibus in Segusiāvōs exercitum dūcit. Hī sunt extrā prōvinciam trāns Rhodanum prīmī.

11. Helvētiī iam per angustiās et fīnēs Sēquanōrum suās
cōpiās trādūxerant, et in Haeduōrum fīnēs pervēnerant eōrumque agrōs populābantur. Haeduī, cum sē suaque ab
eīs dēfendere nōn possent, lēgātōs ad Caesarem mittunt
5 rogātum auxilium: Ita sē omnī tempore dē populō Rōmānō
meritōs esse ut paene in cōnspectū exercitūs nostrī agrī
vāstārī, līberī eōrum in servitūtem abdūcī, oppida expūgnārī nōn dēbuerint. Eōdem tempore Ambarrī, necessāriī et
cōnsanguineī Haeduōrum, Caesarem certiōrem faciunt sēsē
10 dēpopulātīs agrīs nōn facile ab oppidīs vim hostium prohibēre. Item Allobrogēs, quī trāns Rhodanum vīcōs possessiōnēsque habēbant, fugā sē ad Caesarem recipiunt et
dēmōnstrant sibi praeter agrī solum nihil esse reliquī.
Quibus rēbus adductus Caesar nōn exspectandum sibi
15 statuit dum, omnibus fortūnīs sociōrum cōnsūmptīs, in
Santonōs Helvētiī pervenīrent.

12. Flūmen est Arar, quod per fīnēs Haeduōrum et Sēquanōrum in Rhodanum īnfluit, incrēdibilī lēnitāte, ita ut
oculīs in utram partem fluat iūdicārī nōn possit. Id Helvētiī ratibus ac lintribus iūnctīs trānsībant. Ubi per ex-
5 plōrātōrēs Caesar certior factus est trēs iam partēs cōpiārum
Helvētiōs id flūmen trādūxisse, quārtam ferē partem citrā
flūmen Ararim reliquam esse, dē tertiā vigiliā cum legiōnibus
tribus ē castrīs profectus, ad eam partem pervēnit quae
nōndum flūmen trānsierat. Eōs impedītōs et inopīnantēs
10 adgressus māgnam partem eōrum concīdit; reliquī sēsē
fugae mandārunt atque in proximās silvās abdidērunt. Is
pāgus appellābātur Tigurīnus; nam omnis cīvitās Helvētia
in quattuor pāgōs dīvīsa est. Hīc pāgus ūnus, cum domō
exīsset patrum nostrōrum memoriā, L. Cassium cōnsulem
15 interfēcerat et ēius exercitum sub iugum mīserat. Ita sīve

cāsū sīve cōnsiliō deōrum immortālium, quae pars cīvitātis
Helvētiae īnsīgnem calamitātem populō Rōmānō intulerat,
ea prīnceps poenās persolvit. Quā in rē Caesar nōn sōlum
pūblicās sed etiam prīvātās iniūriās ultus est, quod ēius
socerī L. Pīsōnis avum, L. Pīsōnem lēgātum, Tigurīnī eōdem 20
proeliō quō Cassium interfēcerant.

ANNOTATED TEXT

CAESAR, I, CHAPTERS 13-29.

CAESAR CROSSES THE SAÔNE.—THE HELVETII SEND
AN EMBASSY

NOTE.—The meaning of new words is given in the general
vocabulary.

13. Hōc proeliō factō,[1] reliquās cōpiās Helvētiōrum ut
cōnsequī posset, pontem in Ararī faciendum [2] cūrat atque
ita exercitum trādūcit. Helvētiī repentīnō ēius adventū [3]
commōtī, cum id quod ipsī diēbus xx aegerrimē cōnfēcerant,
ut flūmen trānsīrent,[4] illum ūnō diē fēcisse intellegerent, 5
lēgātōs ad eum mittunt; cūius lēgātiōnis Dīvicō prīnceps
fuit, quī bellō Cassiānō dux Helvētiōrum fuerat.[5]

Is ita cum Caesare ēgit: Sī pācem populus Rōmānus
cum Helvētiīs faceret,[6] in eam partem itūrōs [7] atque ibi
futūrōs [7] Helvētiōs ubi eōs Caesar cōnstituisset [8] atque esse 10
voluisset: sīn bellō persequī persevērāret, reminīscerētur [9]
et veteris incommodī populī Rōmānī et prīstinae virtūtis
Helvētiōrum. Quod [10] imprōvīsō ūnum pāgum adortus
esset, cum eī quī flūmen trānsīssent suīs auxilium ferre
nōn possent, nē ob eam rem aut suae māgnopere virtūtī 15
tribueret [11] aut ipsōs dēspiceret: se [12] ita ā patribus māiōribusque suīs didicisse ut magis virtūte contenderent [13] quam
dolō aut īnsidiīs nīterentur. Quā rē nē committeret [14] ut
is locus ubi cōnstitissent ex calamitāte populī Rōmānī

20 et internecīōne exercitūs nōmen caperet aut memoriam
prōderet.

NOTES

[1] See 279. [2] See 241. [3] See 393. [4] **ut . . . trānsīrent** is in apposition with **id.** See 430. [5] The Romans under Cassius were defeated
by the Helvetii 107 B.C. [6] See 548. [7] Supply **esse.** [8] In the direct
discourse addressed to Caesar this would be **cōnstitueris,** a future perfect.
A verb in this tense in a subordinate clause becomes pluperfect subjunctive
in the change from direct to indirect discourse. [9] *he should remember ;*
in direct discourse this would be **reminīscere,** an imperative. See 548.
[10] *As to the fact that.* [11] **nē . . . tribueret,** *he should not attribute it.*
[12] Refers to the Helvetii. [13] A result clause. See 399. [14] **nē . . . committeret,** *he should not allow it to happen,* etc.

TRANSLATE [1]

1. If a bridge shall be built over the Saône, the army
will be led across. 2. He says that if a bridge shall be
built over the Saône, the army will be led across. 3.
When the ambassadors came to Caesar, Divico spoke for [2]
them. 4. The ambassadors came to make peace. 5.
Did Caesar remember the former valor of the Helvetii?

CAESAR'S REPLY TO DIVICO

14. Hīs Caesar ita respondit: Eō [1] sibi minus dubitātiōnis darī,[2] quod eās rēs quās lēgātī Helvētiī commemo-
rāssent memoriā tenēret, atque eō gravius ferre quō minus
meritō populī Rōmānī accidissent; [3] quī sī [4] alicūius iniūriae [5]
5 sibi cōnscius [6] fuisset, nōn fuisse difficile cavēre; sed eō [7]
dēceptum,[8] quod neque commissum [8] ā sē intellegeret quā
rē timēret, neque sine causā timendum [9] putāret. Quod sī
veteris contumēliae oblīvīscī vellet, num [10] etiam recentium

---

[1] The English-Latin vocabulary does not give the meaning of new words
used in the translation exercises of Chapters 13–29. The Latin word must
be recalled from the preceding text, upon which these sentences are
based. [2] **prō.**

iniūriārum, quod eō invītō [11] iter per prōvinciam per vim
temptāssent, quod Haeduōs, quod Ambarrōs, quod Allo- 10
brogēs vexāssent, memoriam dēpōnere posse? Quod [12] suā
victōriā tam īnsolenter glōriārentur, quodque tam diū sē
impūne iniūriās tulisse admīrārentur, eōdem pertinēre.
Cōnsuēsse [13] enim deōs immortālēs, quō [14] gravius hominēs
ex commūtātiōne rērum doleant, quōs prō scelere eōrum 15
ulcīscī velint, hīs secundiōrēs interdum rēs et diūturniōrem
impūnitātem concēdere.

Cum ea ita sint, tamen, sī obsidēs ab eīs sibi [15] dentur, utī
ea quae polliceantur factūrōs intellegat, et sī Haeduōs dē
iniūriīs quās ipsīs sociīsque eōrum intulerint, item sī Allo- 20
brogibus satisfaciant, sēsē cum eīs pācem esse factūrum.
Dīvicō respondit: Ita Helvētiōs ā māiōribus suīs īnstitūtōs
esse utī obsidēs accipere, nōn dare, cōnsuērint; ēius reī
populum Rōmānum esse testem. Hōc respōnsō datō dis-
cessit. 25

NOTES

[1] *the*, with a comparative.   [2] **Eō . . . darī,** *he had the less hesitation.*
[3] **eō gravius . . . accidissent,** *he was the more incensed in that they had
not happened through the fault of the Roman people.*   [4] **quī sī = et sī is.**
[5] See 515.   [6] See 514.   [7] *by this.*   [8] Supply **esse.**   [9] See 481.
[10] See 499.   **num . . . posse?** *could he cease to remember?* etc.   [11] See
279.   [12] **Quod,** *the fact that.*   **Quod . . . admīrārentur,** subject of
pertinēre.   [13] The English order is: **Enim immortālēs deōs cōnsuēsse interdum concēdere secundiōrēs rēs et diūturniōrem impūnitātem hīs, quōs . . . velint, quō . . . doleant.**   [14] See 199.   [15] To
whom does **sibi** refer?

TRANSLATE

1. He remembered the facts that Divico related. 2. We
are not conscious of any wrong. 3. Do you think we
should fear without cause? 4. It happens that they boast
of their victory. 5. The ancestors of the Helvetii were
not accustomed to give hostages.

A CAVALRY SKIRMISH

15. Posterō diē castra ex eō locō movent. Idem facit
Caesar, equitātumque omnem, ad numerum quattuor
mīlium, quem ex omnī prōvinciā et Haeduīs atque eōrum
sociīs coāctum habēbat, praemittit quī videant [1] quās in
5 partēs hostēs iter faciant.[2] Quī cupidius [3] novissimum agmen īnsecūtī aliēnō locō cum equitātū Helvētiōrum proelium committunt; et paucī dē nostrīs cadunt. Quō proeliō
sublātī [4] Helvētiī, quod quīngentīs equitibus [5] tantam multitūdinem equitum prōpulerant,[6] audācius susbistere nōn-
10 numquam et novissimō agmine [7] proeliō nostrōs lacessere
coepērunt. Caesar suōs ā proeliō continēbat, ac satis habēbat [8] in praesentiā hostem rapīnīs,[9] pābulātiōnibus popu-
lātiōnibusque prohibēre. Ita diēs circiter quīndecim iter
fēcērunt utī inter novissimum hostium agmen et nostrum
15 prīmum nōn amplius quīnīs aut sēnīs mīlibus passuum
interesset.[10]

NOTES

[1] See 199. [2] See 502. [3] *too eagerly.* [4] From **tollō.** [5] See 74.
[6] From **prōpellō.** [7] Locative abl. [8] *held it sufficient.* [9] See 448.
[10] See 399.

TRANSLATE

1. Caesar has ordered the lieutenant to move the camp.
2. The camp will be moved the third hour. 3. Having
moved the camp, the soldiers began to lay waste the fields.
4. I fear that the cavalry battle will not be favorable [1] to
our (men). 5. The messenger said that a few of our (men)
fell, because the position [2] was not favorable.[3]

THE HAEDUI FAIL TO FURNISH GRAIN

16. Interim cotīdiē Caesar Haeduōs frūmentum [1] quod
essent pūblicē pollicitī flāgitāre.[2] Nam propter frīgora,

---

[1] **secundus.**   [2] **locus.**   [3] **aliēnus.**

quod Gallia sub septentriōnibus, ut ante dictum est, posita est, nōn modo frūmenta [3] in agrīs mātūra nōn erant, sed nē pābulī [4] quidem satis māgna cōpia suppetēbat; eō autem 5 frūmentō [5] quod flūmine Ararī nāvibus subvēxerat proptereā [6] minus ūtī poterat, quod iter ab Ararī Helvētiī āverterant, ā quibus discēdere nōlēbat. Diem [7] ex diē dūcere [2] Haeduōs; cōnferrī, comportārī, adesse dīcere.[2] Ubi sē diūtius dūcī intellēxit et diem īnstāre quō diē frūmentum 10 mīlitibus mētīrī oportēret, convocātīs eōrum prīncipibus, quōrum māgnam cōpiam in castrīs habēbat, in hīs Dīviciācō et Liscō, quī summō magistrātuī [8] praeerat, quem vergobretum appellant Haeduī, quī creātur annuus et vītae necisque in suōs habet potestātem, graviter eōs accūsat, 15 quod, cum neque emī [9] neque ex agrīs sūmī [9] posset,[10] tam necessāriō tempore, tam propinquīs hostibus, ab eīs nōn sublevētur; praesertim cum māgnā ex parte eōrum precibus adductus bellum suscēperit, multō [11] etiam gravius quod sit dēstitūtus queritur. 20

NOTES

[1] See 534.   [2] See 232.   [3] Notice the plural form, and the special meaning.   [4] See 385.   [5] See 360.   [6] Translate **proptereā** with **quod**, after **poterat**.   [7] **Diem . . . Haeduōs**: *Day after day the Haedui kept putting him off*.   [8] See 379.   [9] Passive present infinitive.   [10] The subject is **frūmentum**, to be supplied.   [11] See 312.

TRANSLATE

1. The Haedui had elected Liscus (as) magistrate.[1] 2. Caesar wishes to use the grain which has been conveyed bys hips. 3. The Haedui promise to give Caesar grain. 4. Why [2] do not the Haedui bring the grain? 5. It is necessary to call the chiefs together in order to find out why the Haedui do not bring [3] the grain.

[1] See 532.   [2] **cūr**, adv., *why?*   [3] See 502.

The Explanation of Liscus

17. Tum dēmum Liscus ōrātiōne Caesaris adductus quod¹ anteā tacuerat prōpōnit: Esse² nōnnūllōs quōrum auctōritās apud plēbem plūrimum valeat,³ quī prīvātim plūs possint³ quam ipsī magistrātus. Hōs sēditiōsā atque
5 improbā ōrātiōne multitūdinem dēterrēre nē frūmentum cōnferant⁴ quod dēbeant: praestāre,⁵ sī iam prīncipātum Galliae obtinēre nōn possint, Gallōrum quam ⁶ Rōmānōrum imperia perferre; neque dubitāre quīn, sī Helvētiōs superāverint Rōmānī, ūnā cum reliquā Galliā Haeduīs ⁷ lībertātem
10 sint ēreptūrī. Ab eīsdem nostra cōnsīlia quaeque in castrīs gerantur hostibus ēnūntiārī; hōs ā sē ⁸ coërcērī nōn posse. Quīn etiam,⁹ quod necessāriō rem coāctus Caesarī ēnūntiārit, intellegere sēsē quantō id cum perīculō fēcerit,¹⁰ et ob eam causam quam diū potuerit tacuisse.

Notes

¹ Pronoun, with antecedent id to be supplied. ² See 548. The subject is nōnnūllōs. ³ See 459. ⁴ nē cōnferant, *from bringing.* ⁵ Used impersonally, *it is better.* ⁶ *Than.* ⁷ Dative case, governed by ēreptūrī, *take away from the Haedui.* ᵇ Refers to the speaker. ⁹ Quīn etiam, *furthermore.* ¹⁰ See 502.

Translate

1. There were some whose influence was very great. 2. Although Liscus was a magistrate, yet he could not restrain these men. 3. If Liscus had kept silent, Caesar would not have been informed. 4. Do ¹ not take away liberty from the Haedui.² 5. Our plans must not be reported to the enemy.

Dumnorix, the Haeduan

18. Caesar hāc ōrātiōne Liscī Dumnorīgem, Dīviciācī frātrem, dēsīgnārī sentiēbat; sed, quod plūribus praesenti-

¹ See 543.   ² See note 7, above.

bus ! eās rēs iactārī nōlēbat, celeriter concilium dīmittit, Liscum retinet. Quaerit ex sōlō [2] ea quae in conventū dīxerat. Dīcit līberius atque audācius. Eadem sēcrētō ab 5 aliīs quaerit; reperit esse [3] vēra: Ipsum esse Dumnorīgem,[4] summā audāciā,[5] māgnā apud plēbem propter līberālitātem grātiā, cupidum rērum novārum.[6] Complūrēs annōs portōria [7] reliquaque omnia Haeduōrum vectīgālia [8] parvō pretiō redēmpta habēre,[9] proptereā quod illō licente contrā 10 licērī audeat nēmō. Hīs rēbus et suam rem familiārem auxisse [9] et facultātēs ad largiendum [10] māgnās comparāsse; māgnum numerum equitātūs suō sūmptū semper alere et circum sē habēre [8] ; neque sōlum domī, sed etiam apud fīnitimās cīvitātēs largiter posse, atque hūius potentiae causā [11] 15 mātrem in Biturīgibus hominī illīc nōbilissimō ac potentissimō collocāsse, ipsum ex Helvētiīs uxōrem habēre, sorōrem ex mātre [12] et propinquās suās nūptum [13] in aliās cīvitātēs collocāsse. Favēre [14] et cupere Helvetiīs propter eam adfīnitātem, ōdisse [15] etiam suō nōmine [16] Caesarem et Rō- 20 mānōs, quod eōrum adventū potentia ēius dēminūta et Dīviciācus frāter in antīquum locum grātiae atque honōris sit restitūtus. Sī quid [17] accidat Rōmānīs, summam in spem [18] per Helvētiōs rēgnī obtinendī [19] venīre; imperiō [20] populī Rōmānī nōn modo dē rēgnō, sed etiam dē eā quam 25 habeat grātiā, dēspērāre. Reperiēbat etiam in quaerendō Caesar, quod proelium equestre adversum paucīs ante diēbus esset factum,[21] initium ēius fugae factum ā Dumnorīge atque ēius equitibus (nam equitātuī, quem auxiliō Caesarī Haeduī mīserant, Dumnorīx praeerat); eōrum fugā reliquum 30 esse equitātum perterritum.

NOTES

[1] *in the presence of many.* See 279.   [2] Supply **eō,** *him.*   [3] Supply **haec** as subject.   [4] **Ipsum . . . Dumnorīgem :** *Dumnorix is the man.* [5] See 464.   [6] See 516.   [7] *customs-duties.*   [8] *taxes.*   [9] **Dumnorīgem** is the subject.   [10] See 239.   [11] **causā** after a genitive means *for the sake, for the purpose.*   [12] **Sorōrem ex mātre,** *half-sister* (on the mother's side).   [13] See 411 and 415.   [14] See 471.   [15] A defective verb. See

App. (43). [16] *on his own account.* [17] Indefinite pronoun. [18] See 344.
[19] See 241. [20] *Under the sway.* [21] quod . . . factum, *in regard to the unsuccessful cavalry battle fought a few days before.*

TRANSLATE

1. When the conference [1] had been broken up (dismissed), Caesar detained Liscus. 2. Caesar perceived that Liscus was not a friend of Dumnorix, the Haeduan. 3. The taxes of the Haedui will be bought up by Dumnorix at a small price. 4. It is said that many Haeduans were desirous of a revolution. 5. If Dumnorix had not been in command of the cavalry, the battle would not have been unsuccessful.

CAESAR SUMMONS DIVICIACUS, THE BROTHER OF DUMNORIX

1 9. Quibus rēbus cōgnitīs, cum ad hās suspīciōnēs certissimae rēs accēderent, quod [1] per fīnēs Sēquanōrum Helvētiōs trādūxisset, quod obsidēs inter eōs dandōs cūrāsset, quod ea omnia nōn modo iniussū suō et cīvitātis sed etiam
5 īnscientibus ipsīs fēcisset, quod ā magistrātū [2] Haeduōrum accūsārētur, satis esse causae arbitrābātur quā rē in eum aut ipse animadverteret aut cīvitātem animadvertere iubēret. Hīs omnibus rēbus ūnum repūgnābat,[3] quod Dīviciācī frātris summum in populum Rōmānum studium, sum-
10 mam in sē voluntātem, ēgregiam fidem, iūstitiam, temperantiam cōgnōverat: nam nē ēius suppliciō Dīviciācī animum offenderet verēbātur. Itaque priusquam [4] quicquam cōnārētur, Dīviciācum ad sē vocārī iubet, et cotīdiānīs interpretibus remōtīs per C. Valerium Procillum, prīncipem
15 Galliae prōvinciae, familiārem suum, cui [5] summam omnium rērum fidem habēbat, cum eō conloquitur; simul commonefacit quae ipsō praesente [6] in conciliō Gallōrum dē

---

[1] See 279.

Dumnorīge sint dicta, et ostendit quae sēparātim quisque
dē eō apud sē dīxerit; petit atque hortātur ut sine ēius offēn-
siōne animī vel ipse dē eō, causā cōgnitā, statuat, vel 20
cīvitātem statuere iubeat.

Notes

[1] The four clauses beginning with **quod** explain **rēs.** See 430. [2] Liscus.
[3] *One fact stood in opposition.* [4] See 472. [5] **cui . . . habēbat,** *in whom
he placed the greatest confidence in all matters.* [6] See **plūribus prae-
sentibus,** chap. 18.

Translate

1. Caesar did not decide about the punishment of
Dumnorix until he had summoned (called) his brother.
2. Caesar sent a messenger to summon Diviciacus. 3. Who
was the messenger whom Caesar sent? 4. He thinks that
Procillus will be Caesar's interpreter. 5. He thought that
Procillus would be Caesar's interpreter.

The Plea of Diviciacus

20. Dīviciācus, multīs cum lacrimīs Caesarem complexus,
obsecrāre coepit [1] nē quid gravius [2] in frātrem statueret:
Scīre sē illa esse vēra, nec quemquam ex eō plūs quam sē
dolōris [3] capere,[4] proptereā quod, cum ipse grātiā plūrimum
domī atque in reliquā Galliā, ille minimum propter adolē- 5
scentiam posset, per sē crēvisset; quibus opibus [5] ac nervīs
nōn sōlum ad minuendam grātiam sed paene ad perniciem
suam ūterētur. Sēsē tamen et [6] amōre frāternō et exīsti-
mātiōne volgī commovērī. Quod [7] sī quid eī ā Caesare
gravius accidisset, cum ipse eum locum amīcitiae apud eum 10
tenēret, nēminem exīstimātūrum nōn suā voluntāte factum;
quā ex rē futūrum utī tōtīus Galliae animī ā sē āvertei entur.[8]
Haec cum plūribus verbīs flēns ā Caesare peteret, Caesar
ēius dextram prēndit; cōnsōlātus rogat fīnem ōrandī faciat; [9]
tantī [10] ēius apud sē grātiam esse ostendit [11] utī et reī pū- 15
blicae iniūriam et suum dolōrem ēius voluntātī ac precibus

condōnet.[12] Dumnorīgem ad sē vocat, frātrem adhibet; quae in eō reprehendat ostendit; quae ipse intellegat, quae cīvitās querātur, prōpōnit; monet ut in reliquum tempus
20 omnēs suspīciōnēs vītet; praeterita [13] sē Dīviciācō frātrī condōnāre [12] dīcit. Dumnorīgī custōdēs pōnit, ut quae agat, quibuscum loquātur, scīre possit.

NOTES

[1] See App. (43). [2] *too severe.* [3] See 385. [4] **nec . . . capere,** *no one was more grieved than he on account of it.* What is the literal translation? [5] See 360. [6] *both.* [7] *And.* [8] **futūrum esse utī āverterentur,** a phrase used instead of the future passive infinitive of **āvertō.** Translate : *for this reason the hearts of all the Gauls would be turned from him.* [9] An imperative when addressed to Diviciacus ; therefore subjunctive when quoted, as here. See 548, note. [10] *so great,* a genitive of *indefinite value.* [11] **tanti . . . ostendit,** *he declares that his influence with him is so great.* [12] **condōnāre,** *pardon* (something, direct obj.), *for the sake of* (something, indirect obj.). [13] *the past* (things bygone).

TRANSLATE

1. No one [1] was more grieved than Diviciacus. 2. Dumnorix increased (in influence) through the popularity of his brother. 3. Procillus spoke with Dumnorix on account of his knowledge [2] of the Gallic [3] language. 4. The soldiers did not know many words of the Gallic language. 5. They will learn more Gallic words if they remain at [4] Geneva.

CAESAR'S PREPARATIONS FOR A BATTLE

21. Eōdem diē ab explōrātōribus certior factus hostēs sub monte cōnsēdisse mīlia passuum ab ipsīus castrīs octō, quālis esset [1] nātūra montis et quālis in circuitū ascēnsus, quī cōgnōscerent [2] mīsit. Renūntiātum est facilem esse.[3]
5 Dē tertiā vigiliā T. Labiēnum, lēgātum prō [4] praetōre, cum duābus legiōnibus et eīs ducibus quī iter cōgnōverant, sum-

---

[1] **Nēmō.** [2] **scientia, -ae,** F. [3] **Gallicus, -a, -um.** [4] See 445, *c.*

mum iugum montis ascendere iubet; quid suī cōnsilī[5] sit[6] ostendit. Ipse dē quārtā vigiliā eōdem itinere quō hostēs ierant ad eōs contendit, equitātumque omnem ante sē mittit. P. Cōnsidius, quī reī mīlitāris perītissimus habē- 10 bātur et in exercitū L. Sullae et posteā in M. Crassī fuerat, cum explōrātōribus praemittitur.

NOTES

[1] See 502. [2] See 199. [3] The subject is **ascēnsum**, to be supplied.
[4] *with the power of.* [5] A predicate partitive genitive. See 518.
[6] **quid . . . sit,** *what his plan is.*

TRANSLATE

1. What is the nature of the mountain? 2. The scouts say that the mountain, at the foot of which the enemy have encamped,[1] is not high. 3. The soldiers are ready to climb[2] the mountain. 4. Having sent the scouts ahead, Caesar followed with the rest of the legions. 5. There is no doubt that Labienus was considered experienced in military matters.[3]

THE ERROR OF CONSIDIUS

22. Prīmā lūce,[1] cum summus mōns ā Labiēno tenērētur,[2] ipse ab hostium castrīs nōn longius mīlle et quīngentīs passibus[3] abesset, neque, ut[4] posteā ex captīvīs comperit, aut ipsīus adventus aut Labiēnī cōgnitus esset, Cōnsidius equō admissō ad eum accurrit; dīcit montem quem ā Labiēnō oc- 5 cupārī voluerit ab hostibus tenērī: id sē ā Gallicīs armīs atque īnsīgnibus cōgnōvisse. Caesar suās cōpiās in proximum collem subdūcit, aciem īnstruit. Labiēnus, ut[4] erat eī praeceptum ā Caesare nē proelium committeret, nisi ipsīus cōpiae prope hostium castra vīsae essent, ut undique ūnō 10 tempore in hostēs impetus fieret, monte occupātō nostrōs

[1] See 548. [2] See 241. [3] Use the singular. What case?

exspectābat proeliōque⁵ abstinēbat.   Multō dēnique diē⁶
per explōrātōrēs Caesar cōgnōvit et montem ā suīs tenērī
et Helvētiōs castra mōvisse et Cōnsidium timōre perter-
15 ritum quod nōn vīdisset prō vīsō⁷ sibi renūntiāsse.   Eō
diē, quō cōnsuērat intervāllō, hostēs sequitur et mīlia passuum tria ab eōrum castrīs castra pōnit.

NOTES

¹ **Prīmā lūce**, *at daybreak*.   ² See 370.   ³ See 311.   ⁴ Notice that
ut is followed by an indicative.   See 556, 6.   ⁵ See 448.   ⁶ **Multō diē**,
late in the day.   ⁷ **prō vīsō**, *as if seen*.

TRANSLATE

1. We shall hold the-top-of the mountain, until the
general comes.   2. The captives said that the arrival of
Labienus was not yet known.   3. Caesar is about to draw
up a line-of-battle.   4. We must make¹ an attack on the
enemy from all sides.   5. Although Considius had been in
many battles, yet he was thoroughly frightened before² the
battle with the Helvetii.

CAESAR GOES TO BIBRACTE FOR SUPPLIES

23. Postrīdiē ēius diēī,¹ quod omnīnō bīduum supererat
cum exercituī frūmentum mētīrī oportēret,² et quod ā
Bibracte, oppidō Haeduōrum longē māximō et cōpiōsissimō,
nōn amplius mīlibus passuum XVIII aberat, reī frūmen-
5 tāriae prōspiciendum³ exīstimāvit; iter ab Helvētiīs āvertit
ac Bibracte⁴ īre contendit.   Ea rēs per fugitīvōs L. Aemilī,
decuriōnis equitum Gallōrum, hostibus nūntiātur.   Helvētiī, seu quod timōre perterritōs Rōmānōs discēdere ā sē
exīstimārent, eō magis, quod prīdiē superiōribus locīs occu-
10 pātīs proelium nōn commīsissent, sīve eō,⁶ quod rē⁷ frūmen-
tāriā interclūdī posse cōnfīderent, commūtātō cōnsiliō atque

¹ What voice must be used in Latin ?   See 478.   ² **antē.**

itinere converso nostros ā novissimo agmine īnsequī ac lacessere coepērunt.

NOTES

[1] **Postrīdiē ēius diēī,** *the next day after that.*   [2] What is the subject of **oportēret?**   [3] See 481.   [4] See 445, a.   [5] See 465, 1.   [6] See 393.   [7] See 448.

TRANSLATE

1. On the next day the army marched twenty miles. 2. We shall reach [1] Bibracte within [2] five hours. 3. Caesar went to Bibracte for-the-purpose of (getting) supplies. 4. When the enemy were informed of this fact, they changed their plan and harassed our men. 5. Did [3] the Helvetians think they had terrified the Romans?

FURTHER PREPARATIONS FOR BATTLE

24. Postquam id animadvertit, cōpiās suās Caesar in proximum collem subdūcit equitātumque quī sustinēret [1] hostium impetum mīsit. Ipse interim in colle mediō [2] triplicem aciem īnstrūxit legiōnum quattuor veterānārum; [3] sed in summō [4] iugō duās legiōnēs quās in Galliā citeriōre 5 proximē cōnscrīpserat et omnia auxilia collocārī, [5] ac tōtum montem hominibus complērī, et intereā sarcinās [6] in ūnum locum cōnferrī, et eum [7] ab hīs quī in superiōre aciē cōnstiterant [8] mūnīrī iussit. Helvētiī cum omnibus suīs carrīs secūtī, impedīmenta [6] in ūnum locum contulērunt; ipsī cōn- 10 fertissimā aciē, rēiectō nostrō equitātū, phalange factā, sub prīmam nostram aciem successērunt.

NOTES

[1] See 199.   [2] *the middle of, half way up.*   [3] See 464.   [4] *the top of.* [5] Depends on **iussit.**   [6] **sarcinae,** the *packs* carried by the soldiers themselves, like our knapsacks ; **impedīmenta,** the *heavy baggage,* tents, provisions, etc., carried by horses and mules.   [7] Supply **locum.**   [8] See 556, 1, *a.*

[1] **perveniō.**   [2] See 159.   [3] See 499.

TRANSLATE

1. Caesar had six legions in all. 2. Two legions are to guard the baggage.[1] 3. Caesar ordered Labienus to lead the troops to the next hill. 4. The scout reports that the enemy will form a phalanx and advance close to [2] our line. 5. Let [3] the whole mountain be filled with men that the Gauls may be terrified.

THE BATTLE

25. Caesar prīmum suō [1] deinde omnium ex cōnspectū remōtīs equīs, ut aequātō omnium perīculō spem fugae tolleret, cohortātus suōs proelium commīsit. Mīlitēs ē locō superiōre pīlīs missīs facile hostium phalangem perfrēgē-
5 runt. Eā disiectā, gladiīs dēstrictīs in eōs impetum fēcē-runt. Gallīs [2] māgnō ad pūgnam erat impedīmentō [3] quod,[4] plūribus eōrum scūtīs ūnō ictū pīlōrum trānsfīxīs et conli-gātīs, cum ferrum sē īnflexisset, neque ēvellere neque sinis-trā impedītā satis commodē pūgnāre poterant, multī ut [5]
10 diū [6] iactātō bracchiō praeoptārent scūtum manū [7] ēmittere et nūdō corpore pūgnāre. Tandem volneribus dēfessī et [8] pedem referre et, quod mōns suberat circiter mīlle passuum, eō [9] sē recipere coepērunt. Captō monte et succēdentibus nostrīs, Bōiī et Tulingī, quī hominum mīlibus circiter xv
15 āgmen hostium claudēbant et novissimīs praesidiō erant, ex itinere nostrōs ab latere apertō adgressī circumvenīre; et id cōnspicātī Helvētiī, quī in montem sēsē recēperant, rūrsus īnstāre et proelium redintegrāre coepērunt. Rōmānī con-versa sīgna bipartītō intulērunt: [10] prīma et secunda aciēs,
20 ut victīs ac submōtīs resisteret; [11] tertia, ut venientēs sus-tinēret.

NOTES

[1] Supply **equō remōtō.** [2] See 525. [3] See 524. [4] The subject of **erat** is **quod neque ēvellere . . . poterant.** [5] *so that many.* [6] Modi-

[1] *for a guard to the baggage.* See 524 and 525. [2] *close to,* **sub.** [3] See 562 *b.*

fies **iactātō.**   [7] See 448.   [8] *both.*   [9] Adverb.   [10] **conversa . . .**
intulērunt, *faced about and charged in two divisions.* What is the literal
translation.   [11] See 471.   Notice the number of times the ablative absolute is used in the chapter.

TRANSLATE

1. Why were the soldiers' horses removed out of sight?
2. Did Caesar encourage his men before he joined battle?
3. Throw the javelins, soldiers, that you may break up the
phalanx of the Gauls.   4. Do not draw your swords until
the signal is given.   5. There were some who were not
able to throw aside the shield from the arm.

DEFEAT OF THE HELVETII

26. Ita ancipitī proeliō diū atque ācriter pūgnātum est.[1]
Diūtius cum sustinēre nostrōrum impetūs nōn possent,
alterī [2] sē, ut coeperant, in montem recēpērunt, alterī [3] ad
impedīmenta et carrōs suōs sē contulērunt. Nam hōc
tōtō proeliō, cum [4] ab hōrā septimā [5] ad vesperum pūgnā-   5
tum sit, āversum hostem vidēre nēmō potuit. Ad multam
noctem [6] etiam ad impedīmenta pūgnātum est, proptereā
quod prō vāllō carrōs obiēcerant [7] et ē locō [8] superiōre in
nostrōs venientēs tēla coniciēbant,[7] et nōnnūllī inter carrōs
rotāsque matarās ac trāgulās subiciēbant [7] nostrōsque vol-   10
nerābant. Diū cum esset pūgnātum, impedīmentīs castrīsque nostrī potītī sunt. Ibi Orgetorīgis fīlia atque ūnus ē
fīliīs captus [9] est. Ex eō proeliō circiter hominum mīlia
cxxx superfuērunt, eāque tōtā nocte continenter iērunt:
nūllam partem noctis itinere intermissō in fīnēs Lingonum   15
diē quārtō pervēnērunt, cum [10] et propter volnera mīlitum
et propter sepultūram occīsōrum nostrī trīduum morātī
eōs sequī nōn potuissent. Caesar ad Lingonēs litterās nūn-
tiōsque mīsit nē [11] eōs frūmentō nēve aliā rē iuvārent: quī
16

20 sī [12] iūvissent, sē eōdem locō quō Helvētiōs habitūrum.
Ipse trīduō intermissō cum omnibus cōpiīs eōs sequī coepit.

Notes

[1] See 428. [2] The Helvetii. [3] The Boii and Tulingi. [4] See 569.
[5] About one o'clock. [6] *Till late in the night.* [7] Notice three compounds of **iaciō**: **obiciō**, *throw in front*, **coniciō**, *throw from above*, **subiciō**, *throw*, or *thrust, from below.* [8] *position.* [9] See 285. [10] See 465. [11] *to warn them not to.* [12] **quī sī**, *for if they.*

Translate

1. The Helvetii fought as [1] fiercely as they could. 2. They feared that the Romans would take away [2] their liberty. 3. They thought they could persuade the Lingones to aid [3] them. 4. Do not aid the Helvetii by (giving) grain. 5. If you aid them, I shall hold you in the same regard (place) as (I do) them.

Surrender of the Helvetii

27. Helvētiī omnium rērum inopiā adductī lēgātōs dē dēditiōne ad eum mīsērunt. Quī [1] cum eum in itinere convēnissent sēque ad pedēs prōiēcissent suppliciterque locūtī flentēs pācem petīssent, atque eōs in eō locō quō tum essent [2]
5 suum adventum exspectāre iussisset, pāruērunt. Eō postquam Caesar pervēnit, obsidēs, arma, servōs quī ad eōs perfūgissent [3] poposcit. Dum ea conquīruntur [4] et cōnferuntur, nocte intermissā, circiter hominum mīlia VI ēius pāgī quī Verbigenus [5] appellātur, sīve timōre perterritī nē armīs trā-
10 ditīs suppliciō adficerentur, sīve spē salūtis inductī, quod in tantā multitūdine dēditīciōrum suam fugam aut occultārī aut omnīnō īgnōrārī posse exīstimārent, prīmā nocte ē cas-

[1] **quam.** See 304. [2] **ēripiō.** [3] In what mood must this be expressed?

trīs Helvētiōrum ēgressī ad Rhēnum fīnēsque Germānōrum
contendērunt.

Notes

[1] **Quī cum = Et cum eī.**   [2] Subjunctive by *attraction;* that is, because
it depends upon the subjunctive **iussisset.**   [3] Subjunctive, because it is
quoted from the words used in making the demand.   [4] See 472, 3.
[5] See 105.

Translate

1. We hear that ambassadors have been sent by the
Gauls because there is no hope of safety.   2. They are
going [1] to speak with the general in-behalf-of [2] those whom
he has conquered.   3. The hostages and slaves, who have
escaped, must be brought back.   4. The slaves attempted to
reach the Rhine.   5. We think we shall be punished if we
give up our arms.

The Helvetii Return to Their Own Territory

28. Quod ubi [1] Caesar resciit, quōrum per fīnēs ierant,
hīs [2] utī conquīrerent et redūcerent, sī sibi [3] pūrgātī esse
vellent, imperāvit; reductōs[4] in hostium numerō habuit;
reliquōs omnēs, obsidibus, armīs, perfugīs trāditīs, in dēditiōnem accēpit.[5] Helvētiōs, Tulingōs, Latobrīgōs in fīnēs   5
suōs, unde [6] erant profectī, revertī iussit; et, quod omnibus
frūgibus [7] āmissīs domī nihil erat quō famem tolerārent,[8]
Allobrogibus imperāvit ut eīs frūmentī cōpiam facerent;
ipsōs [9] oppida vīcōsque quōs incenderant restituere iussit.
Id eā māximē ratiōne fēcit, quod nōluit eum locum unde [6]   10
Helvētiī discesserant vacāre, nē propter bonitātem agrōrum
Germānī, quī trāns Rhēnum incolunt, ē suīs fīnibus in Helvētiōrum fīnēs trānsīrent et fīnitimī Galliae prōvinciae [10] Al-
lobrogibusque essent.   Bōiōs [11] petentibus Haeduīs,[12] quod

[1] See 477.   [2] **prō.**

15 ēgregiā virtūte[13] erant cōgnitī, ut[14] in fīnibus suīs conlocārent, concessit; quibus illī agrōs dedērunt, quōsque posteā
in parem iūris lībertātisque condiciōnem atque[15] ipsī erant
recēpērunt.

NOTES

[1] **Quod ubi = Et ubi id.**   [2] The antecedent of **quōrum.** For case of
hīs, see 471.   [3] See 525.   [4] **reductōs . . . habuit,** a mild way of
stating that he slew them.   [5] **in dēditiōnem accēpit,** *accepted the sur-*
render of.   [6] A relative adverb.   [7] *field products.*   [8] See 459.   [9] The
Helvetii.   [10] Dative, why?   [11] Object of **conlocārent,** put first for
emphasis.   [12] **petentibus Haeduīs concessit,** *to the Haedui, at their*
request, he granted.   [13] See 464.   [14] **Ut . . . conlocārent,** object of
concessit.   [15] **parem atque,** *the same as.*

TRANSLATE

1. Having made peace with the Romans, the Helvetii
returned home.   2. Let[1] us restore the villages that we
have burned.   3. Let the Haedui give part of their territory to the Boii.   4. Since the Helvetii did not have a
supply of grain, their neighbors helped[2] them.   5. The
Germans have been informed of the fertility of the Gallic
fields, and will cross the Rhine to get possession of them.

THE RECORDS OF THE HELVETII

29. In castrīs Helvētiōrum tabulae repertae sunt litterīs
Graecīs cōnfectae[1] et ad Caesarem relātae quibus in tabu-
līs[2] nōminātim ratiō[3] cōnfecta erat, quī numerus[4] domō
exīsset eōrum quī arma ferre possent,[5] et item sēparātim
5 puerī,[6] senēs mulierēsque.   Quārum omnium rērum summa erat capitum Helvētiōrum mīlia CCLXIII, Tulingōrum
mīlia XXXVI, Latobrīgōrum XIIII, Rauracōrum XXIII,
Bōiōrum XXXII; ex hīs quī arma ferre possent[5] ad mīlia
XCII.   Summa omnium fuērunt ad mīlia CCCLXVIII.

---

[1] See 562.   [2] **iuvō.**

Eōrum quī domum rediērunt cēnsū habitō, ut Caesar im- 10
perāverat, repertus est numerus mīlium c et x.

NOTES

[1] *made out*, or *written.*   [2] Notice the repetition of the antecedent of
quibus in the relative clause.   [3] *account.*   [4] **quī numerus,** *showing*
what number.   See 502.   [5] See 459.   [6] Subject of a verb understood,
meaning *were recorded.*

TRANSLATE

1. The Helvetii had made out their records in Greek
letters.   2. Why did they use Greek letters?   3. The Helvetii had fought very bravely, but many were killed.
4. A census was taken (had) in order that Caesar might
find out how many [1] men had returned [2] home.   5. Caesar
conquered the Helvetii in one battle during the consulship
of Lucius Piso and Aulus Gabinius.[3]

---

[1] *how many,* **quot.**   [2] See 502.   [3] See 279.

APPENDIX

NOUNS

1.
First Declension.
Porta, F., *gate.*

SINGULAR.		PLURAL.
NOM.	porta	portae
GEN.	portae	portārum
DAT.	portae	portīs
ACC.	portam	portās
ABL.	portā	portīs

2.
Second Declension.

	Amīcus, M., *friend.*	Puer, M., *boy.*	Ager, M., *field.*	Vir, M., *man.*	Bellum, N., *war.*
			SINGULAR.		
N.	amīcus	puer	ager	vir	bellum
G.	amīcī	puerī	agrī	virī	bellī
D.	amīcō	puerō	agrō	virō	bellō
Ac.	amīcum	puerum	agrum	virum	bellum
AB.	amīcō	puerō	agrō	virō	bellō
			PLURAL.		
N.	amīcī	puerī	agri	virī	bella
G.	amīcōrum	puerōrum	agrōrum	virōrum	bellōrum
D.	amīcīs	puerīs	agrīs	virīs	bellīs
Ac.	amīcōs	puerōs	agrōs	virōs	bella
AB.	amīcīs	puerīs	agrīs	virīs	bellīs

Third Declension.

3. Cōnsul, M., consul.	Legiō, F., legion.	Mercātor, M., merchant.	Pater, M., father.

SINGULAR.

N. cōnsul	legiō	mercātor	pater
G. cōnsulis	legiōnis	mercātōris	patris
D. cōnsulī	legiōnī	mercātōrī	patrī
Ac. cōnsulem	legiōnem	mercātōrem	patrem
Ab. cōnsule	legiōne	mercātōre	patre

PLURAL.

N. cōnsulēs	legiōnēs	mercātōrēs	patrēs
G. cōnsulum	legiōnum	mercātōrum	patrum
D. cōnsulibus	legiōnibus	mercātōribus	patribus
Ac. cōnsulēs	legiōnēs	mercātōrēs	patrēs
Ab. cōnsulibus	legiōnibus	mercātōribus	patribus

4. Lēx, F., law.	Prīnceps, M., chief.	Mīles, M., soldier.	Cīvitās, F., state.

SINGULAR.

N. lēx	prīnceps	mīles	cīvitās
G. lēgis	prīncipis	mīlitis	cīvitātis
D. lēgī	prīncipī	mīlitī	cīvitātī
Ac. lēgem	prīncipem	mīlitem	cīvitātem
Ab. lēge	prīncipe	mīlite	cīvitāte

PLURAL.

N. lēgēs	prīncipēs	mīlitēs	cīvitātēs
G. lēgum	prīncipum	mīlitum	cīvitātum
D. lēgibus	prīncipibus	mīlitibus	cīvitātibus
Ac. lēgēs	prīncipēs	mīlitēs	cīvitātēs
Ab. lēgibus	prīncipibus	mīlitibus	cīvitātibus

5. Flūmen, N.,   **Opus N.,**   **Tempus, N.,**   **Caput, N.,**
river.   *work.*   *time.*   *head.*

SINGULAR.

N. flūmen	opus	tempus	caput
G. flūminis	operis	temporis	capitis
D. flūminī	operī	temporī	capitī
Ac. flūmen	opus	tempus	caput
Ab. flūmine	opere	temporc	capite

PLURAL.

N. flūmina	opera	tempora	capita
G. flūminum	operum	temporum	capitum
D. flūminibus	operibus	temporibus	capitibus
Ac. flūmina	opera	tempora	capita
Ab. flūminibus	operibus	temporibus	capitibus

6. Hostis, M. & F.,   **Nāvis, F.,**   **Mōns, M.,**   **Nox, F.,**
enemy.   *ship.*   *mountain.*   *night.*

SINGULAR.

N. hostis	nāvis	mons	nox
G. hostis	nāvis	montis	noctis
D. hostī	nāvī	montī	noctī
Ac. hostem	nāvim, nāvem	montem	noctem
Ab. hoste	nāvī, nāve	monte	nocte

PLURAL.

N. hostēs	nāvēs	montēs	noctēs
G. hostium	nāvium	montium	noctium
D. hostibus	nāvibus	montibus	noctibus
Ac. hostēs -īs	nāvēs -īs	montēs -īs	noctēs -īs
Ab. hostibus	nāvibus	montibus	noctibus

250 APPENDIX

7. Cubīle, N., _couch_.

	SING.	PLUR.
N.	cubīle	cubīlia
G.	cubīlis	cubīlium
D.	cubīlī	cubīlibus
Ac.	cubīle	cubīlia
Ab.	cubīlī	cubīlibus

Animal, N., _animal_.

SING.	PLUR.
animal	animālia
animālis	animālium
animālī	animālibus
animal	animālia
animālī	animālibus

Fourth Declension.

8. Manus, F., _hand._ **Lacus, M.,** _lake._ **Domus, F.,** _house._ **Cornū, N.,** _horn._

SINGULAR.

N.	manus	lacus	domus	cornū
G.	manūs	lacūs	domūs	cornūs(-ū)
D.	manuī	lacuī	domuī	cornū
Ac.	manum	lacum	domum	cornū
Ab.	manū	lacū	domō(-ū)	cornū

PLURAL.

N.	manūs	lacūs	domūs	cornua
G.	manuum	lacuum	domuum	cornuum
D.	manibus	lacubus	domibus	cornibus
Ac.	manūs	lacūs	domōs(-ūs)	cornua
Ab.	manibus	lacubus	domibus	cornibus

Fifth Declension.

9. Diês, M., _day_.

	SING.	PLUR.
N.	diēs	diēs
G.	diēī	diērum
D.	diēī	diēbus
Ac.	diem	diēs
Ab.	diē	diēbus

Rês, F., _thing_.

SING.	PLUR.
rēs	rēs
reī	rērum
reī	rēbus
rem	rēs
rē	rēbus

Special Nouns.

10. Deus, M., *god.*	Senex, M., *old man.*	Vis, F., *force.*	Iter, N., *way.*
	SINGULAR.		
N. deus	senex	vīs	iter
G. deī	senis	vīs	itineris
D. deō	senī	vī	itineri
Ac. deum	senem	vim	iter
Ab. deō	sene	vī	itinere
	PLURAL.		
N. deī, diī, dī	senēs	vīrēs	itinera
G. deōrum, deūm	senum	vīrium	itinerum
D. deīs, diīs, dīs	senibus	vīribus	itineribus
Ac. deōs	senēs	vīrēs	itinera
Ab. deīs, diīs, dīs	senibus	vīribus	itineribus

ADJECTIVES
First and Second Declensions.

11. **Māgnus,** *large.*

	SINGULAR.			PLURAL.	
M.	*F.*	*N.*	*M.*	*F.*	*N.*
N. māgnus	māgna	māgnum	māgnī	māgnae	māgna
G. māgnī	māgnae	māgnī	māgnōrum	māgnārum	māgnōrum
D. māgnō	māgnae	māgnō	māgnīs	māgnīs	māgnīs
Ac. māgnum	māgnam	māgnum	māgnōs	māgnās	māgna
Ab. māgnō	māgnā	māgnō	māgnīs	māgnīs	māgnīs

Līber, *free.*

	SINGULAR.			PLURAL.	
M.	*F.*	*N.*	*M.*	*F.*	*N.*
N. līber	lībera	līberum	līberī	līberae	lībera
G. līberī	līberae	līberī	līberōrum	līberārum	līberōrum
D. līberō	līberae	līberō	līberīs	līberīs	līberīs
Ac. līberum	līberam	līberum	līberōs	līberās	lībera
Ab. līberō	līberā	līberō	līberīs	līberīs	līberīs

Noster, *our.*[1]

	SINGULAR.			PLURAL.		
	M.	*F.*	*N.*	*M.*	*F.*	*N.*
N.	noster	nostra	nostrum	nostrī	nostrae	nostra
G.	nostrī	nostrae	nostrī	nostrōrum	nostrārum	nostrōrum
D.	nostrō	nostrae	nostrō	nostrīs	nostrīs	nostrīs
Ac.	nostrum	nostram	nostrum	nostrōs	nostrās	nostra
Ab.	nostrō	nostrā	nostrō	nostrīs	nostrīs	nostrīs

12. Alius, *another.*   Alter, *the other* (of two).

				SINGULAR.		
	M.	*F.*	*N.*	*M.*	*F.*	*N.*
N.	alius	alia	aliud	alter	altera	alterum
G.	alīus	alīus	alīus	alterius	alterius	alterius
D.	aliī	aliī	aliī	alterī	alterī	alterī
Ac.	alium	aliam	aliud	alterum	alteram	alterum
Ab.	aliō	aliā	aliō	alterō	alterā	alterō

Neuter, *neither.*   Unus, *one.*

	M.	*F.*	*N.*	*M.*	*F.*	*N.*
N.	neuter	neutra	neutrum	ūnus	ūna	ūnum
G.	neutrīus	neutrīus	neutrīus	ūnīus	ūnīus	ūnīus
D.	neutrī	neutrī	neutrī	ūnī	ūnī	ūnī
Ac.	neutrum	neutram	neutrum	ūnum	ūnam	ūnum
Ab.	neutrō	neutrā	neutrō	ūnō	ūnā	ūnō

13. Third Declension.

Ācer, *sharp.*

	SINGULAR.			PLURAL.		
	M.	*F.*	*N.*	*M.*	*F.*	*N.*
N.	ācer	ācris	ācre	ācrēs	ācrēs	ācria
G.	ācris	ācris	ācris	ācrium	ācrium	ācrium
D.	ācrī	ācrī	ācrī	ācribus	ācribus	ācribus
Ac.	ācrem	ācrem	ācre	ācrēs (-īs)	ācrēs (-īs)	ācria
Ab.	ācrī	ācrī	ācrī	ācribus	ācribus	ācribus

---

[1] Possessive pronoun, used as an adjective.

Fortis, *brave.*

	SINGULAR.		PLURAL.	
	M. & F.	*N.*	*M. & F.*	*N.*
N.	fortis	forte	fortēs	fortia
G.	fortis	fortis	fortium	fortium
D.	forti	fortī	fortibus	fortibus
Ac.	fortem	forte	fortēs (-īs)	fortia
Ab.	fortī	fortī	fortibus	fortibus

Longior, *longer.*

	SINGULAR		PLURAL.	
	M. & F.	*N.*	*M. & F.*	*N.*
N.	longior	longius	longiōrēs	longiōra
G.	longiōris	longiōris	longiōrum	longiōrum
D.	longiōrī	longiōrī	longiōribus	longiōribus
Ac.	longiōrem	longius	longiōrēs	longiōra
Ab.	longiōre	longiōre	longiōribus	longiōribus

Potēns, *powerful.*

	SINGULAR.		PLURAL.	
	M. & F.	*N.*	*M. & F.*	*N.*
N.	potēns	potēns	potentēs	potentia
G.	potentis	potentis	potentium	potentium
D.	potentī	potentī	potentibus	potentibus
Ac.	potentem	potēns	potentēs (-īs)	potentia
Ab.	potentī (-e)	potentī (-ē)	potentibus	potentibus

Vēlōx, *swift.*

	SINGULAR.		PLURAL.	
	M. & F.	*N.*	*M. & F.*	*N.*
N.	vēlōx	vēlōx	vēlōcēs	vēlōcia
G.	vēlōcis	vēlōcis	vēlōcium	vēlōcium
D.	vēlōcī	vēlōcī	vēlōcibus	vēlōcibus
Ac.	vēlōcem	vēlōx	vēlōcēs (-īs)	vēlōcia
Ab.	vēlōcī (-e)	vēlōcī (-e)	vēlōcibus	vēlōcibus

254 APPENDIX

14. Special Adjectives.

Vetus, *old.*

	SINGULAR.		PLURAL.	
	M. & F.	*N.*	*M. & F.*	*N.*
N.	vetus	vetus	veterēs	vetera
G.	veteris	veteris	veterum	veterum
D.	veterī	veterī	veteribus	veteribus
Ac.	veterem	vetus	veterēs	vetera
Ab.	vetere *or* -ī	vetere *or* -ī	veteribus	veteribus

Plus, *more.*

	SINGULAR.		PLURAL.	
	M. & F.	*N.*	*M. & F.*	*N.*
N.	——	plūs	plūrēs	plūra
G.	——	plūris	plūrium	plūrium
D.	——	——	plūribus	plūribus
Ac.	——	plūs	plūrēs	plūra
Ab.	——	plūre	plūribus	plūribus

Duo, *two.*

	M.	*F.*	*N.*
N.	duo	duae	duo
G.	duōrum	duārum	duōrum
D.	duōbus	duābus	duōbus
Ac.	duōs	duās	duo
Ab.	duōbus	duābus	duōbus

Trēs, *three.*

	M. & F.	*N.*
N.	trēs	tria
G.	trium	trium
D.	tribus	tribus
Ac.	trēs, trīs	tria
Ab.	tribus	tribus

15. Regular Comparison.

POSITIVE.	COMPARATIVE.	SUPERLATIVE.
altus, -a, -um, *high*	altior, -ius	altissimus, -a, -um
fortis, -e, *brave*	fortior, -ius	fortissimus, -a, -um
potēns, *powerful*	potentior, -ius	potentissimus, -a, -um
vēlōx, *swift*	vēlōcior, -ius	vēlōcissimus, -a, -um

POSITIVE.	COMPARATIVE.	SUPERLATIVE.
ācer, acris, acre, *sharp*	ācrior, -ius	ācerrimus, -a, -um
liber, -era, -erum, *free*	liberior, -ius	liberrimus, -a, -um
facilis, -e, *easy*	facilior, -ius	facillimus, -a, -um
difficilis, -e, *difficult*	difficilior, -ius	difficillimus, -a, -um
similis, -e *like*	similior, -ius	simillimus, -a, -um
dissimilis, -e, *unlike*	dissimilior, -ius	dissimillimus, -a, -um
humilis, -e, *low*	humilior, -ius	humillimus, -a, -um
gracilis, -e, *slender*	gracilior, -ius	gracillimus, -a, -um

16. Irregular Comparison.

bonus, -a, -um, *good*	melior, melius	optimus, -a, -um
malus, -a, -um, *bad*	pēior, pēius	pessimus, -a, -um
māgnus, -a, -um, *great*	māior, māius,	māximus, -a, -um
multus, -a, -um, *much* } multī, -ae, -a, *many* }	——, plūs	plūrimus, -a, -um
parvus, -a, -um, *small*	minor, minus	minimus, -a, -um
senex, *old*	senior	māximus nātū
iuvenis, -e, *young*	iūnior	minimus nātū
vetus, *old*	vetustior, -ius	veterrimus, -a, -um
(exterus, *outward*)	exterior, *outer,* *exterior*	extrēmus } *outermost,* extimus } *last*
(īnferus, *below*)	īnferior, *lower*	īnfimus } īmus } *lowest*
(posterus, *following*)	posterior, *later*	postrēmus } postumus } *last*
(superus, *above*)	superior, *higher*	suprēmus } summus } *highest*
[cis, citrā, *on this side*]	citerior, *hither*	citimus, *hithermost*
[in, intrā, *in, within*]	interior, *inner*	intimus, *inmost*
[prae, prō, *before*]	prior, *former*	prīmus, *first*
[prope, *near*]	propior, *nearer*	proximus, *next*
[ūltrā, *beyond*]	ūlterior, *further*	ūltimus, *furthest*

17. NUMERALS

CARDINAL.	ORDINAL.	DISTRIBUTIVE.	ADVERBS.
1 ūnus	prīmus	singulī	semel
2 duo	secundus	bīnī	bis
3 trēs	tertius	ternī (trīnī)	ter
4 quattuor	quārtus	quaternī	quater
5 quīnque	quīntus	quīnī	quīnquiēs
6 sex	sextus	sēnī	sexiēs
7 septem	septimus	septēnī	septiēs
8 octō	octāvus	octōnī	octiēs
9 novem	nōnus	nōvēnī	noviēs
10 decem	decimus	dēnī	deciēs
11 ūndecim	ūndecimus	ūndēnī	ūndeciēs
12 duodecim	duodecimus	duodēnī	duodeciēs
13 tredecim	tertius decimus	ternī dēnī	ter deciēs
14 quattuorde-cim	quārtus deci-mus	quaternī dēnī	quater deciēs
15 quīndecim	quīntus deci-mus	quīnī dēnī	quīnquiēs de-ciēs
16 sēdecim	sextus decimus	sēnī dēnī	sexiēs deciēs
17 septendecim	septimus deci-mus	septēnī dēnī	septiēs deciēs
18 duodēvīgintī	duodēvīcēsimus	duodēvīcēnī	duodēvīciēs
19 ūndēvīgintī	ūndēvīcēsimus	ūndēvīcēnī	ūndēvīciēs
20 vīgintī	vīcēsīmus	vīcēnī	vīciēs
21 ūnus et vīgintī (vīgintī ūnus)	vīcēsimus prī-mus	vīcēnī singulī	vīciēs semel
28 duodētrīgintā	duodētrīcēsi-mus	duodētrīcēnī	duodētrīciēs
29 ūndētrīgintā	ūndētrīcēsimus	ūndētrīcēnī	ūndētrīciēs
30 trīgintā	trīcēsimus	trīcēnī	trīciēs
40 quadrāgintā	quadrāgēsimus	quadrāgēnī	quadrāgiēs
50 quīnquāgintā	quīnquāgēsi-mus	quīnquāgēnī	quinquāgiēs

CARDINAL.	ORDINAL.	DISTRIBUTIVE.	ADVERBS.
60 sexāgintā	sexāgēsimus	sexāgēnī	sexāgiēs
70 septuāgintā	septuāgēsimus	septuāgēnī	septuāgiēs
80 octōgintā	octōgēsimus	octōgēnī	octōgiēs
90 nōnāgintā	nōnāgēsimus	nōnāgēnī	nōnāgiēs
100 centum	centēsimus	centēnī	centiēs
101 centum (et) ūnus	centēsimus (et) prīmus	centēnī (et) singulī	centiēs semel
200 ducentī	ducentēsimus	ducēnī	ducentiēs
300 trecentī	trecentēsimus	trecēnī	trecentiēs
400 quadringentī	quadringentē- simus	quadringēnī	quadringentiēs
500 quīngentī	quīngentēsimus	quīngēnī	quīngentiēs
600 sēscentī	sēscentēsimus	sēscēnī	sēscentiēs
700 septingentī	septingentēsi- mus	septingēnī	septingentiēs
800 octingentī	octingentēsi- mus	octingēnī	octingentiēs
900 nōngentī	nōngentēsimus	nōngēnī	nōngentiēs
1000 mīlle	mīllēsimus	singula mīlia	mīlliēs
2000 duo mīlia	bis mīllēsimus	bīna mīlia	bis mīlliēs

PRONOUNS

18. Personal. Reflexive.

Ego, *I.*   **Tū,** *thou.*   **Suī,** *of himself,* etc.

SING.	PLU.	SING.	PLU.	SING.	PLU.
N. ego	nōs	tū	vōs	——	——
G. meī	nostrūm, -trī	tuī	vestrūm, -trī	suī	suī
D. mihi	nōbīs	tibi	vōbīs	sibi	sibi
Ac. mē	nōs	tē	vōs	sē, sēsē	sē, sēsē
Ab. me	nōbīs	tē	vōbīs	sē, sēsē	sē, sēsē

17

19. Demonstrative.

Hīc, *this.*

	SINGULAR.			PLURAL.	
M.	*F.*	*N.*	*M.*	*F.*	*N.*
N. hīc	haec	hōc	hī	hae	haec
G. hūius	hūius	hūius	hōrum	hārum	hōrum
D. huic	huic	huic	hīs	hīs	hīs
Ac. hunc	hanc	hōc	hōs	hās	haec
Ab. hōc	hāc	hōc	hīs	hīs	hīs

Iste, *that* (near you).

	SINGULAR.			PLURAL.	
M.	*F.*	*N.*	*M.*	*F.*	*N.*
N. iste	ista	istud	istī	istae	ista
G. istīus	istīus	istīus	istōrum	istārum	istōrum
D. istī	istī	istī	istīs	istīs	istīs
Ac. istum	istam	istud	istōs	istās	ista
Ab. istō	istā	istō	istīs	istīs	istīs

Ille, *that* (yonder).

	SINGULAR.			PLURAL.	
M.	*F.*	*N.*	*M.*	*F.*	*N.*
N. ille	illa	illud	illī	illae	illa
G. illīus	illīus	illīus	illōrum	illārum	illōrum
D. illī	illī	illī	illīs	illīs	illīs
Ac. illum	illam	illud	illōs	illās	illa
Ab. illō	illā	illō	illīs	illīs	illīs

Is, *this, that, he, she, it.*

	SINGULAR.			PLURAL.	
M.	*F.*	*N.*	*M.*	*F.*	*N.*
N. is	ea	id	eī, iī	eae	ea
G. ēius	ēius	ēius	eōrum	eārum	eōrum
D. eī	eī	eī	eīs, iīs	eīs, iīs	eīs, iīs
Ac. eum	eam	id	eōs	eās	ea
Ab. eō	eā	eō	eīs, iīs	eīs, iīs	eīs, iīs

Īdem, *the same.*

	SINGULAR.			PLURAL.	
M.	*F.*	*N.*	*M.*	*F.*	*N.*
N. īdem	eadem	idem	eīdem	eaedem	eadem
G. ēiusdem	ēiusdem	ēiusdem	eōrundem	eārundem	eōrundem
D. eīdem	eīdem	eīdem	eīsdem	eīsdem	eīsdem
Ac. eundem	eandem	idem	eōsdem	eāsdem	eadem
Ab. eōdem	eādem	eōdem	eīsdem	eīsdem	eīsdem

20. Intensive.

Ipse, *self.*

	SINGULAR.			PLURAL.	
M.	*F.*	*N.*	*M.*	*F.*	*N.*
N. ipse	ipsa	ipsum	ipsī	ipsae	ipsa
G. ipsīus	ipsīus	ipsīus	ipsōrum	ipsārum	ipsōrum
D. ipsī	ipsī	ipsī	ipsīs	ipsīs	ipsīs
Ac. ipsum	ipsam	ipsum	ipsōs	ipsās	ipsa
Ab. ipsō	ipsā	ipsō	ipsīs	ipsīs	ipsīs

21. Relative.

Quī, *who, which, that.*

	SINGULAR.			PLURAL.	
M.	*F.*	*N.*	*M.*	*F.*	*N.*
N. quī	quae	quod	quī	quae	quae
G. cūius	cūius	cūius	quōrum	quārum	quōrum
D. cui	cui	cui	quibus	quibus	quibus
Ac. quem	quam	quod	quōs	quās	quae
Ab. quō	quā	quō	quibus	quibus	quibus

22. Interrogative.

Quis, *who?*

	SINGULAR.	
	M. & F.	*N.*
N.	quis	quid
G.	cūius	cūius

	M. & F.	*N.*
D.	cui	cui
Ac.	quem	quid
Ab.	quō	quō

The plural of the interrogative **quis** is like that of the relative **quī.**

23.   Indefinite.

Aliquis, *some one.*

SINGULAR.

	M.	*F.*	*N.*
N.	aliquis (-quī)	aliqua	aliquid (-quod)
G.	alicūius	alicūius	alicūius
D.	alicui	alicui	alicui
Ac.	aliquem	aliquam	aliquid (-quod)
Ab.	aliquō	aliquā	aliquō

PLURAL.

N.	aliquī	aliquae	aliqua
G.	aliquōrum	aliquārum	aliquōrum
D.	aliquibus	aliquibus	aliquibus
Ac.	aliquōs	aliquās	aliqua
Ab.	aliquibus	aliquibus	aliquibus

VERBS

First Conjugation.

24.   ACTIVE VOICE.—**Laudō,** *I praise.*

PRINCIPAL PARTS : laudō, laudāre, laudāvī, laudātum.

INDICATIVE.		SUBJUNCTIVE.	
Present.		*Present.*	
SINGULAR.	PLURAL.	SINGULAR.	PLURAL.
laudō	laudāmus	laudem	laudēmus
laudās	laudātis	laudēs	laudētis
laudat	laudant	laudet	laudent

INDICATIVE.		SUBJUNCTIVE.	
Imperfect.		*Imperfect.*	
laudābam	laudābāmus	laudārem	laudārēmus
laudābās	laudābātis	laudārēs	laudārētis
laudābat	laudābant	laudāret	laudārent

Future.	
laudābō	laudābimus
laudābis	laudābitis
laudābit	laudābunt

Perfect.		*Perfect.*	
laudāvī	laudāvimus	laudāverim	laudāverimus
laudāvistī	laudāvistis	laudāveris	laudāveritis
laudāvit	laudāvērunt(-ēre)	laudāverit	laudāverint

Pluperfect.		*Pluperfect.*	
laudāveram	laudāverāmus	laudāvissem	laudāvissēmus
laudāverās	laudāverātis	laudāvissēs	laudāvissētis
laudāverat	laudāverant	laudāvisset	laudāvissent

Future Perfect.	
laudāverō	laudāverimus
lavdāveris	laudāveritis
laudāverit	laudāverint

IMPERATIVE.			PARTICIPLE.
SINGULAR.	PLURAL.		*Pres.* laudāns *Fut.* laudātūrus
Pres. laudā	laudāte		

GERUND.

Fut. laudātō laudātōte
    laudātō laudantō

Gen. laudandī
Dat. laudandō
Acc. laudandum
Abl. laudandō

INFINITIVE.

Pres. laudāre
Perf. laudāvisse
Fut. laudātūrus esse

SUPINE.

Acc. laudātum   *Abl.* laudātū

25.   PASSIVE VOICE.—**Laudor,** *I am praised.*

PRINCIPAL PARTS : laudor, audāri, laudātus sum.

INDICATIVE.		SUBJUNCTIVE.	
Present.		*Present.*	
SINGULAR.	PLURAL.	SINGULAR.	PLURAL.
laudor	laudāmur	lauder	laudēmur
laudāris	laudāminī	laudēris (-re)	laudēminī
laudātur	laudantur	laudētur	laudentur

Imperfect.		*Imperfect.*	
laudābar	laudābāmur	laudārer	laudārēmur
laudābāris (-re)	laudābāminī	laudārēris (-re)	laudārēminī
laudābātur	laudābantur	laudārētur	laudārentur

Future.

laudābor	laudābimur
laudāberis (-re)	laudābiminī
laudābitur	laudābuntur

Perfect.		*Perfect.*	
laudātus sum	laudātī sumus	laudātus sim	laudātī sīmus
laudātus es	laudātī estis	laudātus sīs	laudātī sītis
laudātus est	laudātī sunt	laudātus sit	laudātī sint

Pluperfect.		*Pluperfect.*	
laudātus eram	laudātī erāmus	laudātus essem	laudātī essēmus
laudātus erās	laudātī erātis	laudātus essēs	laudātī essētis
laudātus erat	laudātī erant	]audātus esset	laudātī essent

Future Perfect.		INFINITIVE.
laudātus erō	laudātī erimus	*Pres.* laudārī
laudātus eris	laudātī eritis	*Perf.* laudātus esse
laudātus erit	laudātī erunt	*Fut.* laudātum īrī

IMPERATIVE.		PARTICIPLE.
Pres. laudāre	laudāminī	*Perf.* laudātus
Fut. laudātor		*Fut.* laudandus (*Gerundive*)
laudātor	laudantor	

Second Conjugation.

26. ACTIVE VOICE.—**Moneō,** *I advise.*

PRINCIPAL PARTS : moneō, monēre, monuī, monitum.

INDICATIVE.		SUBJUNCTIVE.	
Present.		*Present.*	
SINGULAR.	PLURAL.	SINGULAR	PLURAL.
moneō	monēmus	moneam	moneāmus
monēs	monētis	moneās	moneātis
monet	monent	moneat	moneant

Imperfect.		*Imperfect.*	
monēbam	monēbāmus	monērem	monērēmus
monēbās	monēbātis	monērēs	monērētis
monēbat	monēbant	monēret	monērent

Future.	
monēbō	monēbimus
monēbis	monēbitis
monēbit	monēbunt

Perfect.		*Perfect.*	
monuī	monuimus	monuerim	monuerimus
monuistī	monuistis	monueris	monueritis
monuit	monuērunt (-ēre)	monuerit	monuerint

Pluperfect.		*Pluperfect.*	
monueram	monuerāmus	monuissem	monuissēmus
monuerās	monuerātis	monuissēs	monuissētis
monuerat	monuerant	monuisset	monuissent

INDICATIVE.

Future Perfect.

monuerō	monuerimus
monueris	monueritis
monuerit	monuerint

IMPERATIVE.

SINGULAR.	PLURAL.
Pres. monē	monēte
Fut. monētō	monētōte
monētō	monentō

INFINITIVE.

Pres. monēre
Perf. monuisse
Fut. monitūrus esse

PARTICIPLE.

Pres. monens   *Fut.* monitūrus

GERUND.

Gen. monendi
Dat. monendō
Acc. monendum
Abl. monendō

SUPINE.

Acc. monitum   *Abl.* monitū

27.   PASSIVE VOICE.—**Moneor**, *I am advised.*

PRINCIPAL PARTS : moneor, monērī, monitus sum.

INDICATIVE.

Present.

SINGULAR.	PLURAL.
moneor	monēmur
monēris	monēminī
monētur	monentur

Imperfect.

monēbar	monēbāmur
monēbāris (-re)	monēbāminī
monēbātur	monēbantur

Future.

monēbor	monēbimur
monēberis (-re)	monēbiminī
monēbitur	monēbuntur

SUBJUNCTIVE.

Present.

SINGULAR.	PLURAL.
monear	moneāmur
moneāris (-re)	moneāminī
moneātur	moneantur

Imperfect.

monērer	monērēmur
monērēris (-re)	monērēminī
monērētur	monērentur

INDICATIVE.		SUBJUNCTIVE.	
Perfect.		*Perfect.*	
monitus sum	monitī sumus	monitus sim	monitī sīmus
monitus es	monitī estis	monitus sīs	monitī sītis
monitus est	monitī sunt	monitus sit	monitī sint
Pluperfect.		*Pluperfect.*	
monitus eram	monitī erāmus	monitus essem	monitī essēmus
monitus erās	monitī erātis	monitus essēs	monitī essētis
monitus erat	monitī erant	monitus esset	monitī essent

Future Perfect.		INFINITIVE.
monitus erō	monitī erimus	*Pres.* monērī
monitus eris	monitī eritis	*Perf.* monitus esse
monitus erit	monitī erunt	*Fut.* monitum īrī

IMPERATIVE.		PARTICIPLE.
SINGULAR.	PLURAL.	*Perf.* monitus
Pres. monēre	monēminī	*Fut.* monendus (*Gerundive*)
Fut. monētor		
monētor	monentor	

Third Conjugation.

28. ACTIVE VOICE.—**Regō,** *I rule.*

PRINCIPAL PARTS : regō, regere, rēxī, rēctum.

INDICATIVE.		SUBJUNCTIVE.	
Present.		*Present.*	
SINGULAR.	PLURAL.	SINGULAR.	PLURAL.
regō	regimus	regam	regāmus
regis	regitis	regās	regātis
regit	regunt	regat	regant
Imperfect.		*Imperfect.*	
regēbam	regēbāmus	regerem	regerēmus
regēbās	regēbātis	regerēs	regerētis
regēbat	regēbant	regeret	regerent

INDICATIVE.

Future.

regam	regēmus
regēs	regētis
reget	regent

SUBJUNCTIVE.

Perfect. | *Perfect.*

rēxī	rēximus	rēxerim	rēxerimus
rēxistī	rēxistis	rēxeris	rēxeritis
rēxit	rēxērunt (-ēre)	rēxerit	rēxerint

Pluperfect. | *Pluperfect.*

rēxeram	rēxerāmus	rēxissem	rēxissēmus
rēxerās	rēxerātis	rēxissēs	rexissētis
rēxerat	rēxerant	rēxisset	rēxissent

Future Perfect.

rēxerō	rēxerimus
rēxeris	rēxeritis
rēxerit	rēxerint

IMPERATIVE.

SINGULAR.	PLURAL.
Pres. rege	regite
Fut. regitō	regitōte
regitō	reguntō

INFINITIVE.

Pres. regere
Perf. rēxisse
Fut. rēctūrus esse

PARTICIPLE.

Pres. regēns
Fut. rēctūrus

GERUND.

Gen. regendī
Dat. regendō
Acc. regendum
Abl. regendō

SUPINE.

Acc. rēctum   *Abl.* rēctū

29.   PASSIVE VOICE.—**Regor,** *I am ruled.*

PRINCIPAL PARTS : regor, regī, rēctus sum.

INDICATIVE.		SUBJUNCTIVE.	
Present.		*Present.*	
SINGULAR.	PLURAL.	SINGULAR.	PLURAL.
regor	regimur	regar	regāmur
regeris (-re)	regiminī	regāris (-re)	regāminī
regitur	reguntur	regātur	regantur
Imperfect.		*Imperfect.*	
regēbar	regēbāmur	regerer	regerēmur
regēbāris (-re)	regēbāminī	regerēris (-re)	regerēminī
regēbātur	regēbantur	regerētur	regerentur
Future.			
regar	regēmur		
regēris (-re)	regēmini		
regētur	regentur		
Perfect.		*Perfect.*	
rēctus sum	rēctī sumus	rēctus sim	rēctī sīmus
rēctus es	rēctī estis	rēctus sīs	rēctī sītis
rēctus est	rēctī sunt	rēctus sit	rēctī sint
Pluperfect.		*Pluperfect.*	
rēctus eram	rēctī erāmus	rēctus essem	rēctī essēmus
rēctus erās	rēctī erātis	rēctus essēs	rēctī essētis
rēctus erat	rēctī erant	rēctus esset	rēctī essent
Future Perfect.		INFINITIVE.	
rēctus erō	rēctī erimus	*Pres.* regī	
rēctus eris	rēctī eritis	*Perf.* rēctus esse	
rēctus erit	rēctī erunt	*Fut.* rēctum īrī	

IMPERATIVE.		PARTICIPLE.
SINGULAR.	PLURAL.	
Pres. regere	regiminī	*Perf.* rēctus
Fut. regitor		*Fut.* regendus (*Gerundive*)
regitor	reguntor	

Third Conjugation in -iō.

30. ACTIVE VOICE.—**Capiō**, *I take.*

PRINCIPAL PARTS : **capiō, capere, cēpī, captum.**

INDICATIVE.		SUBJUNCTIVE.	
Present.		*Present.*	
SINGULAR.	PLURAL.	SINGULAR.	PLURAL.
capiō	capimus	capiam	capiāmus
capis	capitis	capiās	capiātis
capit	capiunt	capiat	capiant
Imperfect.		*Imperfect.*	
capiēbam	capiēbāmus	caperem	caperēmus
capiēbās	capiēbātis	caperēs	caperētis
capiēbāt	capiēbant	caperet	caperent
Future.			
capiam	capiēmus		
capiēs	capiētis		
capiet	capient		
Perfect.		*Perfect.*	
cēpī	cēpimus	cēperim	cēperimus
cēpistī	cēpistis	cēperis	cēperitis
cēpit	cēpērunt (-ēre)	cēperit	cēperint
Pluperfect.		*Pluperfect.*	
cēperam	cēperāmus	cēpissem	cēpissēmus
cēperās	cēperātis	cēpissēs	cēpissētis
cēperat	cēperant	cēpisset	cēpissent

INDICATIVE.

Future Perfect.

cēperō   cēperimus
cēperis   cēperitis
cēperit   cēperint

IMPERATIVE.	
SINGULAR.	PLURAL.
Pres. cape	capite
Fut. capitō	capitōte
capitō	capiuntō

INFINITIVE.

Pres. capere
Perf. cēpisse
Fut. captūrus esse

PARTICIPLE.

Pres. capiēns
Fut. captūrus

GERUND.

Gen. capiendī
Dat. capiendō
Acc. capiendum
Abl. capiendō

SUPINE.

Acc. captum   *Abl.* captū

31.   PASSIVE VOICE.—**Capior,** *I am taken.*

PRINCIPAL PARTS : capior, capī, captus sum

INDICATIVE.		SUBJUNCTIVE.	
Present.		*Present.*	
SINGULAR.	PLURAL.	SINGULAR.	PLURAL.
capior	capimur	capiar	capiāmur
caperis	capiminī	capiāris (-re)	capiāminī
capitur	capiuntur	capiātur	capiantur
Imperfect.		*Imperfect.*	
capiēbar	capiēbāmur	caperer	caperēmur
capiēbāris (-re)	capiēbāminī	caperēris (-re)	caperēminī
capiēbātur	cabiēbantur	caperētur	caperentur

INDICATIVE.		SUBJUNCTIVE.

Future.

capiar	capiēmur
capiēris (-re)	capiēminī
capiētur	capientur

Perfect.		*Perfect.*	
captus sum	captī sumus	captus sim	captī sīmus
captus es	captī estis	captus sīs	captī sītis
captus est	captī sunt	captus sit	captī sint

Pluperfect.		*Pluperfect.*	
captus eram	captī erāmus	captus essem	captī essēmus
captus erās	captī erātis	captus essēs	captī essētis
captus erat	captī erant	captus esset	captī essent

Future Perfect.		INFINITIVE.
captus erō	captī erimus	*Pres.* capī
captus eris	captī eritis	*Perf.* captus esse
captus erit	captī erunt	*Fut.* captum īrī

IMPERATIVE.		PARTICIPLE.
SINGULAR.	PLURAL.	*Perf.* captus
Pres. capere	capiminī	*Fut.* capiendus (*Gerundive*)
Fut. capitor		
capitor	capiuntor	

Fourth Conjugation.

32. ACTIVE VOICE.—**Audio,** *I hear.*

PRINCIPAL PARTS : audiō, audīre, audīvī, audītum.

INDICATIVE.		SUBJUNCTIVE.	
Present.		*Present.*	
SINGULAR.	PLURAL.	SINGULAR.	PLURAL.
audiō	audīmus	audiam	audiāmus
audīs	audītis	audiās	audiātis
audit	audiunt	audiat	audiant

INDICATIVE.		SUBJUNCTIVE.	
Imperfect.		*Imperfect.*	
audiēbam	audiēbāmus	audīrem	audīrēmus
audiēbās	audiēbātis	audīres	audīrētis
audiēbat	audiēbant	audīret	audīrent

Future.	
audiam	audiēmus
audiēs	audiētis
audiet	audient

Perfect.		*Perfect.*	
audīvī	audīvimus	audīverim	audīverimus
audīvistī	audīvistis	audīveris	audīveritis
audīvit	audīvērunt (-ēre)	audīverit	audīverint

Pluperfect.		*Pluperfect.*	
audīveram	audīverāmus	audīvissem	audīvissēmus
audīverās	audīverātis	audīvissēs	audīvissētis
audīverat	audīverant	audīvisset	audīvissent

Future Perfect.	
audīverō	audīverimus
audīveris	audīveritis
audīverit	audīverint

IMPERATIVE.

SINGULAR.	PLURAL.
Pres. audī	audīte
Fut. audītō	audītōte
audītō	audiuntō

INFINITIVE.

Pres. audīre
Perf. audīvisse
Fut. audītūrus esse

PARTICIPLE.

Pres. audiēns
Fut. audītūrus

GERUND.

Gen. audiendī
Dat. audiendō
Acc. audiendum
Abl. audiendō

SUPINE.

Acc. audītum   *Abl.* audītū

33. PASSIVE VOICE.—**Audior,** *I am heard.*

PRINCIPAL PARTS : audior, audīrī, audītus sum.

INDICATIVE.		SUBJUNCTIVE.	
Present.		*Present.*	
SINGULAR.	PLURAL.	SINGULAR.	PLURAL.
audior	audīmur	audiar	audiāmur
audīris	audīmini	audiāris (-re)	audiāminī
audītur	audiuntur	audiātur	audiantur
Imperfect.		*Imperfect.*	
audiēbar	audiēbāmur	audīrer	audīrēmur
audiēbāris (-re)	audiēbāminī	audīrēris (-re)	audīrēminī
audiēbātur	audiēbantur	audīrētur	audīrentur
Future.			
audiar	audiēmur		
audiēris (-re)	audiēminī		
audiētur	audientur		
Perfect.		*Perfect.*	
audītus sum	audītī sumus	audītus sim	audītī sīmus
audītus es	audītī estis	audītus sīs	audītī sītis
audītus est	audītī sunt	audītus sit	audītī sint
Pluperfect.		*Pluperfect.*	
audītus eram	audītī erāmus	audītus essem	audītī essēmus
audītus erās	audītī erātis	audītus essēs	audītī essētis
audītus erat	audītī erant	audītus esset	audītī essent
Future Perfect.			
audītus erō	audītī erimus		
audītus eris	audītī eritis		
audītus erit	audītī erunt		

INFINITIVE.

Pres. audīrī
Perf. audītus esse
Fut. audītum īrī

IMPERATIVE.		PARTICIPLE.
SINGULAR.	PLURAL.	*Perf.* audītus
Pres. audīre	audīminī	*Fut.* audiendus (*Gerundive*)
Fut. audītor		
audītor	audiuntor	

34. Active Periphrastic Conjugation.

Laudātūrus sum, *I am about to praise.*

INDICATIVE.		SUBJUNCTIVE.
Pres.	laudātūrus sum	*Pres.* laudātūrus sim
Imp.	laudātūrus eram	*Imp.* laudātūrus essem
Fut.	laudātūrus erō	
Perf.	laudātūrus fuī	*Perf.* laudātūrus fuerim
Plup.	laudātūrus fueram	*Plup.* laudātūrus fuissem
F. Perf.	laudātūrus fuerō	

INFINITIVE.

Pres. laudātūrus esse

Perf. laudātūrus fuisse

35. Passive Periphrastic Conjugation.

Laudandus sum, *I am to be praised.*

INDICATIVE.		SUBJUNCTIVE.
Pres.	laudandus sum	*Pres.* laudandus sim
Imp.	laudandus eram	*Imp.* laudandus essem
Fut.	laudandus erō	
Perf.	laudandus fuī	*Perf.* laudandus fuerim
Plup.	laudandus fueram	*Plup.* laudandus fuissem
F. Perf.	laudandus fuerō	

INFINITIVE.

Pres. laudandus esse

Perf. laudandus fuisse

18

36.   **Deponent Verbs.**

PRINCIPAL PARTS.

CONJ.   I.   hortor, hortārī, hortātus sum, *exhort.*
CONJ. II.   vereor, verērī, veritus sum, *fear.*
CONJ. III.   sequor, sequī, secūtus sum, *follow.*
CONJ. IV.   potior, potīrī, potītus sum, *become master of.*

INDICATIVE.

	I.	II.	III.	IV.
Pres.	hortor	vereor	sequor	potior
	hortāris	verēris	sequeris	potīris
	hortātur	verētur	sequitur	potītur
	hortāmur	verēmur	sequimur	potīmur
	hortāminī	verēminī	sequiminī	potīminī
	hortantur	verentur	sequuntur	potiuntur
Impf.	hortābar	verēbar	sequēbar	potiēbar
Fut.	hortābor	verēbor	sequar	potiar
Perf.	hortātus sum	veritus sum	secūtus sum	potītus sum
Plup.	hortātus eram	veritus eram	secūtus eram	potītus eram
F. P.	hortātus erō	veritus erō	secūtus erō	potītus erō

SUBJUNCTIVE.

Pres.	horter	verear	sequar	potiar
Impf.	hortārer	verērer	sequerer	potīrer
Perf.	hortātus sim	veritus sim	secūtus sim	potītus sim
Plup.	hortātus essem	veritus essem	secūtus essem	potītus essem

IMPERATIVE.

Pres.	hortāre	verēre	sequere	potīre
Fut.	hortātor	verētor	sequitor	potītor

INFINITIVE.

Pres.	hortārī	verērī	sequī	potīrī
Perf.	hortātus esse	veritus esse	secūtus esse	potītus esse
Fut.	hortātūrus esse	veritūrus esse	secūtūrus esse	potītūrus esse

PARTICIPLES.

Pres.	hortāns	verēns	sequēns	potiēns
Fut.	hortātūrus	veritūrus	secūtūrus	potitūrus
Perf.	hortātus	veritus	secūtus	potītus
Ger.	hortandus	verendus	sequendus	potiendus

GERUND.

hortandī   verendī   sequendī   potiendī
hortandō, *etc.*   verendō, *etc.*   sequendō, *etc.*   potiendō, *etc.*

SUPINE.

hortātum, -ū   veritum, -ū   secūtum, -ū   potītum, -ū

Irregular Verbs.

37.   **Sum,** *I am.*

PRINCIPAL PARTS : **sum, esse, fuī.**

INDICATIVE.		SUBJUNCTIVE.	
Present.		*Present.*	
SINGULAR.	PLURAL.	SINGULAR.	PLURAL.
sum	sumus	sim	sīmus
es	estis	sīs	sītis
est	sunt	sit	sint
Imperfect.		*Imperfect.*	
eram	erāmus	essem	essēmus
erās	erātis	essēs	essētis
erat	erant	esset	essent
Future.			
erō	erimus		
eris	eritis		
erit	erunt		

INDICATIVE.		SUBJUNCTIVE.	
Perfect.		*Perfect.*	
fuī	fuimus	fuerim	fuerimus
fuistī	fuistis	fueris	fueritis
fuit	fuērunt (-ēre)	fuerit	fuerint
Pluperfect.		*Pluperfect.*	
fueram	fuerāmus	fuissem	fuissēmus
fuerās	fuerātis	fuissēs	fuissētis
fuerat	fuerant	fuisset	fuissent
Future Perfect.			
fuerō	fuerimus		
fueris	fueritis		
fuerit	fuerint		

IMPERATIVE.

SINGULAR.	PLURAL.
Pres. es	este
Fut. estō	estōte
estō	suntō

INFINITIVE.
Pres. esse
Perf. fuisse
Fut. futūrus esse

PARTICIPLE.
futūrus

38. **Possum,** *I am able, I can.*

PRINCIPAL PARTS : **possum, posse, potuī.**

INDICATIVE.
Pres. possum, potes, potest
possumus, potestis, possunt
Imp. poteram
Fut. poterō
Perf. potuī
Plup. potueram
F. Perf. potuerō

SUBJUNCTIVE.
possim, possīs, *etc.*

possem, possēs, *etc.*

potuerim
potuissem

INFINITIVE.
Pres. posse
Perf. potuisse

PARTICIPLE.
Pres. potēns

39. **Fīō,** *I am made, become.*

PRINCIPAL PARTS : **fīō, fierī, factus sum.**

	INDICATIVE.	SUBJUNCTIVE.
Pres.	fīō, fīs, fit	fīam, fīās, *etc.*
	fīmus, fītis, fīunt	
Imp.	fīēbam	fierem
Fut.	fīam, fīēs, *etc.*	
Perf.	factus sum	factus sim
Plup.	factus eram	factus essem
F. Perf.	factus erō	

	IMPERATIVE.	PARTICIPLE.
Pres.	fī, fīte	*Perf.* factus
		Fut. faciendus (*Gerundive*)
	INFINITIVE.	
Pres.	fierī	
Perf.	factus esse	
Fut.	factum īrī	

40. **Eō,** *I go.*

PRINCIPAL PARTS : **eō, īre, īvī, itum.**

	INDICATIVE.	SUBJUNCTIVE.
Pres.	eō, īs, it,	eam
	īmus, ītis, eunt	
Imp.	ībam	īrem
Fut.	ībō	
Perf.	īvī (iī)	īverim (ierim)
Plup.	īveram (ieram)	īvissem (īssem)
F. Perf.	īverō (ierō)	

	IMPERATIVE.	PARTICIPLE.
Pres.	ī, īte	*Pres.* iēns (*Gen.* euntis)
Fut.	ītō, ītōte	*Fut.* itūrus
	ītō, euntō	

INFINITIVE.		GERUND.
Pres.	īre	eundi, *etc.*
Perf.	īvisse (īsse)	SUPINE
Fut.	itūrus esse	itum, -ū

41.   Ferō, *I bear, carry.*

PRINCIPAL PARTS : **ferō, ferre, tulī, lātum.**

ACTIVE VOICE.

INDICATIVE.		SUBJUNCTIVE.
Pres.	ferō, fers, fert,	feram, ferās, *etc.*
	ferimus, fertis, ferunt	
Imp.	ferēbam	ferrem
Fut.	feram, ferēs, *etc.*	
Perf.	tulī	tulerim
Plup.	tuleram	tulissem
F. Perf.	tulerō	

IMPERATIVE.				PARTICIPLE.
Pres.	fer	ferte	*Pres.*	ferēns
Fut.	fertō	fertōte	*Fut.*	lātūrus
	fertō	feruntō		

GERUND.

ferendī, *etc.*

INFINITIVE.	
Pres.	ferre
Perf.	tulisse
Fut.	lātūrus esse

SUPINE.

lātum, -ū

PASSIVE VOICE

INDICATIVE.		SUBJUNCTIVE.
Pres.	feror, ferris, fertur	ferar, ferāris, *etc.*
	ferimur, feriminī, feruntur	
Imp.	ferēbar	ferrer
Fut.	ferar, ferēris, *etc.*	

INDICATIVE.	SUBJUNCTIVE.
Perf. lātus sum	lātus sim
Plup. lātus eram	lātus essem
F. Perf. lātus erō	

IMPERATIVE.	INFINITIVE.
Pres. ferre, feriminī	*Pres.* ferrī
Fut. fertor	*Perf.* lātus esse
fertor, feruntor	*Fut.* lātum īrī

PARTICIPLE.

Perf. lātus

Fut. ferendus (*Gerundive*)

42. **Volō,** *I am willing;* **Nōlō,** *I am unwilling;* **Mālō,** *I prefer.*

PRINCIPAL PARTS : {
volō, velle, voluī.
nōlō, nōlle, nōluī.
mālō, mālle, māluī.
}

INDICATIVE.

Pres.	volō	nōlō	mālō
	vīs	nōn vīs	māvīs
	volt	nōn volt	māvolt
	volumus	nōlumus	mālumus
	voltis	nōn voltis	māvoltis
	volunt	nōlunt	mālunt
Imp.	volēbam	nōlēbam	mālēbam
Fut.	volam	nōlam	mālam
Perf.	voluī	nōluī	māluī
Plup.	volueram	nōlueram	mālueram
F. Perf.	voluerō	nōluerō	māluerō

SUBJUNCTIVE.

Pres.	velim	nōlim	mālim
Imp.	vellem	nōllem	māllem
Perf.	voluerim	nōluerim	māluerim
Plup.	voluissem	nōluissem	māluissem

IMPERATIVE.

Pres.	nōlī	nōlīte
Fut.	nōlītō	nōlītōte
	nōlītō	noluntō

INFINITIVE.

Pres.	velle	nōlle	mālle
Perf.	voluisse	nōluisse	māluisse

PARTICIPLE.

Pres.　volēns　　　　　　　　　　nōlēns

43. Defective Verbs.

Coepī, *I have begun.*　　**Meminī,** *I remember.*　　**Odī,** *I hate.*

INDICATIVE.

Perf.	coepī	meminī	ōdī
Plup.	coeperam	memineram	ōderam
F.Perf.	coeperō	meminerō	ōderō

SUBJUNCTIVE.

Perf.	coeperim	meminerim	ōderim
Plup.	coepissem	meminissem	ōdissem

IMPERATIVE.

Sing. mementō　　　　　　　*Plur.* mementōte

INFINITIVE.

Perf.	coepisse	meminisse	ōdisse
Fut.	coeptūrus esse		ōsūrus esse

PARTICIPLE.

Perf.	coeptus, *begun*		ōsus
Fut.	coeptūrus		ōsūrus

44.   PREPOSITIONS

I. With the accusative :

ad,	*to*	extrā,	*outside*	prope,	*near*
adversus,	*against*	in,	*into*	propter,	*on account of*
adversum,	*toward*	īnfrā,	*below*	secundum,	*next after*
ante,	*before*	inter,	*among*	sub,	*under*
apud,	*at, near*	intrā,	*inside*	subter,	*beneath*
circā, } circum, }	*around*	iūxtā,	*near*	super,	*above*
		ob,	*on account of*	suprā,	*abcve*
circiter,	*about*	penes,	*in power of*	trāns,	*across*
cis, } citrā, }	*on this side*	per,	*through*	ultrā,	*beyond*
		pōne,	*behind*	versus,	*toward*
contrā,	*opposite*	post,	*after*		
ergā,	*toward*	praeter,	*beyond*		

II. With the ablative :

ā, ab, abs,	*away from, from, by*	prae,	*before, in comparison with*
absque,	*without*	prō,	*before, for*
cōram,	*in the presence of*	sine,	*without*
cum,	*with*	sub,	*under*
dē,	*down from, from*	subter,	*beneath*
ē, ex,	*out of, from*	super,	*above*
in,	*in*	tenus,	*as far as*

NOTE.—**In, sub, subter** and **super** are used with either the accusative or ablative. With the accusative, **in** and **sub** denote *motion to* a place; with the ablative, *rest in* a place.

45. CONJUNCTIONS

I. **Coördinate** (connecting similar constructions).

et, -que, atque (ac), *and*
etiam, quoque, *also*

aut—aut, *either—or*
neque (nec), *and not;* **neque—neque,** *neither—nor*
sīve—sīve, *whether—or*
vel—vel, *either—or*

autem, *moreover;* **enim, nam,** *for;* **sed,** *but*
tamen, *nevertheless*

II. **Subordinate** (connecting subordinate with principal constructions).

1. Temporal, denoting time : **antequam, priusquam,** *before;* **postquam,** *after;* **dum, dōnec, quod,** *while, as long as, until;* **simul,** *as soon as;* **cum, ubi,** *when.*
2. Causal, denoting cause : **cum,** *since;* **quod, quia, quoniam, quandō,** *because.*
3. Conditional, denoting condition : **sī,** *if;* **sīn,** *but if;* **nisi,** *if not, unless.*
4. Concessive, granting something : **cum, etsī, quamquam, quamvīs,** *although.*
5. Comparative, denoting comparison : **quam,** *than;* **ut,** *as.*
6. Final, denoting purpose : **ut (utī), quō** *that;* **nē, quīn, quōminus,** *that not.*
7. Consecutive, denoting result : **ut,** *(so) that.*

PRINCIPAL RULES OF SYNTAX

46. Rules of Agreement.

1. A noun used as an appositive of another noun denoting the same person or thing agrees with it in *case.*

2. Adjectives, whether attributive or predicate, agree with their nouns in *gender, number* and *case.*

3. Pronouns agree with their antecedents in *gender, number* and *person.*

4. A finite verb agrees with its subject in *number* and *person.*

47. Nominative Case.

1. The *subject* of a finite verb is in the nominative case.

2. A *predicate noun* is in the nominative case after the verbs *be, become, seem,* etc., and the passive verbs *be made, be called, be chosen,* etc.*

48. Vocative Case.—The name of the person or thing *addressed* is in the vocative case.

49. Genitive Case.

1. A noun limiting the meaning of another noun, and not meaning the same thing, is in the genitive case. The word in the genitive may denote *possession, description, material,* or *the whole* of which a part is taken.

2. Words denoting a part may be followed by a noun in the genitive denoting *the whole.*

3. An objective genitive is used to complete the meaning of adjectives of *desire, knowledge, memory, skill,* etc.

4. An objective genitive may be used with verbs of *remembering* and *forgetting.*

5. A genitive may be used with verbs of *accusing, condemning,* etc., to denote the charge.

6. A genitive is used with impersonal verbs of *feeling.*

50. Dative Case.

1. The dative denotes the indirect object—

(*a*) With *transitive* verbs in connection with the accusative of the direct.

---

* When these verbs are in the infinitive, a predicate noun agrees with the subject of the infinitive in the accusative case.

(*b*) With verbs meaning *favor, help, please, trust, believe, persuade, command, obey, serve, resist, envy, threaten, pardon, spare.* (These verbs in Latin may be intransitive.)

(*c*) With verbs compounded with *ad, ante, con, dē, in, inter, ob, post, prae, prō, sub, super.*

2. The dative of the *possessor* is used with the verb **sum**.

3. The dative of the *agent* is used with a verb in the passive periphrastic conjugation.

4. The dative is used with adjectives of *nearness, fitness, likeness,* etc., to denote the object toward which the quality is directed.

5. A noun in the dative may denote the *purpose* or *result* of an action.

6. A noun in the dative may denote the object to which something is of interest, and is called a dative of *reference.*

51. Accusative Case.

1. The *direct object* of a verb is in the accusative case.

2. A *predicate* accusative may be used after the active of the verbs *make, call, choose,* etc. (together with a direct object) ; and after the infinitive **esse.**

3. A *secondary object* in the accusative (together with a direct object) may be used with verbs meaning *ask, demand, teach, conceal;* and after transitive verbs compounded with **trāns.**

4. A noun in the accusative may be the object of a preposition.

5. The subject of an infinitive is in the accusative.

6. A noun denoting the *place to which* is in the accusative with **ad** or **in**; but the names of *towns, small islands,* **domus** and **rūs** omit the preposition.

7. A noun denoting *duration of time* is in the accusative.

8. A noun denoting *extent of space* is in the accusative.

52. Ablative Case.

1. A noun in the ablative, with or without **ab, dē** or **ex,** may denote *separation.*

2. A noun in the ablative with the preposition **ab** may denote the *agent* by whom something is done.

3. Comparatives without **quam** are followed by a noun in the ablative.

4. A noun denoting the *means* or *instrument* of an action is in the ablative. This includes the ablative used with **ūtor, fruor, fungor, potior, vēscor.**

5. A noun in the ablative with **cum** may denote the *manner* of an action. (**Cum** may be omitted when there is an adjective modifying the noun.)

6. A noun in the ablative may denote the *cause* of an action.

7. A noun in the ablative with **cum** may denote *the person with whom* anything is done. (*Ablative of accompaniment.*)

8. A noun in the ablative may denote *degree of difference.*

9. A noun in the ablative modified by an adjective may *describe* another noun. (*Ablative of description.*)

10. A noun in the ablative may denote the *respect* in which anything is true. (*Ablative of specification.*)

11. A noun in the ablative, together with a participle, adjective or another noun, may denote the *time, cause* or *condition,* etc., of an action. (*Ablative absolute.*)

12. A noun in the ablative with **in** may denote the *place in which;* but the singular of names of towns, small islands, **domus** and **rūs** is in the locative case.

13. A noun in the ablative, with **ab, dē** or **ex,** may denote the *place from which;* but the preposition is omitted with the names of towns, small islands, **domus** and **rūs.**

14. A noun in the ablative may denote *time when* or *within which*.

NOTE.—The rules for the cases of nouns apply also to pronouns, except when the latter are used as adjectives.

53. The Indicative in Principal Clauses.—The indicative is used in direct statements of fact and questions of fact.

54. The Indicative in Subordinate Clauses.

1. The indicative is used in *relative* clauses that state or determine what person or thing.
2. The indicative is used in *relative* clauses that add a fact not necessary to the main statement.
3. The indicative is used in *causal* clauses beginning with **quod, quia, quoniam** or **quandō,** when the speaker or writer gives his own reason.
4. The indicative is used in *temporal* clauses beginning with **ubi, ut, simul, postquam;** and sometimes **cum, dum, quoad, antequam** or **priusquam.**
5. The indicative is used in *conditional* clauses when the condition is stated as a fact.
6. The indicative is used in *concessive* clauses beginning with **quamquam,** etc.
7. The indicative is used in a *parenthetical* clause or a clause of *comparison* beginning with **ut.**

55. The Subjunctive in Principal Clauses.

1. The subjunctive is used to express an *exhortation* in the first person plural of the present tense.
2. The subjunctive is used to express *command* in the third person of either number, present tense.
3. The subjunctive with **nē** is used to express *negative command* in the second person of either number, present or perfect tense.

4. The subjunctive, generally with **utinam,** is used to express a *wish* or *desire.*

5. The subjunctive may be used to express *a possibility.*

56. The Subjunctive in Subordinate Clauses.

1. The subjunctive with **ut, nē, quī** or **quō** may express *purpose.*

2. The subjunctive with **ut,** or **ut nōn,** may express *result.*

3. The subjunctive with **quī** may *describe* an antecedent not otherwise defined ; that is, may state what sort of person or thing the antecedent is.

4. The subjunctive may be used with **cum, antequam, priusquam, dum, donec, quoad,** to express *time.*

5. The subjunctive may be used with **cum, quod, quia, quoniam** or **quandō** to express *cause.*

6. The subjunctive may be used with **cum, quamvīs,** etc., to express *concession.*

7. The subjunctive is used with **sī** to express a future *condition* less probable, or condition contrary to fact.

8. The subjunctive is used in *indirect questions.*

57. The Imperative.—The imperative is used to express *command* in the second person of the present tense, and the second and third persons of the future.

58. The Infinitive.

1. The infinitive when used as a noun may be a subject, complement, appositive or predicate noun.

2. An infinitive when used as a verb has its subject in the accusative, except that in lively narration the subject may be in the nominative.

59. Indirect Discourse. — In indirect discourse the verb of a principal declarative clause is in the *infinitive ;* the verb of a subordinate clause is in the *subjunctive.*

60. Sequence of Tenses.—Principal tenses follow principal tenses; historical follow historical.

61. Adverbs.—An adverb modifies a verb, adjective or another adverb.

62. Prepositions.—A preposition shows a relation between a noun in the accusative or ablative and some other word.

63. Conjunctions.—A conjunction connects words, phrases or clauses of equal rank ; or principal with subordinate clauses.

LATIN–ENGLISH VOCABULARY

NOTE.—The figure 1 in connection with some verbs indicates that the principal parts are formed like those of **laudō**; 2, that they are formed like the parts of **moneō**; and 4, like those of **audiō**.

A

A., abbreviation for **Aulus**.

ā, ab, prep. with abl., *away from, from, by, on the side of ;* as adv., *off ;* as a prefix, *away.*

abdō, -dere, -didī, -ditum, *put away, hide.*

abdūcō, -dūcere, -dūxī, -ductum [ab + dūcō], *lead away.*

abstineō, -tinēre, -tinuī, -tentum [abs + teneō], *hold from, keep from.*

absum, -esse, āfuī [ab + sum], *be away, be distant.*

ac, *see* **atque** (**ac** is used only before consonants).

accēdō, -cēdere, -cessī, -cessum [ad + cēdō, *make way*], *go to, approach, be added.*

acceptus, -a, -um, p.p. of **accipiō,** as adj., *acceptable, pleasing.*

accidō, -cidere, -cidī [ad + cadō], *fall to, befall, happen.*

accipiō, -cipere, -cēpī, -ceptum [ad + capiō], *take to, receive, accept.*

accurrō, -currere, -currī (-cucurrī), -cursum [ad + currō, *run*], *run to, hasten to.*

accūsō, 1, *accuse, find fault with.*

aciēs, -ēī, F., *edge, line, battle line, army.*

ācriter, adv., *sharply.*

ad, prep. with acc., *to, toward, against, near ;* adv. (with numerals), *about ;* as prefix, *to.*

addūcō, -dūcere, -dūxī, -ductum (ad + dūcō), *lead to, bring to, influence.*

adficiō, -ficere, -fēcī, -fectum [ad + faciō], *do to, affect ;* with **dolor,** *fill with.*

adfīnitas, -ātis, F., *alliance by marriage.*

adgredior, -gredī, -gressus sum [ad + grādior, *step, go*], *go toward, attack.*

adhibeō, -ēre, -uī, -itum [ad + habeō], *bring in, summon.*

admīror, 1, *wonder at, admire.*

admittō, -mittere, -mīsī, -missum [ad + mittō], *send to, let in, let go, allow.*

adolēscentia, -ae, F., *youth.*

adorior, -orīrī, -ortus sum [ad + orior], *rise against, attack.*

adscīscō, -scīscere, -scīvī, -scītum, *take to, receive.*

adsum, -esse, -fuī [ad + sum], *be at hand, be near, be present.*

19

adventus, -ūs, M. [veniō], *a coming
to, arrival, approach.*

advǝrsus, -a, -um, p.p. of advertō,
as adj., *opposite, unfavorable.*

advertō, -vertere, -vertī, -versum
[ad + vertō, *turn*], *turn to, turn
toward.*

aedificium, -ī, N., *a building.*

aegerrimē, adv. (sup. of aegrē),
with the greatest difficulty.

Aemilius, -ī, M., *Lucius Aemilius,*
one of Caesar's officers.

aequō, I, *make equal.*

aestās, -ātis, F., *summer.*

ager, agrī, M., *field, territory.*

āgmen, -inis, N., *an army* (on the
march).

agō, agere, ēgī, āctum, *put in motion, drive, do, discuss.*

aliēnus, -a, -um [alius], *another's,
foreign, unfavorable.*

aliquis (-quī), -qua, -quid (-quod),
some, any.

aliter, adv. [alius], *otherwise.*

alius, -a, -ud, *another, other* (of more
than two).

Allobrogēs, -um, M., a Gallic tribe
between the Rhone and Isère.

alō, alere, aluī, alitum (altum), *nour-
ish, support.*

Alpēs, -ium, F., *the Alps.*

alter, -era, -erum, *the other* (of two) ;
alter—alter, *the one—the other ;*
pl. *one party—the other.*

altitūdō, -inis, F. [altus], *height,
depth.*

altus, -a, -um, *high, deep.*

Ambarrī, -ōrum, M., allies of the
Haedui, on the Saone (Arar).

amīcitia, -ae, F. [amīcus], *friendship.*

amīcus, -a, -um, *friendly ;* as noun,
M., *friend.*

āmittō, -mittere, -mīsī, -missum,
[ā + mittō], *send away, let go,
lose.*

amor, -ōris, M., *love, desire.*

amplius (comp. of amplē), adv., *farther, longer, more.*

amplus, -a, -um, *large, ample.*

anceps, -cipitis [ambō, *both* + caput],
two-headed, twofold, doubtful.

angustiae, -ārum, F. [angustus],
narrowness, a narrow pass.

angustus, -a, -um, *narrow.*

animadvertō, -vertere, -vertī, -ver-
sum [animum advertō], *attend to,
punish.*

animus, -ī, M., *soul, mind, feeling,
spirit, courage.*

annus, -ī, M., *a year.*

annuus, -a, -um, *annual, for a year.*

ante, adv., or prep. with acc., *before.*

anteā, adv., *before, formerly.*

antīquus, -a, -um [ante], *ancient,
former.*

aperiō, -īre, -uī, -tum, *uncover, open,
disclose.*

apertus, -a, -um, p.p. as adj., *open,
exposed, unprotected.*

appellō, I, *call* (by name), *address.*

Aprīlis, -e, *of April.*

apud, prep. with acc., *among, near,
with.*

Aquilēia, -ae, F., *Aquileia* (a town at
the head of the Adriatic).

Aquītānī, -ōrum, M., *the Aquitani,
Aquitanians,* a nation of southern
Gaul.

Aquītānia, -ae, F., *Aquitania.*

Arar, Araris, M., *the Saône* (a river
of Gaul).

arbitror, I, *think, judge.*

Ariovistus, -i, M., a German chief.

arma, -ōrum, N., *arms* (equipment).

ascendō, ascendere, ascendī, ascēnsum, *climb, ascend.*

ascēnsus, -ūs, M., *a climbing up, ascent.*

atque (ac), conj., *and also, as.*

attingō, -tingere, -tigī, -tāctum [ad+tangō, *touch*], *touch upon, border upon, reach.*

auctōritās, -ātis, F., *influence, authority, advice.*

audācia, -ae, F. [audāx], *boldness.*

audācter, adv., *boldly.*

audāx, adj., *bold.*

audeō, audēre, ausus sum, (*be bold*), *dare.*

audiō, 4, *hear.*

augeō, augēre, auxī, auctum, *increase.*

Aulus (abbr. A.), *Aulus,* a Roman name.

aut, conj., aut—aut, *either—or.*

autem, conj., *on the other hand, but.*

auxilium, -ī, N., *help, aid;* pl. *auxiliaries.*

āvertō, -vertere, -vertī, -versum [ā+vertō, *turn*], *turn off, turn away.*

avus, -ī, M., *grandfather.*

Axona, -ae, F., a river of Gaul, *the Aisne.*

B

Belgae, -ārum, M., *the Belgae, Belgians,* a nation of northern Gaul.

bellō, 1, *make war, fight.*

bellicōsus,-a, -um [bellum], *warlike.*

bellum, -ī, N., *war.*

bene, adv. [bonus], *well.*

beneficium, -ī, N., *well-doing, kindness, benefit.*

Bibracte, -is, N., *Bibracte,* a town of the Haedui.

biduum, -ī, N. [diēs], *two days.*

biennium, -ī, N. [bi + annus], *two years.*

bipartītō, adv. [pars], *in two divisions.*

Biturīgēs, -um, M., *the Bituriges,* a tribe of central Gaul.

Bōiī, -ōrum, M., *the Boii,* a tribe of central Gaul.

bonitās, -ātis, F. [bonus], *goodness, fertility.*

bonus, -a, -um, *good.*

bracchium, -ī, N., *the forearm.*

brevis, -e, *short.*

Britannia, -ae, F., *Britain.*

C

C. for G., abbr. of *Gaius.*

cadō, cadere, cecidī, cāsum, *fall.*

Caesar, Caesaris, M., Gāius Iūlius Caesar, a Roman general, statesman and writer ; born 100 (?) B.C., assassinated 44 B.C.; governor of Gaul 58–49 B.C.

calamitās, -ātis, F., *disaster, defeat.*

capiō, capere, cēpī, captum, *take, seize.*

caput, capitis, N., *head.*

carrus, -ī, M., *cart.*

Cassiānus, -a, -um, *Cassian, of Cassius.*

Cassius, -ī, M., *Lucius Cassius,* a Roman general.

castellum, -ī, N., *a fortress, redoubt.*

Casticus, -ī, M., *Casticus,* a chief of the Sequani.

castra, -ōrum, N. [castrum, *fort*], *a fortified camp, camp.*

cāsus, -ūs [cadō], (*a falling*), *accident, calamity, chance.*

Catamantāloedēs, -is, M., a chief of the Sequani.

Caturīgēs, -um, M., *the Caturiges,* · an Alpine tribe.

causa, -ae, F., *cause, reason.*

caveō, cavēre, cāvī, cautum, *take care, be on one's guard.*

celeriter (celerius, celerrimē), adv., *quickly.*

Celtae, -ārum, M., *the Celts,* inhabitants of central Gaul.

cēnsus, -ūs, M., *enumeration.*

centum, indecl. adj., *a hundred.*

certus, -a, -um, *sure, certain;* certiōrem facere, *to inform.*

Ceutronēs, -um, M., *the Ceutrones,* an Alpine tribe.

cibārius, -a, -um, *pertaining to food;* as noun, cibāria, -ōrum, N., *food, provisions.*

circiter, adv., *about.*

circuitus, -us, M. [circum + eō], *a going round, circuit.*

circum, prep. with acc., *around, about;* as prefix, *around.*

circumdūcō, -dūcere, -dūxī, -ductum [circum + dūcō], *lead around.*

circumveniō, -venīre, -vēnī, -ventum [circum + veniō], *surround.*

citerior, -ius, comp. adj. (citrā), *nearer, hither.*

citrā, adv. and prep. with acc., *this side, within.*

cīvitās, -ātis, F., *citizenship, state, citizens.*

claudō, claudere, clausī, clausum, *shut, close.*

cliēns, -entis, M. F., *client, vassal.*

coëmō, -emere, -ēmī, -ēmptum [con + emō, *buy*], *buy up, purchase.*

coepī, coepisse, defect. verb., *began.*

coërceō, -ēre, -uī, -itum, *control.*

cōgō, cōgere, coēgī, coāctum [con + agō], *drive together, collect, compel.*

cōgnōscō, -gnōscere, -gnōvī, -gnitum, *learn;* in perf., *have learned,* hence, *know.*

cohors, cohortis, F., *a cohort* (tenth part of a legion).

cohortor, I, [con + hortor], *exhort, encourage.*

collis, -is, M., *hill.*

colō, colere, coluī, cultum, *till, cultivate.*

combūrō, -ūrere, -ussī, -ūstum [con + ūrō], *burn up, consume.*

commemorō, I [con + memorō], *call to mind, recount, mention.*

commeō, I, *go back and forth;* with ad, *resort to, visit.*

committō, -mittere, -mīsī, -missum [con + mittō], *send together, commit, join, permit.*

commodē, adv., *conveniently.*

commonefaciō, -facere, -fēcī, -factum, *remind.*

commoveō, -movēre, -movī, -mōtum [con + moveō], *move deeply, disturb, alarm.*

commūniō, 4 [con + mūniō], *fortify strongly.*

commūtātiō, -ōnis, F., *change.*

commūtō, I [con + mūtō, *change*], *change entirely.*

comparō, I [con + parō], *get ready, prepare, procure.*

comperiō, -perīre, -perī, -pertum, *ascertain.*

complector, -plectī, -plexus sum, *embrace.*

compleō, -plēre, -plēvī, -plētum, *fill up, fill.*

complūrēs, -a (-ia), *many, very many.*

comportō, ı [con + portō], *bring together.*

con- (com-, comb-), prefix, *together.*

cōnātum, -ī, N., or cōnātus, -ūs, M., *trial, attempt.*

concēdō, -cēdere, -cessī, -cessum [con + cēdō, *make way*], *yield, concede, grant, allow.*

concīdo, -cīdere, -cīdi, -cīsum [con + caedō, *cut*], *cut down, kill.*

conciliō, ı, *bring together, win over, conciliate.*

concilium, -ī, N., *meeting, assembly, council.*

concursus, -ūs, M., *running together, onset.*

condiciō, -ōnis, F., (*a speaking together*), *terms, terms of agreement.*

condōnō, ı [con + dōnō, *give*], *pardon (for the sake of).*

condūcō, -dūcere, -dūxī, -ductum [con + dūcō], *bring together, hire.*

cōnferō, cōnferre, contulī, collātum [con + ferō], *bring together, collect, compare;* sē cōnferre, *to retreat.*

confertus, -a, -um, *crowded, in close order.*

cōnficiō, -ficere, -fēcī, -fectum [con + faciō], *do thoroughly, accomplish, complete.*

cōnfīdō, -fīdere, -fīsus sum [con + fīdō, *trust*], *trust in, rely on.*

cōnfīrmō, ı [con + fīrmō, *strengthen*], *make firm, establish, assure, declare.*

coniciō, -icere, -iēcī, -iectum [con + iaciō], *throw together, hurl.*

coniūrātiō, -ōnis, F. [coniūrō], *conspiracy.*

coniūrō, ı [con + iūrō, *swear together*], *conspire.*

conligō, ı [con + ligō, *bind*], *bind together.*

conlocō [con + locō, *place*], *place together, station;* with nūptum, *give in marriage.*

conloquor, -loquī, -locutus sum [con + loquor], *talk together, confer.*

cōnor, ı, *try, attempt.*

conquīrō, -quīrere, -quīsīvī, -quīsītum [con + quaerō], *search for.*

cōnsanguineus, -a, -um [sanguis, *blood*], *related by blood;* as noun, M., *kinsman.*

cōnscīscō, -scīscere, -scīvī, -scītum [con + scīscō], *decree, resolve :* with mortem, *commit suicide.*

cōnscius, -a, -um, *knowing, conscious.*

cōnscrībō, -scrībere, -scrīpsī, -scriptum [con + scrībō], *write together, enroll, levy.*

cōnsequor, -sequī, -secūtus sum [con + sequor], *follow up, pursue, obtain.*

Cōnsidius, -ī, M., *Considius,* a Roman soldier.

cōnsīdō, -sīdere, -sēdī, -sessum [con + sīdō, *sit down*], *encamp, settle.*

cōnsilium, -ī, N., *counsel, plan.*

cōnsistō, -sistere, -stitī, -stitum [con + sistō, *stand*], *take a stand, stop, remain.*

cōnsōlor, ı, *console, cheer.*

cōnspectus, -ūs, M., (*a looking at*), *sight.*

cōnspiciō, -spicere, -spēxī, -spectum [con + speciō, *look*], *catch sight of, see.*

cōnspicor, ı, *perceive.*

cōnstituō, -stituere, -stituī, -stitū-
tum [con + statuō, *set together*],
arrange, determine, fix.
cōnsuēscō, -suēscere, -suēvī, -suētum,
become accustomed; (in. perf.) *be
accustomed, be wont.*
cōnsul, -ulis, M., *consul.*
cōnsūmō, -sūmere, -sūmpsī, -sūmptum
[con + sūmō], *destroy, consume.*
contendō, -tendere, -tendī, -tentum
[con + tendō, *stretch tight*], *strive,
fight, hasten.*
continēns, -entis, part. as noun, *con-
tinent.*
continenter, adv., *continually.*
contineō, -tinēre, -tinuī, -tentum
[con + teneō], *hold together, restrain, bound* (geographically).
contrā, prep. with acc., and adv.,
opposite, against.
contumēlia, -ae, F., *disgrace, insult.*
conveniō, -venīre, -vēnī, -ventum
[con + veniō], *come together, meet,
assemble :* convenit (impers.), *it is
fitting, it is agreed.*
conventus, -ūs, M., (*a coming together*), *assembly, meeting.*
convertō, -vertere, -vertī, -versum
[con + vertō], *turn :* signa con-
vertere, *wheel about.*
convocō, 1 [con + vocō], *call together,
summon.*
cōpia, -ae, F., *plenty;* pl. *forces,
troops.*
cōpiōsus, -a, -um, *well supplied,
wealthy.*
cornū, -ūs, N., *horn, wing* (of an
army).
cotīdiānus, -a, -um, *daily.*
cotīdiē, adv., *daily.*
Crassus, -ī, M., *Marcus Crassus,*
one of Caesar's lieutenants.

creō, 1, *create, elect.*
cremō, 1, *burn, consume.*
crēscō, crēscere, crēvī, crētum, *grow,
increase.*
cultus, -ūs, M. [colō], *civilization,
culture.*
cum, prep. with abl., *with.*
cum, conj., *when, since, although.*
cupidē, adv., *eagerly.*
cupiditās, -itis, F., *eager desire,
longing.*
cupidus, -a, -um, *desirous of.*
cupiō, -ere, -īvī (-iī), -ītum, *desire,
wish well to.*
cūrō, 1, *care for;* (with gerundive),
have (something done).
custōs, -ōdis, M. F., *guard, spy.*

D

damnō, 1, *condemn.*
dē, prep. with abl., *down from,
from, concerning, of, about;* as
prefix, *down, utterly.*
dēbeō, 2, *owe, ought.*
decem, indecl. adj., *ten.*
decimus, -a, -um, *tenth.*
dēcipiō, -cipere, -cēpī, -ceptum [dē +
capiō], *deceive, entrap.*
decuriō, -ōnis, M., *a decurion, a
commander of cavalry.*
dēditīcius, -a, -um, *surrendered;*
as noun, *prisoner.*
dēditiō, -ōnis, F., (*a giving up*), *surrender.*
dēfendō, -fendere, -fendī, -fēnsum,
keep off, defend.
dēfessus, -a, -um [dēfetīscor], p.p.
as adj , *wearied, exhausted.*
dēiciō, -icere, -iēcī, -iectum [dē + ia-
ciō], *throw down, dislodge, disap-
point.*

deinde, adv., *then, next.*

dēleō, dēlēre, dēlēvī, dēlētum, *blot out.*

dēlīberō, 1, *deliberate, ponder.*

dēligō, -ligere, -lēgī, -lēctum [dē + legō], *choose, select.*

dēminuō, -minuere, -minuī, -minūtum [minus], *lessen, diminish.*

dēmōnstrō, 1, *point out, explain.*

dēmum, adv., *at length.*

dēnique, adv., *at length, lastly.*

dēnsus, -a, -um, *dense.*

depōnō, -pōnere, -posuī, -positum, *lay aside;* with memoria, *blot out.*

dēpopulor, 1 [dē + populor], *ravage, lay waste.*

dēprecātor, -ōris, M., *mediator.*

dēsignō, 1, *indicate, designate.*

dēsistō, -sistere, -stitī, -stitum [dē + sistō, *stand*], *stand away from, abandon.*

dēspērō, 1 [dē + spērō], *be hopeless, despair.*

dēspiciō,-ere, -spēxī, -spectum [dē + speciō], *look down on, despise.*

dēstituō, -stituere, -stituī, -stitūtum [dē + statuō, *set aside*], *abandon.*

dēstringō, -stringere, -strinxī, strictum [dē + stringō, *draw off*], *unsheathe, draw.*

deterreō, 2 [dē + terreō], *frighten off, deter, prevent.*

deus, -ī, M., *a god.*

dexter, -tra, -trum, *right:* dextra (manus), *the right hand.*

dīcō, dīcere, dīxī, dictum, *say, tell, speak.*

dictiō, -ōnis, F., *(a speaking), pleading.*

diēs, -ēī, M. or F., *day, time.*

differō, differre, distulī, dīlātum [dis + ferō, *bear apart*], *differ.*

difficilis, -e [dis + facilis], *not easy, difficult.*

difficultās, -ātis, F., *difficulty.*

dīmittō, -mittere, -mīsī, -missum [dī + mittō, *send apart*], *dismiss, let go.*

dis-, dī-, prefix, *apart, not.*

discēdō, -cēdere, -cessī, -cessum [dis + cēdō, *go apart*], *depart, withdraw.*

discō, discere, didicī, *learn.*

disiciō, -icere, -iēcī, -iectum [dis + iaciō], *throw apart, break, scatter.*

dispōnō, -pōnere, -posuī, -positum, [dis + pōnō, *place apart*], *arrange, station.*

ditissimus, -a, -um (sup. of dīves), *richest.*

diū, adv., *for a long time.*

diūturnus, -a -um [diū], *of long duration, long.*

dīves, -itis, adj., *rich.*

Dīviciācus, -ī, M., a chief of the Haedui.

Dīvicō, -ōnis, M., a chief of the Helvetii.

dīvidō, -videre, -vīsī, -vīsum, *divide, separate.*

dō, dare, dedī, datum, *give.*

doleō, 2, *suffer pain, grieve.*

dolor, -ōris, M., *pain, grief.*

dolus, -ī, M., *treachery, deceit.*

domus, -ūs, F., *house, home;* domī, *at home.*

dubitō, 1, *doubt, hesitate.*

dubitātiō, -ōnis, F., *hesitation.*

dubius, -a, -um, *doubtful.*

ducentī, -ae, -a [duo + centum], *two hundred.*

dūcō, dūcere, dūxī, ductum, *lead, draw, consider.*

dum, conj., *while, until.*

Dumnorīx, -īgis, M., a chief of the Haedui.

duo, duae, duo, *two.*

duodecim [duo + decem], indecl. adj., *twelve.*

duodēvīgintī, indecl. adj., *(two from twenty), eighteen.*

dux, ducis, M. [dūcō], *leader, guide.*

E

ē, ex, prep. with abl., *out of, from;* as prefix, *out, forth.*

ēdūcō, -dūcere, -dūxī, -ductum [ē + dūcō], *lead out.*

effēminō, 1, *weaken, enervate.*

efferō, efferre, extulī, ēlātum [ex + ferō], *bear out, lift up, elate.*

ego, *I.*

ēgredior, -gredī, -gressus sum [ē + gradior, *step*], *go out, march out.*

ēgregius, -a, -um, *uncommon, remarkable.*

emō, emere, ēmī, ēmptum, *buy.*

ēmittō, -mittere, -mīsī, -missum [ē + mittō], *send forth, discharge, let go.*

enim, conj., *for.*

ēnūntiō, 1 [ē + nūntiō], *tell out, report.*

eō, īre, īvī (iī), itum, *go.*

eō, adv., *to that place, thither.*

eōdem, adv., *to the same place.*

eques, equitis, M., *horseman, knight;* pl. *cavalry.*

equester, -tris, -tre [eques], *belonging to a horseman, cavalry.*

equitātus, -ūs, M., *cavalry.*

equus, -ī, M., *horse.*

ēripiō, -ripere, -ripuī, -reptum [ē + rapiō, *seize*], *snatch away, rescue:* sē ēripere, *to escape.*

et, conj., *and.*

etiam, conj., *and also, even.*

etsī, conj., *even if, although.*

ēvellō, -vellere, -vellī, -vulsum [e + vellō, *pluck*], *pull out.*

ex, *see* ē.

exemplum, -ī, N., *example.*

exercitus, -ūs, M. [exerceō, *exercise*], *a trained body, an army.*

exeō, -īre, -īvī (-iī), -itum [ex + eō], *go out.*

exīstimō, 1, *reckon, think.*

exīstimātiō, -ōnis, F., *estimate, opinion.*

expediō, 4 [pēs], *disentangle;* perf. part., *unencumbered, (of troops) without baggage.*

explōrātor, -ōris, M., *scout, spy.*

expūgnō, 1 [ex + pūgnō], *take by storm, capture.*

exsequor, -sequī, -secūtus sum [ex + sequor], *follow out, follow up, enforce.*

exspectō, 1, *look out for, await, expect.*

extrā, adv. and prep. with acc., *outside of, beyond.*

extrēmus, -a, -um, *outermost, farthest, extreme.*

exūrō, -ūrere, -ussī, -ūstum [ex + ūrō, *burn*], *burn up.*

F

facile, adv., *easily.*

facilis, -e, *easy.*

faciō, facere, fēcī, factum, *make, do.*

factiō, -ōnis, F., *faction, party.*

facultās, -ātis, F. [faciō], *opportunity (of doing); means;* pl. *resources.*

famēs, -is, F., *hunger.*

familia, -ae, F., *household, retinue.*

LATIN-ENGLISH VOCABULARY 297

familiāris, -e [familia], *belonging to
the household, private ;* as noun,
friend : rēs familiāris, *private
property.*
faveo, favēre, fāvī, fautum, *favor.*
ferāx, -ācis, adj., *fertile.*
ferē, adv., *almost.*
ferō, ferre, tulī, lātum, *bear, carry,
bring.*
ferrum, -ī, N., *iron.*
fidēs, -eī, F., *faith, confidence, protection.*
fīlia, ae, F., *daughter.*
fīlius, -ī, M., *son.*
fīnis, -is, M., *end, limit, boundary ;*
pl *territory.*
fīnitimus, -a, -um [fīnis], *bordering
upon, adjoining, neighboring :*
fīnitimī, as noun, *neighbors.*
fīō, fierī, factus sum, *be made, be
done, happen.*
fīrmus, -a, -um, *strong, firm.*
flāgitō, ī, *demand earnestly.*
fleō, flēre, flēvī, flētum, *weep.*
flūmen, -inis, N. [fluō], *river.*
fluō, fluere, fluxī, fluxum, *flow.*
fortis, -e, *strong, brave.*
fortiter, adv., *bravely.*
fortitūdō, -inis, F. [fortis], *bravery.*
fortūna, -ae, F., *chance, fortune.*
fossa, -ae, F. [fodiō, *dig*], *ditch,
trench.*
frāter, frātris, M., *brother.*
frāternus, -a, -um, *brotherly, frater-
nal.*
frīgus, -oris, N., *cold, coldness.*
frūctus, -ūs, M., *enjoyment, fruit,
crops.*
frūgēs, -um, F., *crops.*
frūmentārius, -a, -um [frūmentum],
abounding in grain, fruitful.
frūmentor, ī, *gather grain.*

frūmentum, -ī, N., *grain.*
fuga, -ae, F., *flight.*
fugitīvus, -ī, M., *deserter, fugitive.*

G

Gabīnius, -ī, M., *Aulus Gabinius,* a
Roman consul, 58 B.C.
Gāius, -ī, M., a Roman name.
Galba, -ae, M., *Servius Galba,* one of
Caesar's lieutenants.
Gallia, -ae, F., *Gaul.*
Gallicus, -a, -um, *Gallic.*
Gallus, -ī, M., *a Gaul.*
Garumna, -ae, M. or F., *the Garonne,*
a river of Gaul.
Genāva, -ae, F., *Geneva.*
genus, generis, N., *race, tribe, class.*
Germānia, -ae, F., *Germany.*
Germānī, -ōrum, M., *the Germans.*
gerō, gerere, gessī, gestum, *carry on,
wage, do.*
gladius, -ī, M., *sword.*
glōria, -ae, F., *glory.*
glōrior, ī, *boast, glory.*
Grāiocelī, -ōrum, M., *the Graioceli,*
an Alpine tribe.
grātia, -ae, F., *favor, good-will.*
grātulor, ī, *congratulate.*
gravis, -e, *heavy.*
graviter, adv., *heavily, severely :*
graviter ferre, *be annoyed, be vexed.*

H

habeō, 2, *have, hold.*
Haeduī, -ōrum, M., *the Haedui,* a
Gallic tribe.
Haeduus, -a, -um, *of the Haedui,
Haeduan.*
Helvētia, -ae, F., *Helvetia* (now
Switzerland).

Helvētiī, -ōrum, M., *the Helvetii, Helvetians.*

Helvētius (Helvēticus), -a, -um, *of the Helvetii, Helvetian.*

hīberna, -ōrum, N., *winter-quarters* (supply castra).

hīc, haec, hōc, *this.*

hiemō, I, *pass the winter.*

hiems, hiemis, F., *winter.*

Hispānia, -ae, F., *Spain.*

homō, -inis, M. F., *a human being, man.*

honor, -ōris, M., *honor, respect.*

hōra, -ae, F., *hour.*

hortor, I, *urge, encourage.*

hostis, -is, M. F., *stranger,* (public) *enemy ;* pl. *the enemy.*

hūmānitās, -ātis, F., *refinement, civilization.*

I

iaciō, iacere, iēcī, iactum, *throw.*

iactō, I, *toss, discuss.*

iam, adv., *by this time, now, already.*

ibi, adv., *in that place, there.*

Iccius, -ī, M., *a prominent Belgian.*

ictus, -ūs, M., *stroke, blow.*

īdem, eadem, idem, *the same.*

idōneus, -a, -um, *fit, suitable.*

Īdūs, -uum, F., *the Ides.*

īgnis, -is, M., *fire.*

īgnōrō, I, *not know, be ignorant.*

ille, illa, illud, *that* (yonder).

illīc [ille], adv., *there.*

immortālis, -e, *immortal.*

impedīmentum, -ī, N., *hindrance, impediment ;* pl. *baggage, baggage-train.*

impediō, 4 [pēs], *entangle, hinder.*

impendeō, -ēre, *overhang, impend.*

imperium, -ī, N., *command, supreme power.*

imperātor, -ōris, M., *commander-in-chief.*

imperō, I, *command, make requisition for, levy.*

impetrō, I, *obtain* (by request), *accomplish.*

impetus, -ūs, M., *attack.*

impōnō, -ponere, -posuī, -positum [in + pōnō], *place upon, impose.*

importō, I [in + portō], *bring in, import.*

improbus, -a, -um, *base, wicked.*

imprōvīsō, adv. [in + prō + vīsus], *unexpectedly, unawares.*

impūne, adv. [in + poena], *without punishment, with impunity.*

impūnitās, -ātis, F., *freedom from punishment, impunity.*

in, prep. with acc. (of motion), *into, to, against ;* with abl. (of rest), *in, on, over ;* as prefix, *in, into, on ;* negative prefix, *not.*

incendō, -cendere, -cendī, -cēnsum, *set fire to.*

incitō, I, *urge on, incite.*

incolō, -colere, -coluī, -cultum [in + colō], *dwell in, inhabit.*

incommodum, -ī, N., *disadvantage, disaster.*

incrēdibilis, -e [in + crēdō, *believe*], *incredible.*

inde, adv., *from that place, thence.*

indicium, -ī, N., *information, evidence.*

indūcō, -dūcere, -dūxī, -ductum [in + dūcō], *lead into, lead on, induce.*

indulgeo, -dulgēre, -dulsī, -dultum, *favor.*

īnferior, -ius [īnferus], *lower.*

īnferō, īnferre, intulī, illātum, *bring
into, bring upon, wage upon,
attack.*

īnflectō, -flectere, -flēxī, -flexum,
bend, curve.

īnfluō, -fluere, -fluxī, -fluxum, *flow
into, flow.*

inimīcus, -a, -um [in + amīcus], *unfriendly.*

initium, -ī, N., *beginning.*

iniūria, -ae, F. [iūs, *right*], *wrong,
injustice.*

iniussū, adv., *without command.*

inopia, -ae, F., *lack, scarcity.*

inopīnāns, -antis, *not expecting, unaware.*

īnsciēns, -entis [in + sciō], *not knowing, unaware.*

īnsequor, -sequī, -secūtus sum [in +
sequor] *follow up, pursue.*

īnsidiae, -ārum, F., *treachery, am-
buscade, stratagem.*

īnsīgnis, -e, *marked, remarkable :*
Īnsīgne, N., as noun, *sign, decora-
tion.*

īnsolenter, adv., *insultingly.*

īnstituō, -stituere, -stituī, -stitūtum
[in + statuō], *set up, establish,
begin, train.*

īnstitūtum, -ī, N., *custom, institu-
tion.*

īnstō, -stāre, -stitī, -statum [in +
stō, *stand*], *stand near, be near,
press forward.*

īnstruō, -struere, -strūxī, -strūctum,
build, draw up, marshal.

intellegō, -legere, -lēxī, -lēctum
[inter + legō, *gather*], *learn,
know, understand.*

inter, prep. with acc., *between,
among ;* as prefix, *between.*

intercēdō, -cēdere, -cessī, -cessum

[inter + cēdō], *go between, intervene,* (of time) *elapse.*

interclūdō, -clūdere, -clūsī, -clūsum
[inter + claudō, *close*], *cut off,
shut off.*

interdiū, adv. [inter + diū], *during
the day, by day.*

interdum, adv. [inter + dum], *sometimes.*

intereā, adv. [inter + ea], *meanwhile.*

interest, *see* intersum.

interficiō, -ficere, -fēcī, -fectum [inter
+ faciō], *kill.*

interim, adv., *meanwhile.*

intermittō, -mittere, -mīsī, -missum
[inter + mittō], *stop, interrupt,
intervene,* (of time) *let pass.*

interneciō, -ōnis, F., *extermination.*

interpres, -etis, M. F., *interpreter.*

intersum, -esse, -fuī [inter + sum],
be between, intervene ; impers. *it
concerns, it interests.*

intervāllum, -ī, N., *interval.*

invītus, -a, -um, *unwilling.*

ipse, ipsa, ipsum, *himself, herself,
itself.*

is, ea, id, *this, that, he, she, it.*

iste, ista, istud, *that* (of yours).

ita, adv., *so, thus.*

Ītalia, -ae, F., *Italy.*

itaque, conj., *and so, therefore.*

item, adv., *in like manner, likewise.*

iter, itineris, N. [eō], (*a going*), *way,
journey, march.*

iubeō, iubēre, iussī, iussum, *order.*

iūdicium, -ī, N., *judgment, trial.*

iūdicō, I, *judge.*

iugum, -ī, N., *yoke, ridge.*

iūmentum, -ī, N., (*yoke animal*),
beast of burden.

iungō, iungere, iūnxī, iūnctum, *join.*

Iūra, -ae, M., Mount Jura, a mountain range running from the Rhine to the Rhone.

iūs, iūris, N., *right, justice, law.*

iūsiūrandum, iūrisiūrandī, N., *oath.*

iūstitia, -ae, F., *justice.*

iuvō, iuvāre, iūvī, iūtum, *help, aid.*

K

Kalendae (Calendae), -ārum, F., *the Calends* (the first day of a month).

L

L., *see* Lūcius.

Labiēnus, -I, M., *Titus Labienus,* one of Caesar's lieutenants.

lacessō, -ere, -īvī, -ītum, *provoke, assault.*

lacrima, -ae, F., *tear.*

lacus, -ūs, M., *lake.*

largior, 4, *give lavishly, bribe.*

largiter, adv., *lavishly.*

largītiō, -ōnis, F., *giving lavishly, bribery.*

lātē, adv., *broadly, widely.*

lātitūdō, -inis, F. [lātus], *width.*

Latobrīgī, -ōrum, M., *the Latobrigi,* a Gallic tribe.

lātus, -a, -um, *broad, wide.*

latus, -eris, N., *side, flank.*

laudō, 1, *praise.*

lēgātiō, -ōnis, F., *embassy.*

lēgātus, -ī, M., *ambassador, lieutenant.*

legiō, -ōnis, F., *legion.*

Lemannus, -I, M., *Lake Geneva.*

lēnitās, -ātis, F., *smoothness, gentleness.*

lēx, lēgis, F., *law.*

līber, -era, -erum, *free.*

līberālitās, -ātis, F., *liberality.*

līberē, adv., *freely.*

līberī, -ōrum, M. [līber], *children* (free members of a household).

lībertās, -ātis, F. [līber], *freedom, liberty.*

liceor, 2, *bid* (at auction).

licet, licēre, licuit, impers., *it is permitted.*

Lingonēs, -um, M., *the Lingones,* a Gallic tribe.

lingua, -ae, F., *tongue, language.*

linter, lintris, F., *canoe.*

Liscus, -I, M., a chief of the Haedui.

littera, -ae, F., *a letter of the alphabet ;* pl. *a letter* (epistle).

locus, -I, M., pl. loca, ōrum, N., *place.*

longē, adv., *far, by far.*

longitūdō, -inis, F. [longus], *length.*

longus, -a, -um, *long.*

loquor, loquī, locūtus sum, *speak.*

Lūcius, -I (abbr. L.), M., a Roman name.

lūna, -ae, F., *moon.*

lūx, lūcis, F., *light.*

M

M., *see* Mārcus.

magis, comp. adv. (sup. māximē), *more, rather.*

magistrātus, -ūs, M., *magistracy, magistrate.*

māgnopere, adv., *greatly, especially.*

māgnus, -a, -um (comp. māior, sup. māximus), *great, large.*

māiōrēs, -um, C. (māior), *ancestors.*

male, adv., *badly.*

maleficium, -I, N., *mischief, harm.*

malus, -a, -um, *bad.*

mandō, 1, *intrust, order ;* with sē fugae, *take to.*

manus, -ūs, F., *hand, armed force, band.*

Mārcus, -ī, M., a Roman name.

mare, maris, N., *sea.*

matara, -ae, F., *a Gallic javelin.*

māter, mātris, F., *mother, matron.*

mātrimōnium, -ī, N., *marriage.*

Mātrona, -ae, M., *the Marne.*

mātūrō, ī, *hasten.*

mātūrus, -a, -um, *ripe, complete, early.*

māximē, sup. adv. [māgnus], *most, very greatly, especially.*

māximus, *see* māgnus.

medius, -a, -um, *in the middle of.*

memoria, -ae, F., *recollection, memory.*

mēnsis, -is, M., *month.*

mercātor, ōris, M., *merchant, trader.*

mereor, 2, *deserve, merit.*

meritum, -ī, N., *desert, merit.*

Messāla, -ae, M., *Marcus Messala,* a Roman consul 61 B.C.

mētior, mētīrī, mēnsus sum, *measure.*

mīles, -itis, M., *soldier.*

mīlitāris, -e [mīles], *pertaining to a soldier, military.*

mīlle, adj., *a thousand ;* pl. as noun, mīlia, -ium, N. ; mīlia passuum, *miles.*

minimē, adv., *least, by no means.*

minimus, -a, -um (sup. of parvus), *least, very little.*

minor (comp. of parvus), *smaller, less.*

minuō, -ere, -uī, -ūtum [minus], *make smaller, lessen.*

minus, adv. [minor], *less.*

miser, -era, -erum, *wretched, poor.*

mittō, mittere, mīsī, missum, *send.*

modo, adv., *only.*

molō, -ere, -uī, -itum, *grind.*

moneō, 2, *advise, warn, remind.*

mōns, montis, M., *mountain.*

morior, morī, mortuus sum, *die.*

moror, ī, *delay, tarry.*

mors, mortis, F. [morior], *death.*

mōs, mōris, M., *manner, custom ;* pl. *customs, character.*

moveō, movēre, mōvī, mōtum, *move.*

mulier, mulieris, F., *woman.*

multitūdō, -inis, F. [multus], *great number, multitude.*

multus, -a, -um, *much ;* pl. *many.*

mūniō, 4, *fortify.*

mūnītiō, -ōnis, F., *fortification.*

mūrus, -ī, M., *wall.*

N

nam, conj., *for.*

Nammēius, -ī, M., an Helvetian chief.

nātiō, -ōnis, F., *nation.*

nātūra, -ae, F., *nature, character*

nauta, -ae, M., *sailor.*

nāvigō, ī, *sail.*

nāvis, -is, F., *ship.*

nē, conj., *that—not, not to, lest ;* (after words of fearing) *that.*

-ne, enclitic interrog. particle.

nec, *see* neque.

necessāriō, adv., *necessarily.*

necessārius, -a, -um, *necessary;* as noun, M., *kinsman.*

negō, ī, *say not, deny.*

nēmō, -inis, M. F., *no one.*

neque (nec), conj., *and not, and also :* neque — neque, *neither — nor.*

nervus, -ī, M., *sinew ;* pl. *power, strength.*

neuter, -tra, -trum, *neither.*

nĕve (neu), adv., *and not, nor.*
nex, necis, F., *death.*
nihil, indecl. noun, *nothing.*
nisi, conj., *if not, unless.*
nītor, nītī, nīsus or **nīxus sum**, *rely upon, strive.*
nōbilis, -e, *famous, high born, noble.*
nōbilitās, -ātis, F., *nobility, nobles.*
noctū, adv. [nox], *by night.*
nōlō, nōlle, nōluī, *not wish, be unwilling.*
nōmen, -inis, N., *name.*
nōminātim, adv., *by name.*
nōn, adv., *not.*
nōnāgintā, indecl. adj., *ninety.*
nōndum, adv., *not yet.*
nōnnūllus, -a, -um, (*not none*), *some;* pl. as noun, *some.*
nōnnumquam, (*not never*), *sometimes.*
Nōrēia, -ae, F., *Noreia*, a town of the Norici.
Nōricus, -a, -um, *of the Norici, Norican.*
nōs [ego], *we.*
nōscō, nōscere, nōvī, nōtum, *know.*
noster, -tra, -trum [nōs], *our, ours.*
novem, indecl. adj., *nine.*
novus, -a, -um, *new :* **novae rēs,** *new state of affairs, revolution.*
nox, noctis, F., *night.*
nūbō, nūbere, nūpsī, nūptum, *veil one's self* (for marriage), *marry.*
nūdus, -a, -um, *naked, exposed, unprotected.*
nūllus, -a, -um, *not any, no, none.*
num, interrog. particle implying a negative answer.
numerus, -ī, M., *number.*
numquam, adv., *never.*
nūntiō, I, *report, announce.*

nūntius, -ī, M., *messenger, message, news.*
nūper, *recently.*

O

ob, prep. with acc., *on account of;* as prefix, *toward, against.*
obaerātus, -ī, M. [aes, *money*], *debtor.*
obiciō, -icere, -iēcī, -iectum [ob + iaciō], *throw in front, set up, oppose, expose.*
oblīvīscor, oblīvīscī, oblītus sum, *forget.*
obsecrō, I, *beseech, implore.*
obses, -idis, M. F., *hostage.*
obstringō, -stringere, -strinxī, -strictum, *bind.*
obtineō, -tinēre, -tinuī, -tentum [ob + tineō], *hold, possess.*
occāsus, -ūs, M. [cadō, *fall*], *falling, setting.*
occīdō, -cīdere, -cīdī, -cīsum [ob + caedō, *cut*], *kill, slay.*
occultō, I, *hide, conceal.*
occupō, I, *seize, take possession of, occupy.*
occurrō, -currere, -currī, -cursum [ob + currō, *run*], *run to meet, meet.*
Ōceanus, -ī, M., *ocean.*
Ocelum, -ī, N., a town of the Graioceli, in the Alps.
octō, indecl. adj., *eight.*
octōdecim, indecl. adj., *eighteen.*
octōgintā, indecl. adj., *eighty.*
oculus, -ī, M., *eye.*
ōdī, ōdisse, def. verb, *hate.*
offendō, -fendere, -fendī, -fēnsum, (*strike against*), *offend, hurt.*
offēnsiō, -ōnis, F., *offence.*
omnīnō, adv. [omnis], *altogether, in all.*

omnis, -e, *all, every.*

oportet, -ēre, -uit, impers. verb, *it is necessary, one ought.*

oppidum, -ī, N., *town.*

oppūgnō, I, *fight against, storm.*

ops, opis (not used in nom. sing.), *power, strength;* pl. *resources, means.*

opus, -eris, N., *work.*

ōrātiō, -ōnis, F. [ōrō], *speech, address, argument.*

Orgetorīx, -īgis, M., a chief of the Helvetii.

oriēns, -entis, part. as adj. [orior], *rising.*

orior, orīrī, ortus sum, *rise.*

ōrō, I, *speak, plead, entreat.*

ostendō, -tendere, -tendī, -tentum [ob + tendō, *stretch*], *show, point out, declare.*

P

P., *see* Pūblius.

pābulātiō, -ōnis, F., *foraging.*

pābulum, -ī, N., *food, fodder.*

pācō, I [pāx], *pacify, subdue.*

paene, adv., *almost.*

pāgus, -ī, M., *canton, district.*

pār, paris, *equal.*

parātus, -a, -um [parō], *prepared, ready.*

pāreō, 2, *obey.*

pārō, I, *prepare, provide.*

pars, partis, F., *part, direction.*

parvus, -a, -um (comp. minor, sup. minimus), *small, little.*

passus, -ūs, M., *step, pace* (five Roman feet) : mīlia passuum, *mile.*

patēns, -entis, part. as adj., *open, exposed.*

pateō, -ēre, -uī, *lie open, extend.*

pater, patris, M., *father.*

patior, patī, passus sum, *suffer, permit.*

paucī, -ae, -a, *few.*

pāx, pācis, F., *peace.*

pedes, -itis, M., *foot-soldier.*

pellō, pellere, pepulī, pulsum, *drive, beat.*

per, prep. with acc., *through, by means of;* as prefix, *through, thoroughly, very.*

perdūcō, -dūcere, -dūxī, -ductum [per + dūcō], *lead through.*

perfacilis, -e, *very easy.*

perferō, -ferre, -tulī, -lātum [per + ferō], *bear through, endure, suffer.*

perficiō, -ficere, -fēcī, -fectum [per + faciō], *do thoroughly, accomplish, complete.*

perfringō, -fringere, -frēgī, -frāctum [per + frangō, *break*], *break through.*

perfuga, -ae, M., *deserter, fugitive.*

perfugiō, -fugere, -fūgī, *flee, desert.*

perīculum, -ī, N., *danger, risk, peril.*

perītus, -a, -um, *experienced, skilled, skillful.*

permittō, -mittere, -mīsī, -missum [per + mittō, *let through*], *permit, grant, allow.*

permoveō, -movēre, -mōvī, -mōtum [per + moveō], *move thoroughly, rouse, influence.*

perniciēs, -ēī, F., *destruction.*

perpaucī, -ae, -a, *very few.*

perrumpō, -rumpere, -rūpī, -ruptum [per + rumpō, *break*], *break through.*

persequor, -sequī, -secūtus sum [per + sequor], *follow after, pursue.*

persevērō, I, *persist, continue.*

persolvō, -solvere, -solvī, -solūtum [per + solvō], *pay* (in full).

persuādeō, -suādēre, -suāsī, -suāsum, *persuade.*

perterreō, 2 [per + terreo], *frighten thoroughly.*

pertineō, -ēre, -uī [per + teneō], *reach through, extend, pertain.*

perveniō, -venīre, -vēnī, -ventum [per + veniō], *come through, arrive.*

pēs, pedis, M., *foot.*

petō, -ere, -īvī [-iī], -ītum, *attack, aim at, seek.*

phalanx, -angis, F., *phalanx.*

pīlum, -ī, N., *javelin.*

Pīsō, -ōnis, M., *Marcus Piso*, a Roman consul, 61 B.C.

plēbs, plēbis, F., *common people, plebeians.*

plēnus, -a, -um, *full.*

plūrimus, -a, -um, sup. of multus.

plūs, plūris, comp. of multus.

poena, -ae, F., *punishment, penalty.*

polliceor, 2, *promise.*

pōnō, pōnere, posuī, positum, *put, place.*

pōns, pontis, M., *bridge.*

populātiō, -ōnis, F., *ravaging.*

populor, 1, *devastate, ravage.*

populus, -ī, M., *people, nation.*

porta, -ae, F., *gate.*

portō, 1, *carry, bring.*

portōrium, -ī, N., *tax, tariff.*

poscō, -ere, poposcī, *demand.*

possessiō, -ōnis, F., *possession.*

possum, posse, potuī [potis, *able* + sum], *be able, can.*

post, prep. with acc., *behind, after.*

posteā, adv. [post + ea], *afterwards.*

posterus, -a, -um, *following.*

postquam, conj., *after, as soon as.*

postrīdiē, adv., *on the day after.*

potēns, -entis, *powerful.*

potentia, -ae, F., *power, ability.*

potestās, -ātis, F., *power.*

potior, potīrī, potītus sum, *get control of, obtain possession of, secure.*

prae, prep. with abl., *before;* as prefix, *before, over, very.*

praecēdō, -cēdere, -cessī, -cessum [prae + cēdō], *go before, surpass, precede.*

praecipiō, -cipere, -cēpī, -ceptum [prae + capio], *take in advance, order.*

praecipuē, adv., *especially.*

praeda, -ae, F., *booty, plunder.*

praeferō, -ferre, -tulī, -lātum [prae + ferō], *bear before, choose, prefer.*

praeficiō, -ficere, -fēcī, -fectum [prae + faciō], *put before, put over, place in command.*

praemittō, -mittere, -mīsī, -missum [prae + mittō], *send before, send in advance.*

praeoptō, 1 [prae + optō, *choose*], *choose rather, prefer.*

praesens, -entis [praesum], part. as adj., *present.*

praesentia, -ae, F., *the present time.*

praesertim, adv., *especially.*

praesidium, -ī, N., *protection, guard, garrison.*

praestō, -stāre, -stitī, -stitum [prae + stō, *stand*], *stand before, excel, present, furnish;* impers., *it is preferable.*

praesum, -esse, -fuī [prae + sum], *be before, be over, command.*

praeter, prep. with acc., *past, by, beyond, except ;* as prefix, *by, past.*

praetereō, -īre, -īvī (-iī), -itum [praeter + eō], *go by.*

praeterita, -ōrum, N., *the past.*

praeterquam, adv., *except.*

praetor, -ōris, M., *commander, judge.*

prēndō, prēndere, prēndī, prēnsum, *lay hold of, grasp.*

pretium, -ī, N., *price.*

prex, precis, F., *prayer.*

prīdiē, adv., *on the day before.*

prīmum, adv., *in the first place, first.*

prīmus, -a, -um, *first.*

prīnceps, -ipis, adj., *chief ;* as noun, *chief, leader.*

prīncipātus, -ūs, M., *leadership, chief position.*

prīstinus, -a, -um, *former, old.*

prius, comp. adv., *sooner.*

priusquam, conj., *before, sooner than.*

prīvātim, adv., *privately, as private citizens.*

prīvātus, -a, -um, *private, personal.*

prō, prep. with abl., *before, for, in behalf of, in proportion to ;* as prefix, *before, forth, out.*

probō, I, *test, prove, approve.*

Procillus, -ī, M., *Gaius Valerius Procillus,* a Gallic chief.

prōditiō, -ōnis, F., *treason.*

prōdō, -dere, -didī, -ditum, *transmit, hand down.*

proelium, -iī, N., *battle.*

profectiō, -ōnis, F., *setting out, departure.*

proficīscor, proficīscī, profectus sum, *set out, depart.*

prohibeō, 2, *keep from, prohibit, prevent.*

prōiciō, -icere, -iēcī, -iectum [prō + iaciō], *throw forth, hurl, cast down.*

prope, adv., and prep. with acc., *near.*

prōpellō, -pellere, -pulī, -pulsum [prō + pellō], *drive before, rout.*

propinquus, -a, -um, *near, neighboring;* as subst. noun, *relative, kinsman.*

prōpōnō, -pōnere, -posuī, -positum [prō + pōnō], *set forth, declare.*

propter, prep. with acc., *on account of.*

proptereā [propter + ea], adv., *for this reason.*

prōspiciō, -spicere, -spēxī, -spectum, *look forward, look out for.*

prōvincia, -ae, F., *province.*

proximē, adv. [prope], *next, nearest, last.*

proximus, -a, -um, *nearest, last.*

pūblicē, adv., *publicly, on the part of the state.*

pūblicus, -a, -um, *public.*

Pūblius, -ī (abbr. P.), M., a Roman name.

puer, -ī, M., *boy, child.*

pūgna, -ae, F., *fight, battle.*

pūgnō, I, *fight.*

pūrgō, I, *clear, excuse.*

putō, I, *suppose, reckon, think.*

Pȳrēnaeus, -a, -um ; with montēs, *the Pyrenees.*

Q

quā, adv., *by which way, where.*

quadrāgintā, indecl. adj., *forty.*

quadringentī, -ae, -a, *four hundred.*

quaerō, quaerere, quaesīvī, quaesītum, *seek, ask.*

quālis, -e, *of what sort.*

quam, adv. and conj., *how, as, than ;* with sup., *as possible.*

quamquam, conj., *although.*

20

quantus, -a, -um, *how great :* tantus—quantus, *so (as) great—as.*

quā rē, adv., *wherefore, for this reason.*

quārtus, -a, -um, *fourth.*

quattuor, indecl. adj., *four.*

quattuordecim, indecl. adj., *fourteen.*

-que, enclitic conj., *and.*

queror, querī, questus sum, *complain.*

quī, quae, quod, *who, which, that.*

quīdam, quaedam, quoddam, *a certain, certain.*

quidem, *indeed :* nē—quidem, *not even.*

quīn, conj., *that, but that, from :* quīn etiam, *nay more.*

quīndecim, indecl. adj., *fifteen.*

quīngentī, -ae, -a, *five hundred.*

quīnī, -ae, -a, distrib. num. adj., *five each, five.*

quīnquāgintā, indecl. adj., *fifty.*

quīnque, indecl. adj., *five.*

quīntus, -a, -um, *fifth.*

quis, quid, interrog. pron., *who? which? what?* indef. pron., *anyone, anything.*

quisquam, quidquam [quicquam], *any one, any thing.*

quisque, quaeque, quidque [quodque], *each one, every one, each, every.*

quod, conj., *because.*

quoque, conj., *also.*

quot, indec. adj., *how many.*

R

rapiditās, -ātis, F. [rapidus], *swiftness, rapidity.*

rapīna, -ae, F., *plunder, rapine.*

ratiō, -ōnis, F., *reckoning, plan, reason.*

ratis, -is, F., *raft.*

Rauracī, -ōrum, M., *the Rauraci,* neighbors of the Helvetii.

re- (red-), prefix, *back, again.*

recēns, -entis, *fresh, recent.*

recipiō, -cipere, -cēpī, -ceptum [re + capiō], *take back, receive.*

rēda, -ae, F., *wagon.*

redeō, -īre, -iī, -itum [red + eō], *go back, return.*

redimō, -imere, -ēmī, -ēmptum [red + emō], *buy back, buy up.*

redintegrō, 1 [red + integrō], *renew, restore.*

reditiō, -ōnis, F. [redeō], *a going back, return.*

redūcō, -dūcere, -dūxī, -ductum [re + dūcō], *lead back, withdraw.*

referō, -ferre, -tulī, -lātum [re + ferō], *bring back, report.*

rēgnum, -ī, N. [rēx], *sovereignty, royal power.*

regō, 3, *rule.*

reiciō, -icere, -iēcī, -iectum [re + iaciō], *throw back.*

relinquō, -linquere, -līquī, -lictum [re + linquō], *leave behind, abandon.*

reliquus, -a, -um, *the rest of, remaining.*

reminīscor, -ī, *call to mind, remember.*

removeō, -movēre, -mōvī, -mōtum [re + moveō], *move back.*

renūntiō, 1 [re + nūntiō], *bring back word, report.*

repellō, repellere, reppulī, repulsum [re + pellō], *drive back, repulse.*

repentīnus, -a, -um, *sudden, unexpected.*

reperiō, reperīre, repperī, repertum [re + pariō, *procure*], *find out, discover.*

reprehendō, -prehendere, -prehendī, -prehēnsum [re + prehendō, *seize*], *blame, censure.*

repūgnō, I [re + pūgnō], *fight back, resist, be in opposition.*

rēs, reī, F., *thing, affair, fact.*

rescindō, -scindere, -scidī, -scissum [re + scindō], *cut off, break down, destroy.*

rescīscō, -scīscere, -scīvī [sciī], -scītum, *learn.*

resistō, -sistere, -stitī [re + sistō, *stand*], *stand back, stop, resist, withstand.*

respondeō, -spondēre, -spondī, -spōnsum, *answer, reply.*

respōnsum, -ī, N., *reply.*

rēs pūblica, reī pūblicae, F., *state.*

restituō, -uere, -uī, -ūtum [re + statuō], *set up again, restore.*

retineō, -tinēre, -tinuī, -tentum [re + teneō], *hold back, retain.*

revertō, -vertere, -vertī, -versum [re + vertō], *turn back, return :* revertor, -ī, dep., is generally used in the present system.

revocō, I [re + vocō], *call back, recall.*

rēx, rēgis, M., *king.*

Rhēnus, -ī, M., *the Rhine.*

Rhodanus, -ī, M., *the Rhone.*

rīpa, -ae, F., *bank* (of a river).

rogō, I, *ask.*

Rōmānus, -a, -um, *Roman ;* as noun, Rōmānī, -ōrum, M., *the Romans.*

rota, -ae, F., *wheel.*

rūrsus, adv., *again.*

rūs, rūris, N., *the country* (opposed to city).

S

saepe, adv., *often.*

salūs, -ūtis, F., *safety.*

Santonēs, -um [-ī, -ōrum], M., *the Santones,* a Gallic tribe.

sarcinae, -ārum, F., *soldiers' packs, baggage* (carried by soldiers).

satis, adv. and indecl. adj., *enough, sufficiently, sufficient.*

satisfaciō, -facere, -fēcī, -factum [satis + faciō], *do enough, satisfy, make amends.*

scelus, -eris, N., *crime.*

sciō, scīre, scīvī, scītum, *know.*

scūtum, -ī, N., *shield.*

sēcrētō, adv., *secretly, in private.*

secundus, -a, -um, *following, second, favorable.*

sed, conj., *but.*

sēdecim [sex], indecl. adj., *sixteen.*

sēditiōsus, -a, -um, *seditious.*

Segusiāvī, -ōrum, M., *the Segusiavi,* a Gallic tribe.

sēmentis, -is, F., *sowing, planting.*

semper, adv., *always.*

senātus, ūs, M., *senate.*

senex, senis, *old ;* as noun, *old man.*

sēnī, -ae, -a, distrib. num., adj., *six each, six.*

sentiō, sentīre, sēnsī, sēnsum, *feel, perceive, think.*

sēparātim, adv., *separately.*

septentriōnēs, -um (septentriō, -ōnis), M., *seven stars, the Great Bear, the north.*

septimus, -a, -um, *seventh.*

sepultūra, -ae, F., *burial.*

Sēquana, -ae, F. or M., *the Seine.*

Sēquanī, -ōrum, M., *the Sequani, Sequanians,* a Gallic tribe.

sequor, sequī, secūtus sum, *follow.*
servitūs, -ūtis, F., *slavery.*
servus, -ī, M., *slave.*
seu, *see* sīve.
sex, indecl. adj , *six.*
sexāgintā, indecl. adj., *sixty.*
sī, conj., *if.*
sīc, adv., *so, thus.*
sīgnifer, -ferī, M., *standard-bearer.*
sīgnum, -ī, N., *signal, standard.*
silva, -ae, F., *forest.*
similis, -e, *like, similar.*
simul, adv., *at the same time, at once.*
sīn, conj., *but if.*
sine, prep. with abl., *without.*
singulī, -ae, -a, distrib. num. adj., *one at a time, one by one, single.*
sinister, -tra, -trum, *left* (opposed to dexter, *right*).
sīve [seu], conj., *or if ;* sīve—sīve, *whether—or, either—or.*
socer, socerī, M., *father-in-law.*
socius, -ī, M., *ally.*
sōl, sōlis, M., *the sun.*
sōlum, adv., *only.*
solum, -ī, N., *soil, ground.*
sōlus, -a, -um, *alone, only.*
soror, -ōris, F., *sister.*
spatium, -ī, N., *space, period.*
spectō, I, *look, face.*
spērō, I [spēs], *hope, look for.*
spēs, -eī, F., *hope.*
spontis (gen ; sponte, abl.), *of one's own accord, willingly.*
statuō, -uere, -uī, -ūtum, *set up, establish, determine.*
stīpendiārius, -a, -um, *tributary.*
studeō, -ēre, -uī, *be eager for, desire.*
studium, -ī, N., *eagerness, attachment.*

sub, prep. with acc. or abl., *under, near, beneath ;* as prefix, *under.*
subdūcō, -dúcere, -dūxī, -ductum [sub + dūcō], *draw up, withdraw.*
subeō, -īre, -iī, -itum [sub + eō], *go under, go near, undergo.*
subiciō, -icere, -iēcī, -iectum [sub + iaciō], *throw under, discharge, subject, expose to.*
sublevō, I [sub + levō], *lift up, aid.*
submoveō, -movēre, -mōvī, -mōtum [sub + moveō], *remove.*
subsistō, -sistere, -stitī [sub + sistō], *stand still, halt, withstand, resist.*
subsum, -esse, -fuī [sub + sum], *be under, be near.*
subvehō, -vehere, -vēxī, -vectum [sub + vehō], *bring up, convey.*
succēdō, -cēdere, -cessī, -cessum [sub + cēdō], *go under, go near, approach, succeed.*
suī, sibi, sē [sēsē], *himself, herself,* etc.
Sulla, -ae, M., a Roman dictator.
sum, esse, fuī, *be.*
summa, -ae, F., (*highest point*), *sum, total.*
summus, -a, -um [superus], *highest.*
sūmō, sūmere, sūmpsī, sūmptum, *take, claim.*
sūmptus, -ūs, M., *expense.*
super, adv. and prep. with acc., *above, over ;* as prefix, *over.*
superō, I, *surpass, conquer.*
supersum, -esse, -fuī [super + sum], *be over, survive.*
superus, -a, -um (comp. superior, sup. suprēmus, summus), *upper, higher.*
suppetō, -petere, -petīvī, -petītum, *be on hand, be in store.*

suppliciter, adv., *humbly.*
supplicium, -ī, N., *punishment.*
supportō [sub + portō], *bring up,
convey, supply.*
suscipiō, -cipere, -cēpī, -ceptum [sub
+ capiō], *undertake, undergo.*
suspīciō, -ōnis, F., *suspicion.*
sustineō, -tinēre, -tinuī, -tentum
[sub + teneō], *hold up, hold out,
sustain.*
suus, -a, -um, *his, her, its, their.*

T

T., *see* Titus.
tabula, -ae, F., *board, tablet, record.*
taceō, 2, *be silent, keep silent.*
tam, adv., *so.*
tamen, adv., *nevertheless, yet.*
tandem, adv., *at length.*
tantus, -a, -um, *so great.*
tēlum, -ī, N., *weapon, missile, spear.*
temperantia, -ae, F., *self-control,
moderation.*
temperō, 1, *control, refrain.*
tempestās, -ātis, F., *season, weather,
storm.*
temptō (tentō], 1, *try, attempt.*
tempus, -oris, N., *time.*
teneō, tenēre, tenuī, tentum, *hold.*
terra, -ae, F., *earth.*
terreō, 2, *frighten.*
tertius, -a, -um, *third.*
testis, -is, M. F., *witness.*
Tigurīnus, -a, -um, *of the Tigurini:*
Tigurīnī, -orum, M., *the Tigurini,*
a canton of the Helvetii.
timeō, -ēre, -uī, *fear.*
timor, -ōris, M., *fear.*
Titus, -ī (abbr. T.), M., a Roman
name.
tolerō, 1, *endure, support.*

tollō, tollere, sustulī, sublātum, *lift
up, take away, destroy.*
Tolōsātēs, -um, M., *the Tolosates,* a
tribe in southern Gaul.
tōtus, -a, -um (gen. -īus, dat. -ī), *the
whole of, all, entire.*
trādō, -dere, -didī, -ditum, *give over,
hand down, surrender.*
trādūcō, -dūcere, -dūxī, -ductum
[trāns + dūcō], *lead across.*
trāgula, -ae, F., *a Gallic javelin.*
trāns, prep. with acc., *across;* as
prefix, *across, through.*
trānseō, -īre, -iī, -itum [trāns + eō],
go across, cross.
trānsfīgō, -fīgere, -fīxī, -fīxum
[trāns + fīgō], *pierce through.*
trecentī, -ae, -a, *three hundred.*
trēs, tria, *three.*
tribuō, -uere, -uī, -ūtum, *assign,
attribute.*
trīduum, -ī, N., *three days.*
trīgintā, indecl. adj., *thirty.*
triplex, -icis, *threefold, triple.*
tū, *thou, you.*
tuba, -ae, F., *trumpet.*
Tulingī, -ōrum, M., *the Tulingi,* a
German tribe.
tum, adv., *then, at that time.*
turpitūdō, -inis, F. [turpis], *disgrace.*
turris, -is, F., *tower.*
tuus, -a, -um, *thy, your.*

U

ubi, *when, where.*
ulcīscor, ulcīscī, ultus sum, *avenge,
punish.*
ūllus, -a, -um (gen. -īus, dat. -ī),
any.
ulterior, -ius, comp. adj., *farther.*

ultrā, prep. with acc., *beyond.*

ūnā, adv., *together.*

unde, adv., *from which place, whence.*

undique [unde], adv., *from all parts, on all sides.*

ūnus, -a, -um (gen. -īus, dat. -ī), *one.*

urbs, urbis, F., *city.*

ut [utī], conj. with subj., *that, in order that, to ;* with indicative, *as, when.*

uter, -tra, -trum (gen. -īus, dat. -ī), *which of two, which.*

utinam, adv., *O that ! would that !*

ūtor, ūtī, ūsus sum, *use.*

uxor, -ōris, F., *wife.*

V

vacō, 1, *be vacant, be unoccupied.*

vadum, -ī, N., *ford, shoal.*

vagor, 1, *wander.*

valeō, 2, *be strong, be powerful, have influence.*

Valerius, *see* Procillus.

vāllum, -ī, N., *palisade, rampart.*

vāstō, 1, *lay waste, devastate.*

vectīgal, -ālis, N., *tax, revenue.*

vel, *or ;* vel—vel, *either—or.*

vēlōx, -ōcis, *swift.*

veniō, venīre, vēnī, ventum, *come.*

Verbigenus, -ī, M., a canton of the Helvetii.

verbum, -ī, N., *word.*

vereor, 2, *fear, dread.*

vergō, vergere, *incline, slope, lie.*

vergobretus, -ī, M., the title of the chief magistrate of the Haedui.

Verudoctius, -ī, M., an Helvetian chief.

vērus, -a, -um, *true.*

vesper, -erī, M., *evening.*

vester, -tra, -trum, *your, yours.*

veterānus, -a, -um, *old, veteran;* as noun, *veteran soldier, veteran.*

vetus, -eris, *old, former.*

vexō, 1, *harass.*

via, -ae, F., *way.*

victōria, -ae, F., *victory.*

vīcus, -ī, M., *village.*

videō, vidēre, vīdī, vīsum, *see ;* pass., *be seen, seem.*

vigilia, -ae, F., *watch of the night, watch.*

vīgintī, indecl. adj., *twenty.*

vincō, vincere, vīcī, victum, *conquer.*

vinculum, -ī, N., *bond.*

vir, -ī, M., *man.*

virtūs, -ūtis, F., *virtue, valor.*

vīs, vīs, F., *force, violence ;* pl. vīrēs, *strength.*

vīta, -ae, F., *life.*

vītō, 1, *shun, avoid.*

vix, adv., *with difficulty, scarcely.*

vocō, 1, *call, summon.*

Vocontiī, -ōrum, M., *the Vocontii,* a Gallic tribe.

volgus, -ī, N., *the multitude, public, common people.*

volnerō, 1, *wound, injure.*

volnus, -neris, N., *a wound.*

volō, velle, voluī, *wish, be willing.*

voluntās, -ātis, F., *willingness, wish, consent, good-will.*

vōs [tū], *you.*

ENGLISH–LATIN VOCABULARY

A

able, be, *possum.*
about, *circum ;* with numerals, *ad.*
accomplish, *cōnficiō.*
accuse, *accūsō.*
across, *trāns.*
active, *ācer.*
advise, *moneō.*
after, (prep.) *post ;* (conj.) *post-quam.*
aid, *auxilium.*
all, *omnis.*
allow, *concēdō, patior.*
ally, *socius.*
almost, *ferē, paene.*
although, *cum, etsī, quamquam.*
always, *semper.*
ambassador, *lēgātus.*
amends, make, *satisfaciō.*
among, *inter, apud.*
ancestors, *māiōrēs.*
and, *et, -que, ac, atque.*
animal, *animal.*
announce, *nūntiō, ēnūntiō, renūntiō.*
another, *alius.*
anyone, *quis, quisquam.*
appoint, *cōnstituō.*
approach, *accēdō.*
April, *Aprīlis.*
Aquitani, Aquitanians, *Aquītānī.*
are, see be.
arms, *arma.*
army, *exercitus.*

arouse, *commoveō, permoveō.*
arrival, *adventus.*
arrive, *perveniō.*
as—as possible, *quam* with sup., with or without *possum.*
ascent, *ascēnsus.*
ask, *rogō.*
assemble, *conveniō.*
at, *ad.*
attack, (noun) *impetus ;* (verb) *oppūgnō, adorior, adgredior.*
attempt, (noun) *cōnātus ;* (verb) *cōnor.*
auxiliary forces, *auxilia.*
avenge, *ulcīscor.*
away, be, *absum.*

B

baggage, *impedīmenta.*
bank (of a river), *rīpa.*
battle, *proelium.*
be (am), *sum.*
beast of burden, *iūmentum.*
because, *quod.*
before, (prep.) *ante, prō ;* (conj.) *antequam, priusquam.*
began, *coepī.*
beginning, *initium.*
Belgians, *Belgae.*
better, *melior.*
between, *inter.*
blot out, *dēleō.*
boat, *nāvis.*

boldly, *audācter*.
booty, *praeda*.
both—and, *et—et*.
bound (geographically), *contineō*.
boundaries, *jīnēs*.
boy, *puer*.
brave, *fortis*.
bravely, *fortiter*.
bravery, *fortitūdō*.
breadth, *lātitūdō*.
break down, *rescindō*.
break through, *perrumpō*.
bridge, *pōns*.
bring, *portō*, *ferō*.
bring together, *cōgō*, *condūcō*, *conferō*.
bring upon, *īnferō*.
broad, *lātus*.
brother, *frāter*.
building, *aedificium*.
burn, *combūrō*, *exūrō*, *incendō*; burn to death, *cremo īgnī*.
but, *sed*, *autem*.
buy up, *coëmō*.
by, sign of abl.; *ā*, *ab*, with abl.

C

call (by name), *appellō*; (summon), *vocō*.
call together, *convocō*.
camp, *castra*.
can, *possum*.
canoe, *linter*.
canton, *pāgus*.
capture, *expūgnō*, *capiō*.
carry, *portō*.
carry off, *abdūcō*.
carry on (war), *gerō*.
carry out (accomplish), *conficiō*.
cart, *carrus*.
cause, (noun) *causa*; (verb) *cūrō*.

cavalry, (noun) *equitēs*, *equitātus*; (adj.) *equester*.
Celts, *Celtae*.
certain, a, *quīdam*.
chief, *prīnceps*.
children, *līberī*, *puerī*.
choose, *dēligō*.
citizens, *cīvitās*.
city, *urbs*.
civilization, *cultus*.
climb, *ascendō*.
collect, *cōgō*, *condūcō*.
come, *veniō*.
come together, *conveniō*.
command, *imperō*, *iubeō*.
command, be in, *praesum*.
command, put in, *praeficiō*.
commander-in-chief, *imperātor*.
common people, *plēbs*.
compel, *cōgō*.
concerning, *dē*.
congratulate, *grātulor*.
conquer, *vincō*.
consider (regard), *habeō*.
conspiracy, *coniūrātiō*.
conspire, *coniūrō*.
construct, *perdūcō*.
consul, *cōnsul*.
contend, *contendō*.
could, see can.
council, *concilium*.
country, *terra*, *ager*, *fīnēs*; (not city), *rūs*.
courage, *animus*, *virtūs*.
course, *iter*.
cross, *trānseō*.
cultivate, *colō*.

D

daily, *cotīdiānus*.
danger, *perīculum*.

daughter, *fīlia.*
day, *diēs.*
debtor, *obaerātus.*
decide, *cōnstituō, iūdicō.*
deep, *altus.*
defend, *dēfendō.*
demand, *imperō, poscō.*
depart, *discēdō, proficīscor.*
departure, *profectiō.*
deserve, *mereor.*
desire, (noun) *cupiditās;* (verb) *cupiō.*
desirous, *cupidus.*
desist, *dēsistō.*
destroy, *rescindō, cōnsūmō.*
determine, *cōnstituō.*
devastate, *vāstō, populor.*
die, *morior.*
difficult, *difficilis.*
direction, *pars.*
disaster, *calamitās.*
discover, *reperiō.*
disgrace, *turpitūdō.*
dismiss, *dīmittō.*
distant, be, *absum.*
district, *pāgus.*
divide, *dīvidō.*
do, *agō, faciō.*
doubt, there is, *dubium est.*
draw up (troops), *īnstruō.*

E

each other, to, *inter sē.*
eager, *cupidus;* be eager for, *studeō.*
easily, *facile.*
east, *oriēns sōl.*
easy, *facilis.*
eight, *octō.*
eighth, *octāvus.*
eighty, *octōgintā.*
either—or, *aut—aut, vel—vel.*

embassy, *lēgātiō.*
enemy, *hostēs.*
enough, *satis.*
enroll, *cōnscrībō.*
escape, *vītō.*
establish, *cōnfīrmō.*
every, *omnis, quisque.*
excel, *praecēdō, praestō.*
expect, *exspectō.*
extend, *pateō, pertineō.*

F

fact, *rēs.*
famous, *nōbilis.*
farthest, *extrēmus.*
father, *pater.*
favor, *indulgeō.*
fear, (noun) *timor;* (verb) *timeō, vereor.*
fertile, *ferāx.*
few, *paucī;* very few, *perpaucī.*
field, *ager.*
fight, *pūgnō, contendō.*
fire, *ignis.*
first, *prīmus.*
five, *quīnque.*
flight, *fuga.*
flow, *fluō;* flow into, *īnfluō.*
follow, *sequor.*
foot, *pēs.*
footman, *pedes.*
for, prep., sign of dat. case; *prō,* with abl.
foot soldier, *pedes.*
force, *vīs.*
forces, *cōpiae.*
ford, fording, *vadum.*
forest, *silva.*
forget, *oblīvīscor.*
fort, *castellum.*
fortification, *mūnītiō, opus.*
fortify, *mūniō.*

fortify strongly, *commūniō*.
forty, *quadrāgintā*.
four, *quattuor*.
fourth, *quārtus*.
free, *līber*.
friend, *amīcus*.
friendly, *amīcus*.
friendship, *amīcitia*.
from, sign of abl.; *ab, dē, ex*, with abl.

G

Garonne, *Garumna*.
Gaul, *Gallia* ; a Gaul, *Gallus*.
general, *imperātor*.
Geneva, *Genāva*.
Geneva, lake, *Lemannus*.
German, *Germānus*.
get control of, *potior*.
give, *dō*.
go, *eō*.
go across, *trānseō*.
go back and forth, *commeō*.
go forth, *exeō*.
good, *bonus*.
grain, *frūmentum*.
great, *māgnus* ; so great, *tantus*.
guard, *praesidium*.

H

Haeduan, *Haeduus*.
Haedui, *Haeduī*.
hand, *manus*.
harm, *maleficium*.
happen, *accidō, fīō*.
hasten, *contendō, mātūrō*.
have, *habeō*.
he, *is*, or ending of the verb.
hear, *audiō*.
heavy, *gravis*.

height, *altitūdō*.
help, *auxilium*.
Helvetian, *Helvētius*.
her, *ēius* ; her own, *suus*.
high, *altus*.
higher, *superior*.
hill, *collis*.
himself, *ipse, suī*.
his, *ēius* ; his own, *suus*.
hold, *habeō, teneō*.
home, *domus*.
hope, (noun) *spēs* ; (verb) *spērō*.
horn, *cornū*.
horse, *equus*.
horseman, *eques*.
hostage, *obses*.
hour, *hōra*.
house, *domus*.
household, *familia*.
hundred, *centum*.

I

I, *ego*, or ending of the verb.
Ides, *Īdūs*.
if, *sī*.
import, *importō*.
in, sign of abl.; *in* with abl.
in order that, *ut, quō* ; —not, *nē*.
induce, *addūcō, indūcō*.
inflict, *ferō, īnferō*.
influence, (noun) *auctōritās* ; (verb) influence, *addūcō, indūcō*.
inform, *certiōrem faciō*.
informed, be, *certior fīō*.
inhabit, *incolō*.
injury (a wrong), *iniūria*.
intend, *in animō est*, with dat.
into, *in* with acc.
is, see be.
it, demons. pron. or ending of the verb.

J

javelin, *pīlum*.
join, *iungō ;* join (battle), *committō*.
journey, *iter*.

K

keep away (keep off), *prohibeō*.
kill, *concīdō, interficiō, occīdō*.
kindness, *beneficium*.
king, *rēx*.
know, *intellegō, sciō*.

L

lake, *lacus*.
land, *terra*.
language, *lingua*.
large, *māgnus*.
last, *extrēmus*.
law, *lēx*.
lay waste, *vastō, dēpopulor, populor*.
lead, *dūcō*.
lead across, *trānsdūcō*.
lead away, *abdūcō*.
lead out, *ēdūcō*.
leader, *dux*.
learn, *cōgnōscō, discō*.
legion, *legiō*.
length, *longitūdō*.
less, *minus*.
letter, *litterae* (pl.).
levy upon, *imperō*.
lieutenant, *lēgātus*.
like, *similis*.
line (of battle), *aciēs*.
live, *incolō*.
long, *longus* (in space) ; *diūturnus* (in time).
look, *spectō*.
lower, *īnferior*.

M

magistrate, *magistrātus*.
make, *faciō ;* be made *fīō*.
man, *vir, homō*.
many, *multī*.
march, (noun) *iter ;* (verb) *iter faciō*.
Marne, *Mātrona*.
marriage, *mātrimōnium*.
memory, *memoria*.
merchant, *mercātor*.
merit, *meritum*.
message, *nūntius*.
messenger, *nūntius*.
mile, *mīlle passuum*.
mind, *animus*.
mischief, *maleficium*.
month, *mēnsis*.
most, *māximē, plūrimum*, or sup. ending.
move, *moveō*.
mountain, *mōns*.
much, (adj.) *multus ;* (adv.) *multō*.

N

name (noun), *nōmen ;* (verb) *appellō*.
narrow, *angustus*.
narrow-pass, *angustiae*.
nation, *nātiō, genus*.
nature, *nātūra*.
near, *ad, circum*.
nearest, *proximus*.
necessary, it is, *oportet*.
neighbors, *fīnitimī*.
neither, (pron.) *neuter ;* (conj.) *neque*.
next, *proximus*.
new, *novus*.
night, *nox*.
nine, *novem*.
ninth, *nōnus*.

no, (adj.) *nūllus.*
no one, *nēmō, nūllus.*
nobles, the, *nōbilitās.*
none, *nūllus.*
north, *septentriōnēs.*
not, *nōn, nē.*
not only—but also, *nōn sōlum—
    sed etiam.*
not yet, *nōndum.*
nothing, *nihil.*
number, *numerus.*

O

ocean, *Ōceanus.*
of, sign of gen.; *dē, ex,* with abl.
often, *saepe.*
old, *vetus.*
on, *in* with abl.
on account of, *ob, propter.*
on all sides, *undique.*
on this side of, *citrā.*
one, *ūnus.*
opportunity, *facultās.*
or, *aut, vel.*
order, *iubeō, imperō.*
order, in —— that, *ut, quō.*
other, of more than two, *alius ;* the
    other, of two, *alter.*
ought, *dēbeō, oportet.*
our, *noster.*
out of, *ex.*
over, *trāns.*

P

pace, *passus.*
pack animal, *iūmentum.*
part, *pars.*
peace, *pāx.*
people, *populus ;* common people,
    plēbs.
peril, *periculum.*

persuade, *persuādeō.*
pitch (a camp), *pōnō.*
pity, *miseret* (impers. verb).
place, *locus ;* to the same place,
    eōdem.
place over, *praeficiō.*
plan, *cōnsilium.*
pledge, *fidēs.*
popular with, *acceptus.*
possession, get —— of, *potior.*
possible, as—as, *quam* + a superla-
    tive.
powerful, *potēns.*
praise, *laudō.*
prepare, *comparō.*
prevent, *prohibeō.*
private, *prīvātus.*
promise, *polliceor.*
protect, *dēfendō.*
province, *prōvincia.*
public, *pūblicus.*
punish, *ulcīscor.*
punishment, *poena.*
purpose, for the, *causā.*
Pyrenees, *Pȳrēnaeī montēs.*

Q

quickly, *celeriter.*

R

raft, *ratis.*
ravage, *vāstō.*
reach (= arrive at), *perveniō.*
ready, *parātus.*
recall, *revocō.*
receive, *recipiō.*
recent, *recēns.*
recently, *nūper.*
redoubt, *castellum.*
refinement, *hūmānitās.*
remain, *remaneō, relinquor.*

remember, *memoriā teneō, reminiscor.*

reply, *respondeō.*

report, *nūntiō, ēnūntiō, renūntiō.*

resist, *resistō.*

rest, the —— of, *reliquus.*

retainers, *familia.*

retinue, *familia.*

retreat, *recipiō* with *sē,* etc.

return, (noun) *reditiō ;* (verb) *revertō, revertor.*

revolution, *novae rēs.*

Rhine, *Rhēnus.*

Rhone, *Rhodanus.*

right, *iūs.*

right hand, *dextra (manus).*

river, *flūmen.*

road, *via, iter.*

roam about, *vagor.*

Roman, *Rōmanus.*

royal power, *rēgnum.*

S

safety, *salūs.*

sail, *nāvigō.*

sailor, *nauta.*

sake, for the, *causā.*

same, *īdem.*

Saône, *Arar.*

say, *dīcō ;* say—not, *negō.*

scarcity, *inopia.*

scout, *explōrātor.*

second, *alter, secundus.*

see, *videō.*

seek, *petō.*

Seine, *Sēquana.*

seize, *occupō.*

select, *dēligō.*

senate, *senātus.*

send, *mittō.*

separate, *dīvidō.*

Sequani, *Sēquanī.*

Sequanian, *Sēquanus.*

set fire to, *incendō.*

set out, *proficīscor.*

severely, *graviter.*

ship, *nāvis.*

short, *brevis.*

show, *dēmōnstrō, ostendō.*

side, *pars ;* on this —— of, *citrā.*

sides, from all, *undique.*

signal, *signum.*

since, *cum.*

sixth, *sextus.*

skilful, skilled, *perītus.*

slavery, *servitūs.*

small, *parvus.*

so, *ita, tam.*

so that, *ut.*

soldier, *mīles.*

some, *nōnnūllus, aliquis.*

sometimes, *interdum.*

son, *fīlius.*

Spain, *Hispānia.*

spear, *tēlum.*

spend-the-winter, *hiemō.*

spirit, *animus.*

standard, *signum.*

standard-bearer, *signifer.*

station, *dispōnō.*

stone, *lapis.*

storm, (noun) *tempestās ;* (verb) *oppūgnō* (take by storm).

strong, *fortis.*

subdue, *pācō.*

suitable, *idōneus.*

suspicion, *suspīciō.*

swift, *vēlōx.*

sword, *gladius.*

T

take, *capiō.*

take away, *tollō.*

tarry, *moror.*
ten, *decem.*
terrify, *terreō.*
territory, *ager, fīnēs.*
that, (pron.) *is, ille ;* (conj.) *ut,*
   quod, quīn.
their, *eōrum, ipsōrum, suus.*
them, *eos, illōs.*
themselves, *suī,* etc.
there (in that place), *ibi ;* (expletive)
   omit.
these, see this.
they, *eī, illī,* or ending of verb.
thing, *rēs.*
think, *arbitror, exīstimō, putō.*
third, *tertius.*
this, *hīc, is.*
those, see that.
thousand, *mīlle.*
three, *trēs.*
through, *per.*
throw, *iaciō.*
time, *tempus.*
to, sign of dative; sign of inf.; *ad,*
   with acc.; *ut,* with subj.
too, express by ending of a comparative.
tower, *turris.*
town, *oppidum.*
trader, *mercātōr.*
transport, *transportō.*
treason, *prodītiō.*
tribe, *genus, cīvitās.*
trickery, *īnsidiae.*
troops, *cōpiae.*
trumpet, *tuba.*
try, *cōnor.*
turn (aside), *āvertō.*
twenty, *vīgintī.*
two, *duo.*
two hundred, *ducentī.*

U

under, *sub.*
understand, *intellegō.*
undertake, *suscipiō.*
undertaking, *cōnātum.*
unfriendly, *inimīcus.*
until, *dum.*
unwilling, *invītus ;* be unwilling,
   nōlō.
urge, *hortor.*
us, *nōs.*
use, *ūtor.*

V

valor, *virtūs.*
very, superlative ending ; *ipse.*
very few, *perpaucī.*
victory, *victōria.*
village, *vīcus.*

W

wage, *gerō.*
wagon, *carrus.*
wait, *exspectō.*
wall, *mūrus.*
war, *bellum.*
warn, *moneō.*
was, see be.
waste, lay, see lay.
watch, *vigilia.*
way, *via, iter.*
we, *nōs,* or ending of verb.
were, see be.
what ? *quis ?*
when, *cum, ubi.*
where, *ubi.*
whether, *-ne.*
whether—or, *sīve—sīve.*
which, *quī ;* which ? *quis ?;* of two ?
   uter ?

while, *dum.*
who, *quī;* who? *quis?*
whole, *omnis, tōtus.*
why? *cūr.*
wide, *lātus.*
widely, *lātē.*
willing, be, *volō.*
winter, *hiems;* spend the winter, *hiemō.*
winter-quarters, *hīberna.*
wish, *volō.*
with, sign of abl.; *cum,* with abl.
withstand, *resistō.*

within, sign of abl. (time).
without, *sine.*
work, *opus.*
wrong (injustice), *iniūria.*

Y

year, *annus.*
yet, *tamen, autem.*
yoke, *iugum.*
you, *tū, vōs,* or ending of verb.
your, *tuus, vester.*

MAP OF GALLIA

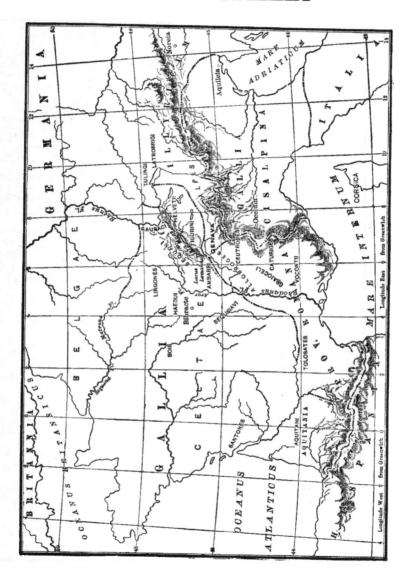

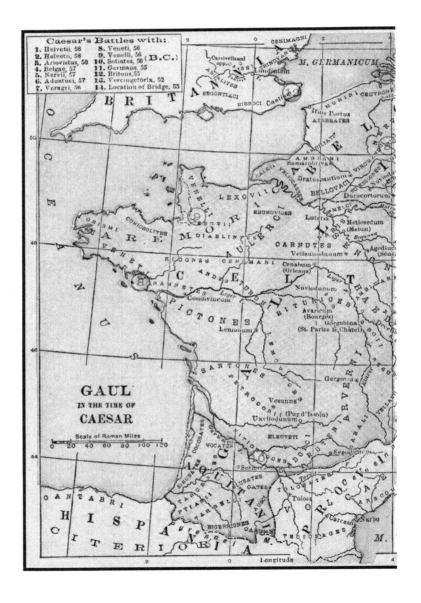

GAUL
IN THE TIME OF
CAESAR

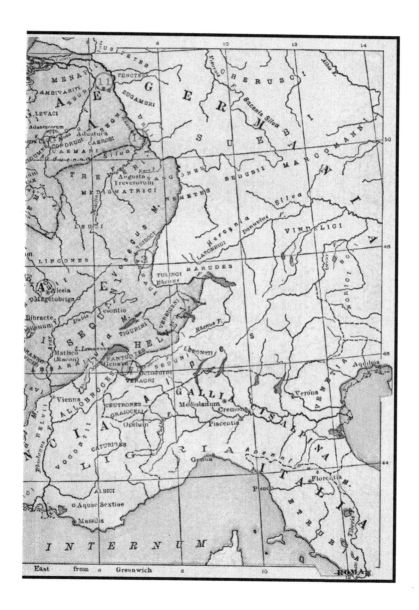

CPSIA information can be obtained at www.ICGtesting.com
Printed in the USA
LVOW04s0831111014

408298LV00027B/308/A